Serials Reference Work

Serials Reference Work

Joseph A. Puccio

1989
LIBRARIES UNLIMITED, INC.
Englewood, Colorado

LIBRARIES UNLIMITED, INC.
P.O. Box 3988
Englewood, Colorado 80155-3988

Library of Congress Cataloging-in-Publication Data

Puccio, Joseph A.
    Serials reference work.

    Includes bibliographical references.
    1. Reference services (Libraries)   2. Reference books
--Bibliography.   3. Serial publications--Bibliography.
4. Serials control systems.   I. Title.
Z711.P85   1989   025.3'432   89-14032
ISBN 0-87287-757-4

*This book is dedicated
to my Mom and Dad*

Contents

Acknowledgments

I am indebted to three of my colleagues, Susan Manakul, Michael Smihula, and Sara Striner, who reviewed each chapter as it was written and whose comments and corrections greatly improved this work. Also, I would like to thank several other staff members at the Library of Congress, including Charles Bean, Louis Drummond, Irene Schubert, and Travis Westly, who answered questions and provided information.

A special note of thanks is extended to all who responded to my letters requesting information. In particular, I am grateful to Marjorie E. Bloss, Kay Gill, Matt Manning, Annette Melville, and Richard H. Oosterom.

I am eternally grateful to Dr. Larry Chrisman, an excellent teacher concerned more with his students than with his tenure.

An extra special thanks for inspiration and stress reduction is owed to Andrew Barnard Katz.

Finally, this book would not have been possible without the help, encouragement, and patience of my wife, Barbara. Thanks.

Introduction

Serials are publications such as newspapers, periodicals, and annuals that are published on a continuing basis, bearing some sort of numerical or chronological designation. They constitute an integral segment of the collections of most libraries. Yet, the field of reference work regarding serials has never been given the attention it deserves. It has always been viewed as a minor portion of either serials work in general or of reference work in general. As such, serials reference work has never been sufficiently addressed in the literature of librarianship.

The purpose of this book is to fill that gap and to act as a practical guide to the tools and techniques of serials reference work. It is intended for librarians, other library support staff who deal with serials, and library school students. All basic serials reference sources are described. In many cases, suggestions are given for the most effective use of these sources. In addition, practical guidance is provided for dealing with various types of common serials reference questions and problems. The primary focus of this book is on serials reference work as it is practiced in the United States.

Chapter 1 provides an introduction to serials and serials reference work, while chapter 2 gives a general introduction to periodicals and reference service related to periodicals. Chapters 3 to 5 cover periodical directories, union lists of periodicals, and periodical indexes and abstracts. The focus of chapter 6 is on the serials of the United States Government and of international governmental organizations. Miscellaneous aspects of reference service with periodicals are covered in chapter 7, while chapter 8 examines reference work relating to annuals, irregular serials, and conference publications. Chapter 9 provides a general introduction to newspapers and reference service relating to them. Chapters 10 to 13 cover newspaper directories, union lists of newspapers, newspaper indexes and abstracts, and miscellaneous aspects of reference work with newspapers. Serials cataloging and processing and their effects on reference service are examined in chapters 14 and 15. Finally, chapter 16 provides a glimpse of the future of serials reference work.

This book is not intended to be a guide to the entire field of serials librarianship, as is Andrew D. Osborn's *Serial Publications: Their Place and Treatment in Libraries*, third edition (Chicago: American Library Association, 1980). Instead, this book covers only reference work related to serials. Although serials cataloging and processing are covered, such coverage is basically from the viewpoint of the effects of these processes on reference service. Likewise, the brief historical surveys of periodical and newspaper publishing are given to enable the reader to place current serials reference work in its appropriate historical perspective.

Directories and union lists of serials, as well as abstracting and indexing services, are constantly changing. These traditional tools of serials reference work have been transformed over the past two decades as they have become available through online databases and, most recently, through CD-ROM systems. The printed versions of these types of works also are prone to great change from one edition to another. In addition, new reference works are continuously being introduced. The information provided in this book regarding these types of sources is current as of late 1988 and is subject to change as later editions of the various works are produced.

1

Introduction to Serials Reference Work

Every reference librarian is a serials librarian. Undoubtedly, many reference librarians would argue that point, but in providing reference service, reference librarians constantly deal with serials. The overwhelming majority of cited literature is from serials. Much of the reference collection in any library is comprised of serials. A large portion of every library's budget is appropriated for serials.

Yet, many reference librarians try to distance themselves, psychologically, if not physically, from serials. Complaints by the user on dealing with serials abound. Unfortunately, complaints of this type are usually justified. Serials can be difficult and frustrating to use. Correspondingly, it can often be difficult to provide reference service for serials.

Richard DeGennaro has written that "serials are ... the most used and the most bibliographically complex materials in the library."[1] That concisely states the situation that arises for reference librarians. The most bibliographically complex items in the library are also those that are used the most. The problems that result are attributable to the high level of use and high level of bibliographical complexity. Obviously, if nobody was using *Saturday Review*, nobody would have cared when it split into four different titles (*Saturday Review of the Arts, Saturday Review of Education, Saturday Review of Science* and *Saturday Review of Society*), then ceased publication, then revived as yet another title, *Saturday Review/World*, in the 1970s.[2]

However, readers did, and still do, have citations to *Saturday Review* articles under its various titles. Even a sophisticated library user can become frustrated or stymied when confronted with a complex and confusing bibliographic situation such as the one that has been created by the *Saturday Review*. Should readers not abandon the search and head out the door confused and unsatisfied, they will probably seek assistance from a reference librarian or other reference staffer. The purpose of this book is to provide the reference librarian and other reference staff with a basis for assisting readers in need of serials aid.

The Serials Mystique

Through the years a "serials mystique" has developed, giving birth to the notion that serials and their associated problems and complexities are too special and unique to be understood or handled by anyone but a serials librarian. This, of course, is a belief not based in reality. As was noted in an article on this subject, "serials are not mystical."[3] As in any field, the more one knows about a subject, the less "mystical" that subject seems to be.

Therefore, to provide effective serials reference service, the library staffer must have a well-rounded knowledge of the subject. The nature of serials must be appreciated, and the role that serials play in libraries should be understood. Becoming familiar with basic reference sources such as union lists, directories, and indexing and abstracting services is necessary. The effects upon reference service of serials cataloging and of processing should also be understood. Increased knowledge about serials and the reference sources devoted to them will make answering the reference questions about them easier. Appreciating serials as a vibrant publishing form grows as comfort with them grows.

What Is a Serial?

The question, "What is a serial?" may seem to be rather insignificant. Surprisingly, though, quite a bit of time and effort has been expended in trying to define the term "serial." In his landmark work, *Serial Publications: Their Place and Treatment in Libraries*, Andrew D. Osborn devotes an entire chapter to this subject, examining and rejecting numerous definitions. He finally pronounces "that a serial is any item which lends itself to serial treatment in a library."[4] Bill Katz, another renowned serials expert has stated that Osborn's definition is "lucid and logical."[5]

The *Anglo-American Cataloguing Rules, Second Edition (AACR2)* defines "serial" as:

> A publication in any medium issued in successive parts bearing numerical or chronological designations and intended to be continued indefinitely. Serials include periodicals; newspapers; annuals (reports, yearbooks, etc.); the journals, memoirs, proceedings, transactions, etc. of societies; and numbered monographic series.[6]

Paul S. Dunkin points out that there are basically two main characteristics of serials. First, a serial "appears in parts for an indefinite period of time." Second, it "may successively be prepared by different authors, compilers or editors."[7]

Serials also are characterized by a title that is continued from issue to issue and some sort of successive numbering scheme. Multiple authorship is another key element that defines serials.

The main disagreement in defining a "serial" concerns its relation to the term "periodical." It has been argued that "periodical" is preferred to "serial." Further, it has also been argued that it is impossible to make distinctive definitions of these two terms. Recently, though, the term "serial" has come to the forefront as the descriptor of choice for this type of publication.

In common usage, "periodical" has come to define a subset of publication types beneath the "serial" umbrella. *The ALA Glossary of Library and Information Science* provides the following definition of "periodical":

> A serial appearing or intended to appear indefinitely at regular or stated intervals, generally more frequently than annually, each issue of which is numbered or dated consecutively and normally contains separate articles, stories or other writings. Newspapers disseminating general news, and the proceedings, papers, or other publications of corporate bodies primarily related to their meetings, are not included in this term.[8]

Clearly, then, "periodical" is subordinate to "serial" in current library usage, and for the purposes of this book.

Classified as major subsets of serials are periodicals (including magazines, journals, and newsletters), newspapers, and a final class composed of annuals, biennials, occasional publications and publications issued on an irregular basis but not more frequently than once a year. Publications such as gazettes and house organs are types of serials, and transactions and proceedings are, in some instances, considered to be serials.

How Many Serials Are There?

Nobody knows how many serials are currently being published in the world, nor how many have been published throughout history. Certainly, major scholarly journals, popular magazines, and other periodicals can be identified and counted. The 1988-89 edition of *Ulrich's International Periodicals Directory*, which is the first edition to combine the information from *Irregular Serials and Annuals* with the customary information about periodicals traditionally given in *Ulrich's*, contains 108,590 titles. Sixty-one thousand publishers from 197 countries are listed.[9] The 1988-89 edition of *The Serials Directory*, published by EBSCO, provides information on over 118,000 serial titles published internationally.[10] *The Standard Periodical Directory*, which lists titles published in the United States and Canada only, contains entries for 65,000 periodicals in its 1988 edition.[11]

So, allowing for duplication among these directories, roughly 150,000 current serial publications are covered in these three major sources. These titles would comprise the majority of that part of the serials publishing world that is well documented. However, there is another segment of the serials publishing world that is not well documented. A huge number of serials exist in this "unknown" world in which every title is a mystery for the reference staffer to handle. Many library patrons and some novice reference staffers will assume that if a title does not appear in the major directories, it does not exist. This is not always the case; don't assume it is so.

In serials publishing much of what is produced is of interest to a narrow band of people or institutions. Publications aimed at these smaller markets generally do not achieve a great circulation or any widespread notoriety. They are often not listed in any of the standard serials reference sources. It is likely that tens of thousands of newsletters are composed on a typewriter or on a word processor and then "published" on a photocopy machine. The resulting twenty-five or fifty or one hundred copies are then distributed within an office, or a company, or to members of an organization or to a select group of people with a very specific interest.

In most cases, these publications present no problems for a reference librarian since they are not known and library users are not requesting information about them. However, if one of these "unknown" publications is quoted in a newspaper article or is mentioned on a television talk show, the resulting inquiries can prove to be quite vexing and frustrating.

Since it cannot be accurately determined at any one time how many serial titles are being published, it is also impossible to know how many such publications have existed throughout history. Such estimates range from one million to five million titles.[12] The low range of that scale is probably much too conservative. In conjunction with planning for the United States Newspaper Program, it was estimated that more than 300,000 newspapers have been published in the United States alone.[13] Perhaps, then, five million might be closer to the actual number of serials that have existed.

The Problem(s) with Serials

It has been noted that "serials and monographs represent two different worlds of reality in the library."[14] Once published, the monograph does not change. A cataloger can depend on the item remaining the same for all time unless it physically deteriorates. The author will not change. The place of publication will not change. The title will not change.

Serials do represent a totally different world—the world of the living. Serials are remarkably like people in that they are born, change names, marry, divorce, have offspring, and finally die. Serials also have been known to come back from the dead and resume living, often in a different format or with a different focus. As changing entities, serials are inherently more complex and, subsequently, more difficult to handle. It is almost impossible for library cataloging to properly describe most currently published serials since they are in a constant state of flux. In fact, a serial can only be fully cataloged or described once it has ceased publication. At that point, however, most of the demand for any serial will be on the decline.

One of the most intimidating problems regarding serials is the title change. From the viewpoint of the librarian, title changes, in most instances, are needless and just serve to confuse readers and cause more work for librarians. It is doubtful that many publishers consider librarians when making title changes. Publishers are concerned with sales or in more accurately describing the contents of the publication. Since they have no voice in the matter, librarians have had to learn to live with, and accommodate, title changes. There are cases, though, when one wonders what the publisher is thinking.

For example, *Knit Directions* existed under that title from volume 1, 1966, through volume 8, number 2, second quarter, 1973. Then, in three successive issues, it had three title changes, transforming *Knit Directions* to *Knit/Textile Directions* to *Textile/Knit Directions* to *Textile Directions*.[15]

More recently, one computer publication has had six different titles in less than three years. This periodical started life with volume 1, number 1, March/April 1984 as *Microthought, The Journal of Financial Software*. With volume 1, number 4, September/October 1984, the title changed to *The Journal of Financial Software*. Tiring of that name after two issues, the publisher then changed it to *The Journal of Financial Software and Hardware*. That title lasted for three issues and was replaced with *The Journal of Financial Computing* beginning with volume 2, number 4, July/August 1985. After four issues, it was changed to *The Journal of Corporate Computing* starting with volume 3, number 2, March/April 1986. In January 1987, the title was changed, once more, to *The CIO Letter* (the CIO stands for Chief Information Officer), and this time the frequency was changed to monthly, and the volume numbering started all over again. Single title changes can create problems for readers and librarians, but multiple title changes such as those noted above cause greater troubles. By using appropriate reference sources, though, a librarian can identify serial title changes and solve many mysteries that arise from title changes.

Some publications have such peculiar titles to begin with that it is not necessary for them to change to create confusion and problems. For some inexplicable reason, some publishers run words in titles together. Thus, we must deal with titles such as *InformationWeek, NewYork Woman*, and *Woodenboat*. Another common occurrence is the use of initialisms in titles. Sometimes it is unclear whether the initials are part of the logo or design, or if they are actually part of the title itself. Even the venerable *Library Journal* provided problems of this sort. In issues of 1974 through 1976, the title pages carried a succession of different entries that included *LJ, LJ/Library Journal*, and, finally, *Library Journal*.[16]

Some serials have identity problems manifested in numerous titles found within, or on the cover of, the same issue of a publication. Sanford Berman found a magazine that displayed all of the following titles in its December 1978 issue:

Sea

Sea Magazine

Sea Combined with Rudder

Sea for the Inland Boatman

Sea: Inland Edition

Inland Sea[17]

In response to a letter from Berman, the executive editor of the periodical provided plausible reasons for all of the titles being present. He added, "And if you think it is confusing cataloging this gem, think what it must be like to produce it."[18]

Another title-related problem is the generic title. The challenge for the library patron or reference staffer is to identify the specific publication and publisher being sought. The titles *Bulletin* and *Journal* leap to mind as prime examples. However, with the proliferation of serials publishing, some less common words have been overused as titles. A 1970 article noted that *New Serial Titles, 1961-65* listed thirteen publications with the title *Challenge*, and the *Union List of Serials in Libraries of the United States and Canada* listed several more.[19] A recent search of the current serials accessioning file at the Library of Congress showed entries for twenty-one different publications titled *Challenge*. In general, serial publications with the same title are differentiated by place of publication. This is not a foolproof system, though, since the place of publication may change during the life of a serial. If one has a citation to a volume number and a date, then a valid identification can often be made by comparing check-in records.

Serials numbering can also cause significant problems. There is a whole range of numbering oddities that frequently occur. The following list of notes used in actual serials cataloging records attests to this.

Vol. 2, no. 1 called also consecutive issue no. 3.

Issues for July and Nov. 1977 called v.175, no. 7 and 10 but constitute v. 176, no. 1 and 5.

Vol. 1, no. 1 preceded by a "Pilot issue" called v. 1, no. 0.

Issues for Apr. 1977, Dec. 1977, and Mar. 1978 unnumbered but constitute vol. 1, no. 1-3.

Vol. 5 omitted in numbering.

Vol. for 1978 called also 1979 on cover.[20]

Numbering oddities are part of the serials territory. The examples cited above are not at all uncommon, and such oddities are not limited to obscure publications. For instance, in 1988, *New Statesman* and *New Society*, two well-known English periodicals, merged to form *New Statesman Society* (also known as *New Statesman & Society*). The new publication carried three separate numbering schemes, one for both of the prior titles and one for the new title. Thus, the July 22, 1988, issue was numbered:

Volume 1, no. 7 (*New Statesman Society*)

Volume 116, no. 2990 (*New Statesman*)

Volume 84, no. 1333 (*New Society*)

Quarterly publications dated by the season of the year, rather than by a month or range of months, present another serious numbering problem. The check-in clerk must decide if "Winter 1989" refers to January 1989 or December 1989. If accessioned improperly, a nonexistant gap in the holdings will appear on the record, and any resulting reference service based on that information will be incorrect. Seasonal dating can also create misunderstandings since seasons in the Northern and Southern Hemispheres are reversed. There have been appeals from librarians for publishers to discontinue seasonal dating, but it remains a fairly common practice.

This short review of serials-related problems shows what librarians dealing with serials must face on a regular basis. Unfortunately, the accumulation of problems pushes some librarians to the edge of despair. Articles occasionally surface in the literature in which authors plead with publishers for a change in publishing habits to ease librarians' jobs. For instance, one article suggested all periodicals publish only one volume per year and volume changes should take place only in January.[21] An article published in 1970 called for government enforcement, through the U.S. Post Office, of a standard for periodicals publishing. Under this suggested plan, publication titles could never vary and an advisory board of librarians would need to approve all title changes.[22]

Any library staffer working with serials must come to the realization that there is never going to be complete standardization in this field. Title changes, numbering errors, and other oddities are a way of life. In providing reference service for serials, a multitude of problems can arise. Only the major serials-related problems have been mentioned here. Further on, more specific examples and practical solutions will be provided.

The Library User and Serials

The library user is generally not concerned with title changes, numbering problems, or with the definition of "serial." The user is only interested in obtaining a certain article or in locating an article on a particular subject. Everything else is irrelevant. The only relevant questions are, "Does the library have the needed publication and issue, and are the pages still intact?" The intricacies and complexities of serials are not of interest to most patrons. Their only goal is to complete the search successfully and to find a copy of the article.

Often, the reader will arrive at the library without a reference to an article. Indexes may then be used to obtain a citation to an article on a particular subject. Once the citation is obtained, the reader must determine if the library has the publication cited and if the holdings include the particular issue that is needed. If the library is supposed to have the issue, then the location for the item must be identified.

In an open stack system, the patron will then proceed to the appropriate area and try to find the loose issue, bound volume, or microform. In a closed stack system, a request will be submitted, and the retrieval of the loose issue, bound volume, or microform becomes the responsibility of the library staff. Once the item is in the reader's hands, the article is then located and either read on the spot, photocopied, or checked out. A successful search has been completed.

In real life, though, things can go wrong at any of these steps. If reference staff are not consulted at the beginning of a search, an entirely inappropriate index may be used. Many library users know of only one index, the *Readers'*

Guide to Periodical Literature, and they use that index exclusively. The reader may search for a subject in several volumes with no luck, become frustrated, and leave the library. An assumption may be made on the reader's part that there are no articles on a particular topic since none could be located in the *Readers' Guide.*

For readers who do have citations to articles, the retrieval process can come to a stop at any point because of the following reasons:

The library does not have the title that is needed.

The library has the title but does not have the issue needed.

The library has the title and issue needed, but the loose issue or bound volume or microform is not on the shelf.

The material has been checked out of the library.

The issue has been sent to the bindery.

The issue is located, but the needed pages have been ripped out.

The issue is located, but the article is not on the pages that were referred to in the index.

All of these dead ends are all too familiar to those who work with serials. This is an area that can be terribly frustrating to the reader, expecially for unsophisticated library users who may expect the retrieval process to be rather simple.

One factor that is a constant frustration to library patrons everywhere is that no library can possibly have available all of the serials that are covered in the various abstracting and indexing services. Many patrons make the natural assumption that if a library has an index that includes citations to a particular periodical, then the library must also have that periodical. Being informed otherwise can be a rude awakening to a reader who has spent a large block of time transcribing citations to articles that can only be obtained through interlibrary loan or by a visit to another library.

The Art of Serials Reference

Empathy is the foremost quality that a reference librarian must feel and project in working with frustrated or novice serials users. Compared to book searching, serials searching is much more complex, and the chance for failure is much greater. Those who do not seek help from the library staff often find serials searches impossible to complete successfully. Unsophisticated library users may give up on a search for an article after the first or second roadblock, and the failure will never come to the attention of the reference staff.

Another class of novice library user is composed of those who are the opposite of the type just described. This type of patron will ask what seems to be dozens of questions in an attempt to become familiar with serials and the associated reference tools. At a busy reference desk, the librarian may become irritated with a user who is constantly reappearing and asking questions. This is particularly true when the questions are repeated, and the user doesn't seem to be listening to the answers.

In cases such as these, the librarian's empathy should come into play. The user may be totally unfamiliar with libraries, let alone with serials. A cursory explanation of the *Readers' Guide* or of the serials catalog may not be comprehended by the user. The concept of a bound volume of periodical issues may be alien to a user who has never seen such a thing. What the reference staffer perceives as "not listening to the answer" may actually be a case of the user not understanding the answer. Instead of viewing this patron as a problem, the reference staff should view this user as a challenge. Such opportunities for the librarian to teach and instruct should be seized instead of avoided.

Another type of frustrated serials user is the sophisticated library patron who runs into roadblocks in a serials search. Of course, people react in different ways to this kind of frustration. Some take it stoically and leave the library without saying anything to the reference staff. Such users may return to the library at a later date and try the search again, or they may find an alternative source or library for the item that they need. Others who run into roadblocks approach the reference staff, explain the problem politely, and then ask what can be done. If nothing can be done, or if nothing can be done immediately, this patron may then become a member of another class — the frustrated and angry serials user. This can be a very unpleasant situation for the reference staff.

Yes, empathy can help in dealing with all of these types of serials users. If librarians can put themselves in the patron's shoes, a new perception may arise. Even though this probably will not make a missing issue appear, it may help let the reader know that the library staff does care.

The Tools of Serials Reference

The more a reference librarian knows about serials and serials reference sources, the better equipped that librarian will be to deal with frustrated serials users and with all serials inquiries. Some reference librarians shy away from serials because of problems associated with them. Admittedly, it is a rare occurrence when a patron can go into any library with a list of ten citations and emerge an hour or two later with copies of all ten articles not having run into any difficulties.

As with any field of endeavor, the experts more easily handle the problems. Problems common to serials are handled more effectively by librarians and library staffers who are familiar with the appropriate reference sources and tools. Some apparent serials problems may not be problems at all to a librarian who has the proper background, knowledge, and experience. For example, a library patron may have searched for an article in a scholarly journal and found that the pages that include the article have been ripped out.

The patron is understandably upset and wonders what can be done. An uninformed reference staffer may tell the reader that nothing can be done until the library obtains a replacement copy of the article. A knowledgeable staffer will know that there are probably several alternatives available to the reader.

The three major classes of serials reference tools—union lists, directories, and indexes—can then be consulted. A union list may turn up a nearby library with the needed journal. A periodical directory may list a phone number for the publisher, who might supply a photocopy of the article to the patron. A directory may also list alternate means of obtaining this article, such as online retrieval or a document delivery service. Finally, the user may not necessarily need that particular article, but will accept any article that provides the same type of information. Consulting an indexing or abstracting service might uncover other similar articles.

So, the patron is presented with a range of alternatives. Although this isn't as good as supplying a copy of the needed article, it is better than staring at the mutilated issue and saying, "Well, we might be able to get replacement pages through interlibrary loan in a month or so."

The Provision of Serials Reference

Serials reference has received very little attention in libraries. Only the largest libraries devote entire staff positions to this task. Indeed, in many instances, the job of serials reference falls either to "regular" reference staff, who often have little serials experience, or to serials staff, who often have little reference experience. Some libraries provide a little of both, with a minimal level of reference service being provided by the serials department in a periodicals reading room, while full-scale reference service can be obtained from the reference staff in the reference room.

Helen M. Grochmal has written, "One of the most important and neglected units of the process that makes up the total serials service in libraries is its reference service."[23] Serials departments generally provide the processing functions (including check-in and maintenance of serial records) and sometimes the cataloging functions for serials. In most libraries, the serials department is part of technical services. As such, librarians assigned to these departments are usually processing or cataloging specialists. Although some degree of reference service may be provided, this is not the major focus of a serials department or of the normal serials librarian.

On the other hand, reference departments generally provide access to and reference service concerning indexing and abstracting services, union lists, directories, and other serials reference sources. Reference librarians who have had no experience working in a serials department may feel uncomfortable with serials. Also, in-depth knowledge about the peculiarities of serials may be missing.

In other words, unless a serials reference specialist is employed by a library, the quality of serials reference service is probably inadequate. Since there has been no great trend to start hiring serials reference specialists, present staffing patterns will probably continue. Serials reference will continue to be either split between serials and reference departments or be handled entirely by reference librarians who are not serials specialists. To add to the serials reference dilemma, much of serials reference service is provided by nonlibrarians such as technicians and student assistants.

Serials reference work has been ignored both in libraries and in the literature of librarianship. Since serials comprise such a vital component of any library, this might seem surprising. However, given the fact that serials reference has been a "stepchild" in most library settings, it is understandable that the literature on this subject has not been abundant.

The purpose of this book is to fill that gap in the literature of librarianship and to serve as a guide to sources and procedures in serials reference work. It is intended for all practitioners of serials reference (be they serials librarians, reference librarians, technicians, student assistants, etc.) and for library school students studying reference and serials librarianship.

Allen B. Veaner has written that "the serial ranks as one of the greatest social and technological inventions of modern times."[24] Perhaps that lofty description should be kept in mind the next time a patron complains about a missing issue, or an incorrect citation, or ripped out pages, or an abbreviation that cannot be deciphered, or issues that are at the bindery, or....

Notes

[1]Richard DeGennaro, "Wanted: A Minicomputer Serials Control System," *Library Journal* 102 (15 April 1977): 879.

[2]*Title Varies* 1 (1 February 1974): 5.

[3]Don Lanier and Glenn Anderson, "Dispelling the Serials Mystique," *The Serials Librarian* 5 (Summer 1981): 17.

[4]Andrew D. Osborn, *Serial Publications: Their Place and Treatment in Libraries*, 3d ed. (Chicago: American Library Association, 1980), 14.

[5]Bill Katz, "Osborn and That Elusive Definition," *The Serials Librarian* 6 (Winter 1981/Spring 1982): 144.

[6]Michael Gorman and Paul W. Winkler, eds., *Anglo-American Cataloguing Rules, Second Edition* (Chicago: American Library Association, 1978; Ottawa: Canadian Library Association, 1978), 570.

[7]Paul S. Dunkin, *Cataloging U.S.A.* (Chicago: American Library Association, 1969), 36-37.

[8]Heartsill Young, ed., *The ALA Glossary of Library and Information Science* (Chicago: American Library Association, 1983), 166.

[9]*Ulrich's International Periodicals Directory 1988-89*, 27th ed. (New York: R. R. Bowker, 1988), vii.

[10]*The Serials Directory 1988-89*, 3d ed. (Birmingham, Ala.: EBSCO Publishing, 1988), vii.

[11]*The Standard Periodical Directory*, 11th ed. (New York: Oxbridge Communications, 1988), unnumbered page in prefatory section.

[12]Donald Davinson, *The Periodicals Collection*, rev. and enl. ed. (Boulder, Colo.: Westview Press, 1978), 14.

[13]George Clack, "Preserving Yesterday's News," *Humanities* 8 (January/February 1987): 25.

[14]Benita M. Weber, "Education of Serials Librarians: A Survey," *Drexel Library Quarterly* 11 (July 1975): 72.

[15]"Break It to 'em Gently," *Title Varies* 4 (March/May 1977): 10.

[16]Howard W. Robertson, "What Every Serials Publisher Should Know about Unnecessary Title Changes," *The Serials Librarian* 3 (Summer 1979): 419.

[17]Sanford Berman, *The Joy of Cataloging: Essays, Letters, Reviews and Other Explosions* (Phoenix, Ariz.: Oryx Press, 1981), 35.

[18]Ibid., 36.

[19]Huibert Paul, "Serials: Chaos and Standardization," *Library Resources & Technical Services* 14 (Winter 1970): 21.

[20]David E. Griffin and Jim E. Cole, "Notes Worth Noting: Notes Used in AACR2 Serials Cataloging," *Serials Review* 9 (Fall 1983): 53-55.

[21]K. C. Garg and R. K. Dua, "A Plea for the Rationalizing of the Publication Schedules of Periodicals," *The Serials Librarian* 9 (Summer 1985): 95-96.

[22]Paul, "Serials," 26-27.

[23]Helen M. Grochmal, "The Serials Department's Responsibilities for Reference," *RQ* 20 (Summer 1981): 403.

[24]Allen B. Veaner, "Into the Fourth Century," *Drexel Library Quarterly* 21 (Winter 1985): 6.

2
Periodicals and Their Place in the Library

Brief History of Periodicals

The forerunners of serial publishing existed for three thousand years before Gutenberg's invention of the printing press. Annals transcribed on tombs of Egyptian kings who reigned from 2750 to 2625 B.C. are described as being possibly the earliest serial.[1] Various precursors of newspapers are also known to have existed. In particular, the Roman Empire gave birth to manuscript newspapers that reported the proceedings of the senate and other news. A Chinese newspaper has been reported as having been published in the seventh century A.D.[2] After the introduction of the printing press, newspapers became more common.

Periodical publishing, as it is known today, developed in the seventeenth century. A community of scientists, or "natural philosophers," began to come together into scientific and academic societies. Communication between members was by letter. In that manner, ideas and information could be exchanged with relative speed. However, this form of written communication was rather restrictive.

> The practice of communication by letter was restricting in that the information could be disclosed to only one person at a time or to a very limited number if copyists were employed. Publication in conventional book form was cumbersome, time consuming and uneconomic as the author was forced to delay until he had gathered enough material to justify publication.[3]

Newspapers were not the appropriate means for disseminating this kind of information, either. A new type of publication was needed to cover the middle ground between newspapers and books and to replace letters written between individuals with similar interests. The periodical was thus born.

On 5 January 1665, the first issue of the *Journal des Scavans* was published, becoming the first of its kind. The purposes of this publication ranged from presenting information about new books and publicizing experiments to providing obituaries of notable people. In a publishing field where hundreds of thousands (if not millions) of other titles have come and gone, this periodical has survived into the 1980s. It changed titles in 1816 to *Journal des Savants*, resuming publication after having been suspended since 1792.

A few months after the introduction of this journal, a second periodical publication emerged. It began life with the title, *Philosophical Transactions: Giving Some Account of the Present Undertakings, Studies, and Labours of the Ingenious in Many Considerable Parts of the World*, and later became the official organ of the Royal Society of London. Except for a few years when it was temporarily suspended, the *Philosophical Transactions* has also been continuously published up to the present. Shortly after the introduction of these first two periodicals, others of a lighter nature began to appear including the French *Le Mercure Galant* (later titled *Mercure de France*) and *The Athenian Gazette* from England (also titled *The Athenian Mercury*).

Four main periods in the history of serials have been identified. The first period is characterized by the establishment of the first serials, most notably, those mentioned above. The second period of serials history encompasses the years 1700 through 1825. At that time, literary periodicals and gentleman's magazines came into prominence.[4] Influential English periodicals of this period include Sir Richard Steele's *The Tatler, The Spectator* (produced by Steele and Joseph Addison), Daniel Defoe's *Review*, and Edward Cave's *The Gentleman's Magazine*. American magazine publishing began in 1741 with Andrew Bradford's *The American Magazine* and Benjamin Franklin's *The General Magazine*. Although many American periodicals were established during the 1700s, most were short-lived. The eighteenth century also saw the establishment of hundreds of learned societies which began publishing their own journals.[5] Over seven hundred scientific and medical periodicals published through the close of the eighteenth century have been identified.[6]

The third period of serials history covers the years 1825 through 1890. This period was characterized by technological improvements and the establishment of numerous general interest and special interest magazines. It has been noted that "the rapid spread of education, the reduction of illiteracy, the improvements in printing machinery, and the rise of the cities" created a climate in which the magazine business could expand into mass market size.[7] In the United States, *The Saturday Evening Post* and the *Youth's Companion* achieved great popularity. Illustrated magazines flourished worldwide, with *The Illustrated London News, Leslie's Weekly,* and *Harper's Weekly* all beginning in the mid-nineteenth century. Women's periodicals also thrived, with one of the most popular being the monthly *Godey's Lady's Book*. Literary and scientific periodicals abounded in this period, including *The Edinburgh Review, Blackwood's Edinburgh Magazine, The North American Review, Atlantic, Nature,* and *Scientific American*.

The final period of serials history covers from 1890 to the present, a time in which serials have become a part of the mass communications process and have become big business. General interest and special interest periodicals have proliferated to the point where virtually every interest, regardless of how narrow it might be, has a periodical devoted to it. This period has also seen the emergence of advertising as a prime force in the economics of periodicals publishing.

Women's magazines such as *Good Housekeeping* and *Vogue* have multiplied. Mass circulation news magazines, most notably *Time* and *Newsweek*, were established in the 1920s and 1930s and have become fixtures in the publishing world. Photo magazines enjoyed an era of prominence in the mid-twentieth century with popular titles such as *Life* and *Look*. Specialized magazines also have achieved great popularity, perhaps most significantly in the field of business (*Business Week, Fortune*, etc.). Journal and scholarly periodical publishing has expanded to the extent that every known discipline and subdiscipline is covered.

As noted in chapter 1, the 1988 edition of *The Standard Periodical Directory* lists 65,000 periodicals published in the United States and Canada alone, while the 1987-88 edition of *Ulrich's International Periodicals Directory*, which was the last edition that included only periodicals, listed 70,800 periodicals published worldwide.[8] Numbers alone do not tell the story, but an examination of the subject headings in these directories and some of the titles under each subject does indicate that virtually every interest, hobby, or academic discipline has at least one periodical to cover it. Of course, many subjects have far too many periodicals devoted to them. This dilutes the quality of contributions. So, instead of one or two top flight periodicals in a certain subject area, there may be one good periodical and half a dozen mediocre titles.

Are there too many periodicals? Peter Gellatly has written that "it may be true that there can never be too much of a good thing, but the problem seems to be that not every magazine, and certainly not every new one, merits the time, effort, money, and paper used to produce it."[9] This is borne out by the many periodicals that cannot attract enough readers or advertisers and must cease publication, often after only a year or two of existence. In some cases a publication might exist for only an issue or two. For every publication that goes out of business, however, there is another one starting up. Periodicals publishing is a vibrant, dynamic business that is constantly changing.

It is inconceivable that the state of periodicals publishing will change drastically any time in the near future, thus no one library can aspire to collect any more than a fraction of the total number of titles published. And there will continue to be "too many" periodicals in that no directory will ever be able to list them all and provide correct addresses, phone numbers and other salient information. However, each periodical published has a purpose for existing and an active readership. Even if the purpose is quite modest, and the readership is very limited, each has a place in the periodicals world. Apparently, there is always room for one more.

This section has provided a very brief history of periodicals and has touched only on the most important events and trends in that history. For more detailed coverage of the history of periodicals, one may consult:

A History of American Magazines. 5 vols. By Frank Luther Mott. Cambridge, Mass.: Harvard University Press, 1938-1968.

A History of Scientific & Technical Periodicals: The Origins and Development of the Scientific and Technical Press, 1665-1790. 2d ed. By David A. Kronick. Metuchen, N.J.: Scarecrow Press, 1976.

Women's Magazines, 1693-1968. By Cynthia L. White. London: Michael Joseph, 1970.

Magazines in the Twentieth Century. 2d ed. By Theodore B. Peterson. Urbana, Ill.: University of Illinois Press, 1964.

Types of Periodicals

As discussed in chapter 1, periodicals form a large subset in the field of serials. Characteristically, periodicals are published more than once a year, and each issue is consecutively numbered or dated. Each issue normally contains numerous articles or stories written by a variety of authors.

Magazines, journals, and newsletters are types of periodicals. Newspapers that disseminate general news, such as *The Washington Post* or *The New York Times*, are not periodicals. They comprise a separate subset of serials. Confusion often arises over what is or is not a newspaper. Readers will often assume that anything published on newsprint or in tabloid format is a newspaper, regardless of content. To these readers such a publication may well be a "newspaper," but to the library world, any publication that has a subject orientation and is reporting something other than general news is not a newspaper. Thus, *Computerworld*, which is in tabloid format, is classified as a periodical. Likewise, the horse racing publication, the *Daily Racing Form*, is also considered to be a periodical. This is true even though it is published daily and has the appearance of a newspaper.

Other types of serials that are not periodicals include annual publications and titles published less frequently than once a year. Proceedings and publications emanating from meetings of corporate bodies (societies, associations, and other such groups) are not considered to be periodicals.

Magazines

The ALA Glossary of Library and Information Science defines "magazine" as "a periodical for general reading, containing articles on various subjects by different authors."[10] The term seems to have evolved from the original meaning of magazine as a warehouse or storehouse of goods or of military supplies. *The Oxford English Dictionary* indicates that the word magazine, as related to publishing, was first used in titles of books that were printed as storehouses of information on a particular subject. Later, the word came to describe a type of periodical intended usually for a general readership. The first noted use of the word magazine in this sense occurred in 1731 in the periodical title, *The Gentleman's Magazine.*[11]

There is no confusion amongst readers as to what a magazine is, since these publications are omnipresent in our society. Every street corner newsstand sells a variety of magazines. They may be purchased in convenience stores and at airports, railway and bus stations. The waiting rooms of dentists and doctors are stocked with magazines. Advertisements for magazines assault us on television and radio. The sweepstakes mailings never seem to stop arriving, with their ultimate goal of getting the public to subscribe to magazines. There are magazines for every interest and for every market ranging from *Reader's Digest, Family Circle*, and *Boys' Life*, to *Cosmopolitan, Car and Driver*, and *Penthouse.*

Magazines are an extremely pervasive printed medium in today's society. A blockbuster bestselling book may sell a few million copies, and then its sales life is finished, in most cases. A magazine, though, performs as a continuing bestseller, generally on a monthly or weekly basis. In 1985, *Reader's Digest* had a United States circulation of 17,657,011 copies per issue.[12] That multiplies out to nearly a quarter of a billion copies of issues circulated during the year! *TV Guide*, published weekly, circulated over 870 million copies of issues in that same year.[13]

These facts would indicate that magazines are very popular with the public. There are a number of reasons for this. First, most magazines aspire to be a source of entertainment for their intended audiences. The entertainment can be supplied by quality writing, interesting stories or articles, and good illustrations and photographs. Of course, each magazine must entertain a different type of audience, and what is fascinating to a *Gourmet* subscriber may be deadly boring to a *Motor Trend* reader. A magazine that fails to be consistently entertaining to its intended audience will soon be out of business.

In addition to being entertaining, most magazines also provide some kind of essential or useful information to its readership. One of the largest selling magazines of all, *TV Guide*, provides its readership with information about television programming. These readers can use the schedules printed in *TV Guide* to plan their television watching. This is essential information to a large segment of the American population. Virtually all magazines provide their readers with information that is "essential" to some degree. Certainly, the recipes in *McCalls* or the answers in the "Playboy Advisor" column could qualify as "essential" information.

Another factor that enhances the popularity of magazines is that an issue can be read in segments. The normal magazine is comprised of a number of articles, stories, columns, features, and filler. Unlike books, which are designed to be read starting with the first page and progressing through to the end, a magazine can be read piecemeal and in any order desired. Also, magazine items do not demand the long-term attention that a book requires. In addition, magazines are viewed as terrific time-killers. This is why they can be found in waiting rooms of all types and why they are sold in airports.

Judging by their numbers, magazines are also popular with publishers. There is a sound reason for this, and that reason is profit. Magazine publishing can be quite lucrative. Well-managed new magazines apparently start to show a profit in the fourth year of publication, and the failure rate for new magazines is very low as compared to other new businesses.[14] Another incentive for magazine publishers is that start-up costs can be very inexpensive.

Benjamin M. Compaine, in his book, *The Business of Consumer Magazines*, has written:

> Magazine publishing is an easy entry business. It requires little
> capital equipment, as printing and even typesetting may be handled
> by outside suppliers. By relying on free-lance writers and an
> advertising sales force compensated largely by commission, fixed
> costs can be held to a minimum.[15]

Successful magazines provide revenue to the publisher through subscription and single copy sales. More significantly, though, revenue is generated through the sale of advertising space in the magazine. Through the past few decades, the ratio of advertising to editorial material in magazines has balanced at roughly fifty-fifty.[16] Compaine has stated that the magazine business is based on selling an audience to advertisers. The essential nature of magazine publishing is to attract and hold readers with an editorial product.[17] In general, then, magazines provide readers with entertainment and information, while providing publishers with a profit and advertisers with an audience.

Magazines are usually classified in two categories — general interest and special interest. General interest magazines are intended for a mass audience, and achieve the greatest circulation of all magazines. Although some general interest magazines have a specific subject interest (for example, *TV Guide*), the articles and advertisements carried within these publications are aimed at the general market. Editorial material is geared to a "passive" interest on the part of the reader. Special interest magazines cater to those taking an "active" interest in some subject or pursuit.[18] In so doing, special interest magazines present articles dealing with participation in whatever interest that particular magazine happens to cover. Special interest magazines are embraced by advertisers as a means to reach targeted markets. Thus, such magazines will carry advertisements for products that can be used in the pursuit of that interest.

Journals

Another type of periodical, with a very different purpose, is the journal. Whereas the magazine exists to entertain the reader and to provide an audience for advertisers, the journal exists primarily to serve as a conduit for the exchange of scholarly or research information. "Journal" is defined as "a periodical, especially one containing scholarly articles and/or disseminating current information on research and development in a particular subject field."[19]

The typical journal finds its readership within a clearly defined field, that may well be quite narrow. Circulation of journals is minuscule as compared to the circulation of magazines. It is not unusual for a scholarly journal to have a circulation of just a few thousand. Generally, the physical appearance of the journal is lackluster, with none of the gloss of magazines. The articles are usually academic or technical in nature. Information transfer, not entertainment, is the goal.

If advertising is included in a journal, it will most often be for another journal or for a book in the same or a related field. Since advertising is not a major source of income, journal publishers can realize a profit only through the subscription price. As acquisitions librarians know, journals can be extremely expensive. Subscription prices can run into the hundreds of dollars per year for one title. Journal publishers also add to their profit margins by not paying for the articles that they publish. The only payment that an author can expect to receive may be a few copies of the journal issue or reprints of the article. Authors, though, do not intend to make money from their articles. In the "publish or perish" atmosphere that prevails in many academic environments, it is necessary for promotion and tenure to have a constantly expanding resume of published works. A published journal article means much more to the author than any token payment that the journal publisher might be able to offer.

Although journals do act as a proving ground for academics anxious to keep their jobs or to be promoted, the main purpose of the journal is to provide a means for the rapid transmission of information. As was discussed earlier, the first printed serials were established as a way for academics to communicate with each other and their respective communities in a more efficient manner than by letter. To this day, the journal enables scholars or researchers to communicate ideas, to describe and publicize their work, and to be involved in a "continuous critical examination of scientific hypotheses and theories."[20]

Readers use journals to:

Keep current in the field and identify significant developments in related fields.

Expedite the retrieval of data and information.

Focus on relevant material and bypass irrelevant material.

Get ideas for future research.

Identify others with similar interests and follow the progress of colleagues.[21]

The published journal also has another important effect. Even those who are not associated with a certain field still have access to the developments in that field. Charles B. Osburn has written:

The need to exchange ideas is fundamental to the notion of science and scholarship operating as a community, in which the journal not only is a repository of completed work, but also is consulted by practitioners in all fields in order to learn of work in progress. Those who are not participants in the inner circles of the community, which is referred to frequently as the 'invisible college,' still are afforded by the journal an avenue to exposure for their ideas and a means of access to information and because of that mechanism those scholars are not isolated completely.[22]

The magazine is often thought of as the middle ground between the newspaper and the book. Along those lines, the journal would need to be viewed, not as a middle ground, but as the starting point for books. The new ideas, experiments, and information that are in today's journals will serve as the basis for the books of tomorrow.

Newsletters

A quite different type of periodical is the newsletter. It is defined as "a serial consisting of one or a few printed sheets containing news or information of interest chiefly to a special group."[23]

The quintessential classic newsletter is *The Kiplinger Washington Letter*:

> Its four 8½x11 inch size pages are stapled and have the appearance of being typewritten. The right margin is ragged and there are numerous underlinings to highlight important points. The sentences are short and often incomplete, giving the impression that only essential information is being reported. First published in 1923, *The Kiplinger Letter* is one of the oldest continuously published newsletters. With a circulation over 400,000 it is also one of the most successful.[24]

The history of newsletters actually begins in the thirteenth through seventeenth centuries, before the introduction of printed serials. Large mercantile houses of the period were responsible for producing handwritten manuscript newsletters. These letters would emanate from correspondents in the commercial centers of Europe and would convey business information along with reporting the notable events of the day.[25] A complex network of correspondents existed to gather and disseminate news, not unlike the correspondents for modern newspapers and wire services.[26] The most extensive of these newsletters were from the Fugger merchant banking house. Some 17,600 issues were written on 35,230 pages from 1568 through 1605.[27]

The modern newsletter is almost as popular in today's society as is the magazine. It seems as if every organization, association, company, group, and special interest has its own newsletter. Anyone with access to a typewriter or a word processor and a photocopy machine can publish a newsletter. The recent introduction of desktop publishing through the use of personal computers should also have a pronounced effect by enabling an increasing number of individuals to produce professional-looking newsletters at a low cost. Although many newsletters have a wide circulation and are very profitable for the publisher, a great percentage of newsletters have a limited circulation and are more concerned with passing on information than with making money.

The 1988 edition of the *Oxbridge Directory of Newsletters* lists fifteen thousand newsletters published in the United States and Canada alone.[28] This is just a fraction of the total number published, since newsletters are published throughout the world. Also, there are undoubtedly a significant number of currently published United States and Canadian newsletters not listed in this source, as many newsletters are very difficult to track down owing to their limited circulation. Thus, an undeterminable, huge number of newsletters are currently produced in the United States and worldwide.

Periodicals in Libraries

Periodicals comprise a significant portion of the collections of most libraries and obligate a large percentage of the budgets of those libraries. In 1985-1986, university library members of the Association of Research Libraries reported median current serials subscriptions of 20,537 titles and median expenditures of $1,496,774 for current serials.[29] In libraries of all types, outlays for periodicals are a recurring expense that can be draining on a budget.

Whereas a book is paid for once, a periodical must be repurchased every year. Once a periodical subscription is entered by a library, it takes on a life and inertia of its own. Traditionally, except in severe budget cutbacks, periodical subscriptions are seldom cancelled. It is easier in the library environment to start a periodical subscription than it is to cancel such a subscription. Recently, though, libraries have started a trend toward the wholesale cancellation of periodical subscriptions due to tight budgets and increasing subscription rates.

In addition to the recurring annual subscription price, funds must be allocated for the continuous processing of periodical issues. Check-in, or accessioning, clerks must log in each issue and claim those that do not arrive. Money must also be appropriated for the collation and binding of loose issues into bound volumes. Missing and mutilated issues must be replaced. In many cases, duplicate subscriptions are entered for the same title, one being a subscription for the current hard copies and the second subscription for a permanent copy in microform or in pre-bound volumes. The inevitable nature of periodicals to change titles also necessitates the allocation of staff time to recatalog and revise previous cataloging.

With all of these costs involved, it might seem that periodicals are not worth the money. Why then do libraries subscribe to periodicals in such great numbers? Basically, libraries have no choice. As Osborn has pointed out, the overwhelming majority of cited material is from serials.[30] So, bibliographies, footnotes, indexes and abstracts lead the researcher or student to periodicals. Another factor was noted by the National Enquiry into Scholarly Communication. On the average, it reported that a scholar "scans seven journals, follows four or five regularly, and reads three to five articles a week."[31] A separate study of graduate students has shown that 60 percent of them used periodical literature at least once a week.[32] In essence, the teacher, student, scholar and researcher present a continuing demand for journals and research periodicals. Other types of more general interest magazines are needed by those who require information on a subject but do not wish to use, or cannot understand, the academic periodicals in a particular subject area. There is also the constant demand on the library for items of light reading or entertainment. The need for periodicals exists in the academic community because they are a means to communicate new knowledge in a rapid manner. They are also a rich source of materials for students in any discipline. In the nonresearch and nonacademic environment, periodicals are viewed in many different ways, from sources of entertainment to sources of instruction. However, the demand for periodicals is present in all types of libraries.

Elements of Periodicals
Reference Service

The description of serials reference work in chapter 1 applies in total to periodicals reference service. Probably the most basic building block in periodicals reference service is the librarian's knowledge of the periodicals collection in the library. This depth of knowledge does much to determine the resulting reference service. Reference personnel should strive to know not only the titles in the collection but also the general contents of those periodicals. Granted, the larger the periodicals collection, the more difficult it is to be familiar with the entire collection. However, it should be possible to start with the most popular periodicals and work toward the more obscure titles, in a continuing effort to be acquainted with the collection. A guide such as *Magazines for Libraries*, by Bill Katz and Elizabeth Sternberg Katz, can be of help in this process (see chapter 3 for a description of this guide). The wise library administrator will encourage the reference staff in this endeavor.

With a basic knowledge of the titles in the library, and with a grounding in the contents of the most popular periodicals in the collection, a reference staffer can provide much more efficient and accurate reference service. Familiarity with the collection allows the staffer to conduct a better reference interview. It also leads to more appropriate uses of indexes and abstracts, union lists, and periodical directories. A working knowledge of these types of periodicals reference tools is required for the provision of periodicals reference.

Periodicals reference service differs from other types of reference service in that much of it concerns locating an article or an issue of a periodical. While other types of reference deal with finding an answer to a question or in accessing bits of information, much of periodicals reference is consumed with physically locating a known item. A relatively recent study in a large academic library had 31 students search for five cited articles from titles held by the library. Out of the 155 citations, only 55 percent were retrieved by the students. Fifteen percent were not retrieved due to user error (did not use serials directory, used serials directory incorrectly, etc.). Thirty percent were not retrieved because of errors that could be attributed to the library (ripped out articles, incomplete volumes, volumes at bindery, etc.).[33]

Many of the questions received by those who are responsible for periodicals reference regard the failure of library patrons to locate certain periodicals or issues of periodicals, as the study just described would tend to support. The inability of a library patron to find an issue of a periodical can eventually require the reference staffer to employ all types of reference tools and techniques. The following five chapters address this common periodical problem, as well as all other aspects of periodicals reference.

Notes

[1]Andrew D. Osborn, *Serial Publications: Their Place and Treatment in Libraries*, 3d ed. (Chicago: American Library Association, 1980), 24.

[2]Bernard Houghton, *Scientific Periodicals: Their Historical Development, Characteristics and Control* (London: Clive Bingley, 1975), 11.

[3]Ibid., 12.

[4]Osborn, *Serial Publications*, 31.

[5]Ibid.

[6]Fielding H. Garrison, "The Medical and Scientific Periodicals of the Seventeenth and Eighteenth Centuries," *Bulletin of the History of Medicine* 2 (July 1934): 300.

[7]John Tebbel, *The American Magazine: A Compact History* (New York: Hawthorn, 1969), 47.

[8]*Ulrich's International Periodicals Directory 1987-88*, 26th ed. (New York: R. R. Bowker, 1987), vi.

[9]Peter Gellatly, "Too Many Magazines?" *The Serials Librarian* 7 (Spring 1983): 1.

[10]Heartsill Young, ed., *The ALA Glossary of Library and Information Science* (Chicago: American Library Association, 1983), 137.

[11]*The Compact Edition of the Oxford English Dictionary* (Oxford: Oxford University Press, 1971), 1690.

[12]*The World Almanac and Book of Facts 1987* (New York: World Almanac, 1987), 368.

[13]Ibid.

[14]James B. Kobak, "New Magazine Myths," *Folio: The Magazine for Magazine Management* 7 (October 1978): 35.

[15]Benjamin M. Compaine, *The Business of Consumer Magazines* (White Plains, N.Y., and London: Knowledge Industry Publications, 1982), 16.

[16]Ibid., 19.

[17]Ibid., 55.

[18]Ibid., 5-6.

[19]Young, *ALA Glossary*, 125.

[20]Houghton, *Scientific Periodicals*, 19.

[21]Wayne I. Boucher, "The Place of the Author in the Coming Information Society," in *Strategies for Meeting the Information Needs of Society in the Year 2000* (Littleton, Colo.: Libraries Unlimited, 1981), 124.

[22]Charles B. Osburn, "The Place of the Journal in the Scholarly Communications System," *Library Resources & Technical Services* 28 (October/December 1984): 320.

[23]Young, *ALA Glossary*, 153.

[24]Brigitte T. Darnay and John Nimchuk, eds., *Newsletters Directory*, 3d ed. (Detroit: Gale Research, 1987), 10.

[25]Osborn, *Serial Publications*, 26-27.

[26]Donald Davinson, *The Periodicals Collection*, rev. and enl. ed. (Boulder, Colo.: Westview Press, 1978), 25.

[27]Osborn, *Serial Publications*, 27.

[28]*Oxbridge Directory of Newsletters*, 1988 ed. (New York: Oxbridge Communications, 1988), preface.

[29]Nicola Daval and Alexander Lichtenstein, comps., *ARL Statistics 1985-86* (Washington, D.C.: Association of Research Libraries, 1987), 25-26.

[30]Osborn, *Serial Publications*, 40.

[31]*Scholarly Communication: The Report of the National Enquiry* (Baltimore, Md., and London: Johns Hopkins University Press, 1979), 43.

[32]Stephen L. Peterson, "Patterns of Use of Periodical Literature," *College & Research Libraries* 30 (September 1969): 427.

[33]Marjorie E. Murfin, "The Myth of Accessibility: Frustration & Failure in Retrieving Periodicals," *The Journal of Academic Librarianship* 6 (March 1980): 17.

3

Periodical Directories and Other Sources of Current Periodical Information

Many inquiries regarding periodicals can be answered by using current periodical directories. The range of such inquiries is indicated by the following list of sample questions. The answers to these questions can be found by using the major directories.

What periodicals are published by the United Nations?

Is *Religious Education* available on microfilm? If so, who produces the microfilm edition?

Is there a list of periodicals that are published on a daily basis?

What is the circulation of *Rolling Stone*?

What would it cost to place a full-page advertisement in the *Army Times*?

Where is *PC Week* indexed, and what is its ISSN?

Is there a list of all United States magazines about horses?

Who is the editor of *Organic Gardening*?

What periodicals are available online?

Whatever happened to *Mechanix Illustrated*?

In general, directories fulfill three main purposes. First, directories perform a grouping function by arranging periodicals into subject categories or by place of publication. A second major function is to provide publishing data regarding individual periodicals such as:

Name, address, and phone number of the publisher.

Subscription price.

Frequency of publication.

Special features included such as book reviews or advertising.

Other formats in which the publication may be available, generally either microform or online.

Circulation.

Information regarding where the periodical is indexed or abstracted.

The third function of periodical directories is to provide bibliographic data. Such data is usually quite limited and in no way compares with a cataloging record. However, most general periodical directories do provide one or more of the following categories of bibliographic data:

Year the periodical was first published.

International Standard Serial Number (ISSN).

Classification numbers (Dewey, Library of Congress, etc.).

Variant forms of title.

Former title(s).

Titles of periodicals that have merged into the present title.

Each major periodical directory also offers special features or unique coverage. Unfortunately, for library users, librarians, and library budgets, there is no one periodical directory that "does it all." It is therefore desirable for libraries to own a number of different current periodical directories in order to attain the most complete coverage. Since each directory is different, it is necessary for reference staff to understand what each can provide.

The remainder of this chapter is devoted to descriptions of the most useful directories and other reference sources that provide current information about periodicals. These works fall into a number of categories, generally defined by the scope of the publication, and have been arranged into the following groupings.

Directories with an international scope.

Directories covering a single region or country.

Newsletter directories.

Directories covering periodicals in a specific subject or interest area.

Reference works that are not periodical directories but that do contain such information.

Miscellaneous sources of periodical information.

International Periodical Directories

Ulrich's International Periodicals Directory. New York: R. R. Bowker.

For years, *Ulrich's International Periodicals Directory* has been the primary source for information about current periodicals. First published in 1932, this directory is now updated annually. Traditionally, this directory provided coverage of periodicals only, while a companion publication, *Irregular Serials and Annuals,* covered serials published once a year or less frequently. Effective with the twenty-seventh edition, 1988-89, of *Ulrich's,* these two directories have merged into one publication under the *Ulrich's* title. This merger was evidently brought about by competition from a similar, new publication titled, *The Serials Directory* (described later in this chapter).

The twenty-seventh edition contains 108,590 titles categorized under 554 subject headings. *Ulrich's* is produced from the Bowker International Serials Database, which includes information from 61,000 publishers in 197 countries.[1] A continual program of updating the information in the database is accomplished through yearly international mailings to all of the included publishers. Personal contacts are also maintained in publishing houses around the world.[2]

Beginning with the 1988-89 edition, *Ulrich's* is printed in three volumes. The entries for the serials are arranged under broad subject categories in the first two volumes. Various indexes, including a title index, and other lists comprise the third volume.

Individual entries in the first two volumes all provide the following:

Title.

Frequency of publication.

Publisher name and address.

Country of publication code.

Dewey Decimal classification number.

The following information is provided when available:

Telephone number (generally for United States and Canadian publishers).

ISSN.

CODEN.

Subscription price.

Year first published.

Language of text.

Special features such as book reviews and availability of commercial advertising.

Where indexed or abstracted and if the periodical produces its own index.

Corporate author.

Former title(s).

Variant forms of title.

Availability in other formats such as microform or online.

Circulation.

Library of Congress classification number.

Brief description of contents.

In addition to the title index, there is also an index to international congress proceedings that are published as serials. Separate indexes are also included for serials of:

—International organizations.

—European Communities.

—United Nations.

A separate section groups together, in one listing, all serials known to be available online. This is followed by a listing, arranged by online vendor, of these same publications. A "cessations" section lists all titles which have ceased publication in the past three years. Titles in this section can be accessed through the title index, where they are interfiled with active titles. Publications that have undergone a title change (or merged or incorporated, etc.) are listed under the current title with the former title being listed in the entry and used as an access point in the title index. An ISSN index is provided which lists titles from the Bowker database with such a number, including publications that have ceased and are not otherwise listed in this directory. The 1988-89 edition lists nearly 100,000 ISSNs.

Ulrich's is supplemented by the quarterly publication, *Ulrich's Update*, which formerly was titled, *The Bowker International Serials Database Update*.

The Serials Directory. Birmingham, Ala.: EBSCO Publishing.

In direct competition with *Ulrich's* is *The Serials Directory*, published by EBSCO Publishing. EBSCO Industries is most widely known as a subscription agent for libraries. Its annual *Librarians' Handbook*, a detailed catalog of serials titles available through its subscription services section, has served for a number of years as a fairly complete title listing of current serials that are in print and readily available (see a complete description later in this chapter).

In 1986, the premiere edition of *The Serials Directory* was published in three volumes and marketed as a viable alternative to, and improvement over, the two Bowker directories, *Ulrich's* and *Irregular Serials and Annuals*, which were then published separately. The third edition, 1988-89, of *The Serials*

Directory lists over 118,000 serial publications from around the world. Periodicals, newspapers, annuals, and other serial publications are combined in one directory.

Information in this directory is collected from three main sources. The primary source is the CONSER database (see description of CONSER in chapter 14). EBSCO's internal title file database, developed through their years as a subscription agency and containing more than 195,000 serial titles, is the second source of information for this directory. Finally, for further information and authentication, publishers are contacted directly by questionnaire.[3]

The serial title entries are arranged in broad subject categories. Listings include all of the following data elements, when available:

Title statement.

Key title.

Main entry when it is a conference, meeting or corporate name.

Series statement.

Variant forms of title.

Dates of publication and volume information.

ISSN.

Country of publication.

Language.

Frequency.

Price.

Publisher's name, address, and telephone/telex number.

Editor(s).

Where indexed or abstracted and if the periodical produces its own index.

Library of Congress classification number.

Dewey Decimal classification number.

Universal Decimal classification number.

National Library of Medicine classification number.

CODEN.

Availability of advertising and book reviews.

Circulation.

Availability in other formats.

Description of content as provided by the publisher.

Former title.

The entries for individual serial publications are contained in the first two volumes, while the third volume is comprised solely of indexes. There are three different indexes—a title index, a ceased title index, and an ISSN index. Although there is a separate ceased title index, the actual entries for these titles are interfiled with the active titles, with the word "ceased" in boldface.

The filing rules are a bit odd and can be quite confusing. In particular, serial titles with geographic designations given in parentheses to differentiate publications with the same title are filed as if the geographic designation was part of the title. For example, in the title index there are a few publications with the one word title *Film*. Instead of being grouped together, they are dispersed throughout the section of titles beginning with the word "film." This results in the following filing for one of the titles in question:

Film Criticism

Film Culture

Film (Denver, Colo.)

Film Directions

So, in referring users to this directory, be certain to mention the filing arrangement.

The Serials Directory is supplemented by issues of *The Serials Directory Update*.

Bowker versus EBSCO

Upon publication of the Premiere Edition of *The Serials Directory* in 1986, EBSCO mounted an advertising campaign to convince librarians that their directory was preferable to the two Bowker directories. In response, Bowker attempted to show that their products were superior and went on to merge them into one directory. In so doing, Bowker was able to also state that they included all types of serials, except for newspapers, in one directory. This eliminated one of the major advantages claimed by EBSCO for its directory. With other improvements and additions to *Ulrich's* some other advantages originally claimed for *The Serials Directory* are now shared by both publications.

However, the following distinct advantages can still be claimed by *The Serials Directory:*

Includes authenticated MARC serial record and CONSER file data.

Includes Universal Decimal and National Library of Medicine classification numbers.

For its part, Bowker notes that it has had a long track record of serials coverage, and that *Ulrich's* provides the following unique features:

Data is compiled directly from the publishers.

Separate sections list periodicals available online and online vendors with the titles they offer.

Their coverage is available in a number of different formats.

Due to budget constraints, most libraries will likely need to decide between *The Serials Directory* and *Ulrich's*. At least for the present, *Ulrich's* would seem to be preferable, if one must make that choice. The competition from EBSCO has resulted in a greatly improved *Ulrich's*. From the reference standpoint, though, it would be best to have both *The Serials Directory* and *Ulrich's* available. Each publisher does provide unique special features that can be useful in various reference situations. Also, although there is tremendous overlap in the coverage of titles, undoubtedly a certain percentage of titles will be found only in *The Serials Directory*, and a certain percentage will be found only in *Ulrich's*.

Reliability of data found within directories is always a major concern. The Bowker information has proven to be quite reliable. Only through years of use in libraries will the ultimate level of reliability be fixed for *The Serials Directory*.

When using any periodical directory that is arranged by subject, such as the two already described, it is sometimes difficult to identify the subject under which a particular class of periodicals might be listed. This usually arises when a patron asks for a list of all periodicals on a specific subject. For example, the patron may want to know if there are any periodicals devoted to the subject of convenience stores. In cases such as this, it can be maddening to determine what subject heading such periodicals might be classified under in any particular directory. Instead of trying to locate the proper subject heading, search in the title index under "convenience stores," or whatever the specific subject may be. In most cases when the subject is sufficiently broad, there will be one or two publications with those words as the title or as the beginning of the title. The page number will then be supplied, and when it is turned to, the title entry will be found along with other related publications under the same subject heading.

Benn's Media Directory: International. Tonbridge, U.K.: Benn Business Information Services.

Benn's Media Directory is published annually in two volumes, one of which covers the United Kingdom (described later in this chapter), and this volume, which covers the rest of the world. This directory traces its history back to the publication, in 1846, of the *Newspaper Press Directory.* In the late 1970s, the title was changed to *Benn's Press Directory*, and, with the 134th edition for 1986, the title was changed once again to *Benn's Media Directory.*

Covered in the International volume are 197 countries with over thirty thousand press entries included in the 1988 edition. It is noted that the "whole volume has been planned with the outward-looking British businessman especially in mind."[4] Much of the information presented reflects this. The directory is arranged by broad geographic area, with subdivisions such as "Africa/Middle East" and "The Americas." These area listings are followed by the country sections. Each broad area and country section includes listings of national news agencies and broadcasting organizations and their British offices (if any). Newspapers are then listed, with periodicals listed last, arranged by subject category. (The newspaper aspects of this directory will be described in chapter 10.) The periodical entries provide title, frequency, address, and circulation. Publications of the United Kingdom are included, but not to the extent that they are covered in the separate United Kingdom volume.

There is no title index in this directory, and the index of countries giving appropriate page numbers is difficult to locate since it is neither at the rear, nor the front, of the volume. The lack of any type of worthwhile index limits the usefulness of this directory. However, this directory can be used as a survey of major periodicals available from various countries; more countries are covered in this work than in the other comparable British directory, *Willings Press Guide.* Some coverage of the Soviet Union is provided by *Benn's*, whereas *Willings* provides none.

Willings Press Guide. East Grinstead, U.K.: British Media Publications.

The 1988 printing of *Willings Press Guide* was the 114th edition of this annual publication. Primarily, the focus of *Willings* is on the press of the United Kingdom, but coverage is provided for major publications from different areas of the world. (See chapter 10 for the newspaper aspects of this directory.)

One section is devoted to publications of the United Kingdom, and it provides extensive coverage with 7,699 periodicals listed in the 1988 edition. Another 1,084 annuals and over 1,700 newspapers are interfiled in the same section. The periodical entries include title, publisher, editor, address, telephone number, year first published, frequency, subscription price, circulation, and, in some cases, a very brief description of contents.

The "Overseas Section" lists newspapers and periodicals from most of the countries of the world, with the Soviet Union being a notable exception. The publications are arranged by country within broad geographic designations ("The Americas," "Far East," etc.). A table of contents at the beginning of the section provides page numbers for the various countries. Approximately 7,800 periodicals are listed in this section, and the entries are similar to those in the United Kingdom section. Another section lists English publishers (both of newspapers and periodicals), along with the titles they produce.

A classified index is provided which divides periodicals into broad subject categories. A title index is not provided. *Willings* is a very handy directory since it lists both newspapers and periodicals virtually worldwide in a single volume. Its coverage of English periodicals is excellent. For periodicals of the rest of the world, though, this directory should be used in the same manner as the *Benn's* international volume. It provides a good listing of the major periodicals of many countries of the world, but in no way provides comprehensive international coverage as does *Ulrich's* or *The Serials Directory*.

Gale International Directory of Publications. Detroit: Gale Research.

The first edition of this directory has recently been published and is dated, "1989-90." It is intended to serve as an international companion volume to the *Gale Directory of Publications* (described later in this chapter) and thus contains selective listings of both periodicals and newspapers circulating primarily outside the United States and Canada. Entries for 2,748 periodicals from 132 countries are included in the first edition.

The arrangement of this directory is by country, then subdivided by cities and towns. Under each city or town is an alphabetical title list of the publications produced in that locale. Individual entries may include some, or all, of the following data elements: address, telephone and telex numbers, brief description, date established, frequency, language, format, advertising rates and closing deadline, contacts, United States source, ISSN, subscription price, and circulation. Three indexes are provided, one each for newspaper titles and periodical titles, and one combined alphabetical title and keyword index.

Since so few periodicals are included in this directory, be certain to describe its limitations when referring a patron to it. However, the advantage it does provide is that it lists, geographically, the periodicals and newspapers of individual nations and localities. The ultimate value of this directory cannot be determined, though, until it has been used in reference situations for an extended period of time.

The International Directory of Little Magazines & Small Presses. Edited by Len Fulton. Paradise, Calif.: Dustbooks.

First published in 1965 as the *Directory of Little Magazines*, this work annually provides a valuable service by listing small, and sometimes very obscure, magazines that may not be listed in other periodical directories. Basically, this directory contains entries for small presses (book publishers) and little magazines or periodicals. Magazine entries include:

Title, name of press, editor, address, and telephone number.

Type of material published.

Other comments by editor about recent contributions.

Year founded.

Price.

Average number of pages.

Production method.

Circulation.

Other information of interest to possible contributors.

There is a fairly detailed subject index, and a regional index arranged by state for United States publishers and arranged by country for publishers from other countries. In examining the regional index, it becomes apparent that perhaps three-fourths of the entries in this directory are for United States publishers. So, do not expect an exhaustive listing of foreign small presses and magazines. Although no total is provided, it appears that perhaps two thousand to three thousand periodicals are listed in this directory. This work could be described as a *Writer's Market* for small magazines and small presses. Much of the information included in the entries is provided for writers who are trying to find a publisher.

It is very important for serials reference staff to be familiar with this directory, since many of the periodicals listed here will be found in no other directory.

Sources of Serials. New York: R. R. Bowker.

This irreplaceable directory was first published in 1977, and updated with a second edition in 1981. There have been no further revisions published. The value of this directory is the fact that it lists, by publisher, serials produced worldwide. For each country, serials publishers are listed, along with the titles they publish (also providing frequency of publication notations and ISSNs). The addresses of the publishers are given, too. The second edition includes 65,000 publishers and corporate authors arranged under 180 countries. Listed are 96,600 serial titles. An alphabetical index of publishers is provided.

For a reference librarian, this work can be a lifesaver. In all too many cases, a requester may know the name of the publisher but not the name of the periodical for which they are searching. In some cases, a library patron may want to have a complete list of all the periodicals published by a certain company or organization. In these types of situations, *Sources of Serials* has been the main source to use. However, as with any directory, the older it gets, the less useful it is. Hopefully, Bowker will publish a revised edition soon.

In the meantime, if this source does not provide the needed information, other less comprehensive directories do provide some listings of serials by publisher. These works include *MIMP: Magazine Industry Market Place* (for United States magazines); *Bacon's Publicity Checker*, volume 1, *Magazines* (for American and Canadian magazines); *Business Publication Rates and Data; Newsletters in Print* (for United States and Canadian newsletters); *Hudson's Newsletter Directory* (for newsletters worldwide); and *Willings Press Guide* or *Benn's Media Directory: United Kingdom* (for English serials). All of these directories are described elsewhere in this chapter.

Periodical Directories Covering a Single Region or Country

Gale Directory of Publications. Detroit: Gale Research.

Over the past century, librarians have come to rely on the *Ayer Directory of Publications* as a primary source of current information regarding American newspapers and periodicals. In the 1980s, this publication has changed titles three times, first to *The IMS Ayer Directory of Publications*, then to *The IMS Directory of Publications*, and finally to the *Gale Directory of Publications*, effective with the 119th edition, 1987. Beginning with the 120th edition for 1988, this directory is being published in two volumes, instead of the traditional single volume.

Regardless of title, this annual publication continues to be one of the standard sources for information about newspapers of the United States and Canada. (See chapter 10 for a description of its newspaper aspects.) Since this directory has been readily available in libraries for so long, many have come to depend on this publication for American periodicals information, too. The *Gale Directory* can be used for this purpose, but it should be realized that this directory does not attempt to present an exhaustive listing of periodicals, and that it is not the best source for the most comprehensive listing of periodicals.

The *Gale Directory* provides coverage of the United States (including Puerto Rico) and Canada. The 1988 edition lists a total of 12,309 periodicals (11,229 from the United States, 1,077 from Canada, and three from Puerto Rico). This total, then, is just a fraction of the 65,000 titles listed in *The Standard Periodical Directory* (described next in this chapter). The publishers have even stated that the *Gale Directory* "is not intended to be a compilation of anything and everything in print at some moment in time."[5] So, users must understand that this is not a complete list of all United States periodicals in print. This message doesn't always get across, though. Evidence of this is that the *Statistical Abstract of the United States* provides the numbers from this directory to be the total number of periodicals in the United States.[6] It should be noted that the new publishers of this directory do intend to increase the number of periodicals and newspapers covered.[7]

However, for the periodicals that are covered, this is a very useful and reliable directory. Volume 1, the *Catalog of Publications*, is the main body of this work. This section is arranged by state and city (or by province and city). For each state or province, general census and directory-type data are provided. Each city or town is described, also, including population and location. Coordinates are given in order to locate each locale on maps within the directory. The newspapers and periodicals of the city or town are then listed in one alphabetical arrangement by title. Periodical entries include the following items:

Title, editor, publisher, address and phone number.

Format.

Year established.

Frequency.

Brief description in a few words.

Subscription price.

Advertising rates.

Circulation.

Some of the most valuable features of this directory can be found in the extensive cross-reference sections located in volume 2, *Indexes and Maps.* The "Index to Classifications" is basically an index to the cross-reference sections, indicating page numbers for the hundreds of different classifications employed. Two different sections group agricultural publications, first by state or province and then according to subject classification. Other cross-reference sections include:

College publications.

Foreign language publications.

Jewish publications.

Women's publications (new with the 1988 edition).

Hispanic publications (new with the 1988 edition).

Fraternal publications.

Religious publications.

Newsletters.

Magazines of general circulation.

Daily periodicals.

Many of these sections interfile newspaper and periodical entries, just as they are interfiled in the main body of the work. Serials reference personnel should become quite familiar with these sections, since they can answer many queries. Of special interest is the section covering foreign language publications. These, of course, are foreign language newspapers and periodicals that are published in the United States and Canada.

An alphabetical title and keyword index of each publication listed completes this directory. Beginning with the 1988 edition, recently discontinued titles are listed in this index, and this is the only place in the directory where such titles are listed. Another enhancement is that each entry in volume 1 is now numbered, thus making access from the various indexes in volume 2 much easier. Also, a supplement and an updating service have been instituted.

The *Gale Directory of Publications* is an outstanding source, although somewhat limited for periodicals information.

The Standard Periodical Directory. New York: Oxbridge Communications.

The Standard Periodical Directory was first published in an edition dated 1964/65, and new editions are now being produced annually. The eleventh edition, 1988, provides data on 65,000 periodicals from the United States and Canada. According to the publishers, this is the most comprehensive directory of American and Canadian periodicals available. For the purposes of this directory, "periodical" is applied to any serial published at least every two years. So, annuals are listed, and there is a separate section devoted to newspapers.

The entries are arranged into 239 broad subject areas that are spelled out in the table of contents. A subject index provides cross references from terms that are not used to terms that are used. Individual entries provide a wealth of data, including:

Title and previous title (if any).

Publisher's name, address, and phone number.

Sponsoring group (if any).

Editor and other important staff members.

Short description of editorial content.

Availability of book reviews.

Where indexed or abstracted.

Year established.

Frequency.

Subscription and single copy prices.

Circulation.

Production information.

Page rate for black and white advertising.

Availability in other formats.

ISSN.

As with all directories, not every entry includes complete information. *The Standard Periodical Directory* states that this is "due to failure of the periodical to provide it."[8] In some cases, where the data can only be supplied by the publisher, then incomplete entries can be blamed on the response from the periodical. This directory, on the other hand, claims to provide indexing and abstracting information, which is of great significance from a reference standpoint. However, such information is given in relatively few entries. For instance, the 1988 edition's entry for *Business Week* shows no sources where this periodical is abstracted or indexed.[9] This can be confusing or misleading to someone not familiar with periodicals or with that particular widely-indexed publication. Unless relatively complete abstracting and indexing information can be provided for all periodicals listed, then this "feature" should be eliminated from this directory.

The primary source of current information and updating is a questionnaire that Oxbridge mails out to all periodicals listed in the previous edition. Various other sources of information are employed to keep their files up to date. In comparison with the previous edition, the 1988 edition had the following changes:

6,100 new titles were added.

29,000 entries were revised.

5,700 periodicals that ceased publication or could not be located
   were deleted.[10]

Librarians should be aware that the information about government publications in *The Standard Periodical Directory* is updated every two years in contrast to the yearly updating of information about the other periodicals in this directory.[11] So, this would not be the best source of information regarding government periodicals (see chapter 6 for other suggestions).

In summary, *The Standard Periodical Directory* is, by its own claim, the most comprehensive source for data about periodicals published in the United States and Canada. It lists many publications that are not found elsewhere. Thus, it serves as a reliable complement and backup to the international directories such as *Ulrich's* and *The Serials Directory*.

The National Directory of Magazines. New York: Oxbridge Communications.
   The first edition of this directory, which the publishers plan to issue annually, was published in 1988 with the claim of being the "largest single source of information available on the American magazine industry."[12] Produced by the same company that publishes *The Standard Periodical Directory*, this publication seems to be slanted toward the smaller library market. The working definition of "magazine" for this directory includes tabloids but does not include newsletters. Journals are also excluded, except for those that accept advertising and appear more frequently than four times a year. In the first edition, the scope was limited to United States magazines, but it is anticipated that Canadian magazines will be included in future editions. Although the total number of titles is not given, the "listings" section in the first edition is 673 pages with approximately twenty entries on each page.

The individual title listings are arranged under general subject headings. They include the publisher's name, address, telephone number, ISSN, circulation data, and advertising information, among other data elements. Most listings also provide a brief description of the periodical. A title index is included.

Since this directory is produced from the same database used to produce *The Standard Periodical Directory*, much of the information is duplicated. However, it is unlikely that a single library will purchase both of these directories. Taken by itself, *The National Directory of Magazines* is quite an impressive work and does seem to live up to its subtitle, *The Most Comprehensive Guide to American Magazines.*

The Working Press of the Nation. Volume 2, *Magazine Directory*; Volume 5, *Internal Publications Directory.* Chicago: National Research Bureau.

The Working Press of the Nation is an annual directory, published in five volumes. Volume 1 is a newspaper directory (see chapter 10). Volume 4 is a directory of feature writers and photographers (see chapter 13), and volume 3 is a radio and television directory. Volume 2, *Magazine Directory*, lists more than 5,400 United States magazines in its 1989 edition. All five volumes of *The Working Press* are "designed for persons needing information for contacting media personnel or for mailing list compilation, media selection or market analysis."[13] The entries are arranged into broad publication types ("farm and agricultural," "consumer," etc.), and then subdivided into specific subjects. An alphabetical title index and a cross index of subjects are provided.

This directory strives to present comprehensive listings for the magazines covered. All of the normal directory-type information is given (publisher, address, phone number, year established, frequency, etc.). In addition, the following special elements are provided:

Types of publicity materials accepted.

Freelance pay scale.

Fairly detailed reader profile.

Fairly detailed description of editorial content.

Deadlines for submissions.

These special data elements are what add significance to this directory.

Volume 5, *Internal Publications Directory*, lists internal and external publications of more than 2,800 United States companies, government agencies, clubs, and other groups. Internal publications of companies, also known as house organs, are notoriously difficult to track down. Some may be found listed in general periodical or newsletter directories. This *Working Press* volume is devoted to internal publications, so it should always be consulted in such a search.

The main body of volume 5 arranges the listings by the sponsors of the publication. Thus, one can look under "General Motors" and find a list of their house organs. Indexes are provided that list the publications by title and by industry. A third index lists sponsors by editorial interest.

The complete listings in the main body of the work include:

Sponsor name, address, and phone number.

Industry affiliation.

Publication name and editor.

Frequency.

Size.

Publicity materials accepted.

Freelance pay scale.

Deadline for submissions.

Encyclopedia of Associations. Association Periodicals. Detroit: Gale Research.
    The first edition of this work was issued in the following three separate volumes during 1987 and 1988:

Volume 1 — *Business, Finance, Industry and Trade*

Volume 2 — *Science, Medicine, and Technology*

Volume 3 — *Social Sciences, Education, and Humanities*

Each volume covers approximately four thousand periodicals. The scope of this publication includes all serials produced by national organizations of the United States. The arrangement, in each volume, is by subject keywords. Individual entries include serial title, organization name, address, phone number, brief description, special features, special issues published, indexing information, editor(s), year first published, frequency, price, ISSN, circulation, and availability in other formats. Two indexes are included, one of associations and another of keywords.

MIMP: Magazine Industry Market Place. New York: R. R. Bowker.
    First published in 1980 and updated annually, *MIMP* is a directory for the entire American periodical industry. It is not strictly a directory of periodicals, although nearly half of this work is given over to that type of data. The remainder of the volume provides information of interest to those who publish periodicals. Such information includes lists of advertising agencies, lists of companies providing publishing services and supplies, and a lengthy "Names and Numbers" section providing addresses and phone numbers for individuals and companies in the industry.

The first section of the 1987 edition of *MIMP* lists over 3,500 United States magazines that have a circulation of at least 5,000. Entries for individual periodicals include the usual directory-type information, such as publishing company, address and phone number, along with the names and titles of key staff members. Advertising rates are given, as well as a short description of the publication. This section includes two indexes, one which classifies the titles by type ("consumer," "farm," etc.), and the other by subject category. A list of recent cessations and a list of recent mergers and acquisitions are also provided.

The second section of the work is comprised of a list of publishers who publish three or more periodicals, along with the titles of those periodicals. This can be very helpful in that the major, comprehensive work that gives this type of listing, *Sources of Serials* (described earlier in this chapter), has not been updated in many years.

Another section of *MIMP* is a directory of micropublishers.

Bacon's Publicity Checker. Volume 1, *Magazines.* Chicago: Bacon's Publishing.

This annual directory is intended for the public relations market and provides information suited to that audience. The 1988 edition lists over 7,200 American and Canadian business, trade, industrial, professional, farm, and consumer magazines. They are arranged into 195 market classifications and subgroups. Volume 2 of this directory lists newspapers (see chapter 10). Only those magazines known to use publicity materials are listed. The stated purpose is to simplify work in preparing news release lists. Each entry provides the address and phone number of the publication and also includes specific information on the kinds of publicity releases accepted and used.

Also included is an alphabetical title index and a list of multiple magazine publishers with the titles they produce.

Gebbie Press All-In-One Directory, edited by Amalia Gebbie. New Paltz, N.Y.: Gebbie Press.

First published in 1972, this annual directory is intended for the use of public relations personnel. It covers in detail ten major fields of media in the United States available to the public relations practitioner. These fields include television and radio stations, newspapers, general magazines, business and trade periodicals, and farm publications. (The newspaper aspects will be described in chapter 10.) Business "papers," the trade press, farm publications, and general consumer magazines comprise the four broad categories in the first section (or "White Pages") of the directory. The entries are further subdivided by more specific categories. Data in the entries include:

Title, editor, address and phone number.

Frequency.

Circulation.

Description of readership of the publication.

A separate title index is provided at the beginning of the "White Pages" section.

This directory is a bit confusing to use despite its claim that it is "so clear and simple that directions for using the book are superfluous."[14] The value of this directory stems from its comprehensiveness in providing public relations personnel with a directory of thousands of media outlets to which press releases may be sent.

Benn's Media Directory: United Kingdom. Tonbridge, U.K.: Benn Business
    Information Services.

This is the companion volume to *Benn's Media Directory: International* edition (described earlier in this chapter). The United Kingdom edition covers England, Wales, Scotland, Northern Ireland, the Isle of Man, and the Channel Islands. This volume serves as a newspaper and a periodical directory as well as a guide to broadcast and electronic media. (The newspaper aspects will be described in chapter 10.)

The 1988 edition lists over eight thousand periodicals in two separate sections. One small section lists consumer magazines that are distributed free of charge, while the other, much larger section lists all other periodicals. The entries include the normal directory-type data including name of publishing company and address, along with a description of the publication and its readership. All the periodical titles from both sections are included in a subject index that precedes these two sections. Also, a master index of all publications (both periodicals and newspapers) listed in this work is provided.

Along with *Willings Press Guide*, this volume provides an in-depth, authoritative listing of British periodicals.

Canadian Serials Directory, 1987. 3d ed. Edited by Gordon Ripley. Toronto:
    Reference Press.

Published irregularly (the second edition was published in the mid-1970s, and the fourth edition is planned for 1989), this work lists most types of serials, including periodicals, daily newspapers, and annual publications published in Canada. The main body of the work is an alphabetical list of serials, providing name of editor and publisher, address, frequency of publication, year established, ISSN, indexing information, and subscription price. A subject index and a publisher index are included. Although the exact number of entries is not given, this directory appears to cover approximately 2,500 to 3,000 serials.

Current British Journals, 1986. 4th ed. By David P. Woodworth and Christine M. Goodair. Boston Spa, U.K.: British Library Document Supply Centre.

This directory is published irregularly, with the first edition having appeared in 1970 under the title, *Guide to Current British Journals.* Approximately 7,500 British periodicals of all types, not just academic or scholarly journals as the title would seem to indicate, are included in the 1986 edition. The title listings are broadly classified under the Universal Decimal Classification system numbers. Individual entries include year of first issue, frequency of publications, publisher, address, telephone number, subscription price, ISSN, and a very brief description. A title index and a subject index are provided.

There are numerous other periodical directories that cover the publications of a single region or country. A selected list of these publications, arranged by country, follows. Most of these directories are published in the predominant language of the nation, although many of the non-English publications have introductions and headings translated into English.

Australia:	*Australian Periodicals in Print.* Melbourne: D. W. Thorpe.
Brazil:	*Anuario Brasiliero de Midia.* São Paulo: Editora Meio & Mensagem.
China:	*China Press and Publishing Directory 1985.* Beijing: Modern Press.
East and West Germany:	*Stamm Leitfaden durch Presse und Werbung.* Essen, W. Germany: Stamm-Verlag GMBH.
France:	*Annuaire de la Presse de Publicite et de la Communication.* Paris: Ecron Publicite.
Italy:	*Guida della Stampa Periodica Italiana.* Rome: Unione Stampa Periodica Italiana.
Japan:	*Zasshi Shimbun Sokatarogu.* Tokyo: Media Risachi Senta.
Netherlands:	*Handboek van de Nederlandse Pers en Publiciteit: Gedrukte Media.* Schiedam: Nijgh Periodieken.
South Africa:	*Promadata, Promotion, Marketing & Advertising Data.* Rosebank: Clarion Communications Media.

Directories exist for other nations and regions, too. In addition, there are other directories for some of the countries listed above. Some, though, have not been revised for many years. The best source for identifying these directories is Eugene P. Sheehy's *Guide to Reference Books*, tenth edition, 1986 (Chicago: American Library Association).

Newsletter Directories

Oxbridge Directory of Newsletters. New York: Oxbridge Communications.
This directory was originally titled, *The Standard Directory of Newsletters* and began publication, on an irregular basis, in 1971. Recently, it has begun publishing on an annual basis. Oxbridge is a well-known name in the field of serials directories, being the publisher of *The Standard Periodical Directory* (described earlier in this chapter) and other directories. This newsletter directory, in its 1988 edition, contains entries for fifteen thousand newsletters published in the United States and Canada. They are arranged into 167 subject categories. Individual title entries provide the following information:

Title, publishing company, address, and phone number.

Editor, publisher, and other important members of the publishing staff.

Short description of editorial content.

Availability of book reviews.

Year established.

Frequency.

Subscription and single copy price.

Circulation and distribution of readership.

Physical size.

Method of printing.

Average number of pages.

Use of color.

Availability in other formats.

ISSN.

Primary readership.

A title index is included.
This directory claims to be the most comprehensive source for information about newsletters. In addition to subscription newsletters, both association and corporate newsletters are listed. With fifteen thousand entries, this directory has far more entries than any other directory devoted solely to newsletters. It should be noted, however, that most of the newsletters listed here are also listed in the *Standard Periodical Directory*. This observation is based on a sampling of titles from the indexes of the 1988 editions of these two directories.

Newsletters in Print. Detroit: Gale Research.

First published in 1966 as the *National Directory of Newsletters and Reporting Services*, and later as the *Newsletters Directory, Newsletters in Print* is Gale's entry into the newsletter directory field. The subtitle of this publication identifies its scope, *A Descriptive Guide to More Than 10,000 Subscription, Membership, and Free Newsletters, Bulletins, Digests, Updates, and Similar Serial Publications Issued in the United States and Canada and Available in Print or Online.*

The newsletter entries are arranged into thirty-two general subject categories. Three indexes are included, one of which is a title index, giving past, present, and alternate names of newsletters. Another index lists all publishers appearing in the directory, and a comprehensive subject index lists nearly four thousand terms and cross-references for searching the newsletters. The entries include title, publisher, editor, address, phone number, intended audience, types of illustrations, frequency, year first published, size, price, circulation, ISSN, online availability, and a description, in a few sentences, of the editorial content. Two separate sections list "Online Newsletters" and "Free Newsletters."

Supplements are issued as an update service between the published regular editions. At present, the frequency of publication of the regular edition and the supplements seems to be irregular or not yet established. The fourth edition was published to cover 1988-1989.

Hudson's Newsletter Directory. Rheinebeck, N.Y.: Hudson's Newsletter Directory.

This directory began publication in 1977 and was formerly titled *The Newsletter Yearbook Directory*. Newsletters published worldwide are included, but this is not an exhaustive directory. Although the exact number of entries is not provided, there appear to be somewhere near four thousand titles listed in the 1988 edition. Only newsletters available by subscription are listed. All information in the entries has been verified by the listed publishers.

The main portion of the directory is arranged by general subject categories. Entries include:

Title, publishing company, address, and phone number.

Editor, and/or publisher.

Subscription rate.

Frequency.

Types of press releases that the publisher is interested in receiving.

Year first published.

Availability in "electronic edition."

An alphabetical title index and a geographic index are included. A separate section lists publishers of multiple newsletters along with the titles they publish. "Newsletters: A Continuing History" takes up forty pages and provides a wealth of background material about newsletters.

Although most of the entries are for American newsletters, a number of publications from other countries are also included. Since the *Oxbridge Directory of Newsletters* and *Newsletters in Print* cover only the United States and Canada, this is a prime source for searching international newsletters that are not listed in any of the international periodical directories. It is also of use to public relations people who are trying to identify publications that will accept and use their materials.

Periodical Directories in Specific Subject or Interest Areas

An entire book would be required to list and describe the multitude of periodical directories and bibliographies that fall into this category. Many of these directories are retrospective listings of periodicals that have been published through the years covering a certain subject or interest. An example of such a directory is *American Indian and Alaska Native Newspapers and Periodicals* (New York: Greenwood Press), a three volume set that lists such publications from 1826 through 1985. There have been a large number of such directories published. Since the focus of this chapter is on current information, these retrospective directories will not be included. The current directories included here comprise a selected list of such works, and account for just a portion of such publications available.

MLA Directory of Periodicals: A Guide to Journals and Series in Languages and Literatures. New York: Modern Language Association of America.

This directory, updated biennially, is a companion volume to the *MLA International Bibliography* and contains information on all journals and series in that bibliography's master list. The *MLA Directory* is published in a clothbound volume, which lists over 3,100 titles, and in a paperbound volume, which lists only titles published in the United States and Canada, approximately one-third of the total. The publications eligible for inclusion are in the subject areas of language, literature and folklore.

The title entries are listed in alphabetical order, and the standard directory data such as address and phone number are given. Other information included is:

Availability in microform.

Availability of advertising.

Editorial description.

Detailed requirements for submission of manuscripts.

Indexes to subjects, sponsoring organizations, editorial personnel, and languages are provided.

Annotated Bibliographies of Serials: A Subject Approach. Series editor, Norman Frankel. New York: Greenwood Press.

Greenwood Press is currently in the midst of an ambitious project to produce annotated bibliographies of serials in various subject areas. Some of the titles in this series already published are:

Agricultural and Animal Science Journals and Serials: An Analytical Guide

Dentistry Journals and Serials: An Analytical Guide

Economics Journals and Serials: An Analytical Guide

Education Journals and Serials: An Analytical Guide

Financial Journals and Serials: An Analytical Guide to Accounting, Banking, Finance, Insurance, and Investment Periodicals

History Journals and Serials: An Analytical Guide

Library and Information Science Journals and Serials: An Analytical Guide

Philosophy Journals and Serials: An Analytical Guide

English language serials from around the world are included. Entries in the books of this series provide the usual directory-type information, including indications of where the publication is indexed or abstracted. An extensive annotation of a paragraph or two is given for each serial. Various types of indexes are provided in each volume.

Books and Serials in Print. New York: R. R. Bowker.

R. R. Bowker has taken advantage of its various bibliographic databases to produce a continuing series of large, current subject bibliographies. Some of the publications in this series are:

Business and Economics Books and Serials in Print

Computer Books and Serials in Print

Law Books and Serials in Print

Medical and Health Care Books and Serials in Print

Religious and Inspirational Books and Serials in Print

Scientific and Technical Books and Serials in Print

The thousands of serials titles in each of these directories are selected from the database used to produce *Ulrich's International Periodicals Directory.* Entries are arranged into subject categories and look the same as the entries in *Ulrich's.* Title indexes are provided.

Business Organizations, Agencies, and Publications Directory. Detroit: Gale Research.

This two-volume work, formerly titled *Business Organizations and Agencies Directory*, contains approximately 24,000 entries covering specific types of organizations, agencies, or publications of interest to the business community. The entries for individual national and international associations provide, when available, the titles of the publications of that association, along with the frequency of publication. Another section lists approximately one thousand general business and finance periodicals, trade journals, and government business periodicals, giving the publisher address and phone number. Over 1,300 newsletters are listed and described in another separate section.

Business Publication Rates and Data. Wilmette, Ill.: Standard Rate & Data Service.

This directory is actually a monthly periodical published in three parts. Its main purpose is to give detailed information about advertising in the publications listed. The first and largest part is comprised mostly of entries for individual American business publications (practically all of them being periodicals), arranged into market groups. Although no total is given, there appear to be about two thousand or three thousand entries. Each entry contains publisher information and a list of personnel and representatives or branch offices. The remainder of each lengthy entry provides extremely detailed advertising and circulation information. The other two parts provide data on classified and direct response ad rates. A small section of international business publications is included as is a section that lists publishers of multiple business publications. Title indexes are available.

Although this directory is complex and difficult to use, it does provide a wealth of information. A similar monthly publication from the same publisher is *Consumer Magazine and Agri-Media Rates and Data.* This publication covers general magazines and farm publications.

Catholic Press Directory. Rockville Centre, N.Y.: Catholic Press Association.

First published in 1923, this directory covers American and Canadian Catholic newspapers, periodicals, and general publishers. In the 1988 edition, the magazines section contains entries for approximately four hundred to five hundred periodicals. A separate section lists newsletters. Listings in the periodicals and newsletters sections are alphabetical. These entries include the publisher's name, address, and phone number, as well as a sentence or two describing the publication. The key personnel of the publication are listed. A separate section lists periodicals in languages other than English. An index of titles is included. The lengthy newspapers section is arranged geographically. The publications listed here, although referred to as "newspapers," would actually be handled as periodicals in most libraries.

The Directory of Literary Magazines. New York: Coordinating Council of
Literary Magazines.

This small annual directory provides information about American literary
magazines. Over four hundred titles are listed in the 1988-89 edition.
Addresses, phone numbers, and other basic information is given, along with a
description of the content of the magazines. An index by state is provided.

Directory of the College Student Press in America. New York: Oxbridge.

This directory, which was first published in an edition dated 1967/68 and
updated irregularly, currently lists over six thousand newspapers, magazines,
and other serials published on United States college and university campuses.
The arrangement of this work is geographical by states, and then subdivided
into an alphabetical listing of the colleges and universities within the state.
General information about the listed institutions and specific data about the
publications are provided.

*Guide to the American Ethnic Press: Slavic and East European Newspapers
and Periodicals.* By Lubomyr R. Wynar. Kent, Ohio: Center for the
Study of Ethnic Publications, 1986.

Published at Kent State University, this valuable guide lists 580 publications for seventeen different Slavic and East European ethnic groups. In
addition to giving addresses and phone numbers, the entries provide a translated title (if the original is not in English), sponsor, language(s), a brief
annotation, and a list of libraries with holdings of the publication. Title and
geographical indexes are included. A statistical analysis of individual Slavic
and East European presses is also provided.

The Oxbridge Directory of Ethnic Periodicals. Edited by Patricia Hagood.
New York: Oxbridge Communications, 1979.

Approximately 3,500 newspapers, magazines, journals, newsletters,
bulletins, directories, yearbooks, and other publications published in the
United States and Canada are included. The listings for these titles are
arranged into some seventy different ethnic group categories. The standard
directory information is given, plus a short description of the publication.
Although published in 1979, this is the most recent directory that attempts
comprehensive coverage of this field. This work can still be used with the
knowledge that much of the information is no longer current.

*Encyclopedic Directory of Ethnic Newspapers and Periodicals in the United
States.* 2d ed. By Lubomyr R. Wynar and Anna T. Wynar. Littleton,
Co.: Libraries Unlimited, 1976.

This work is also no longer current, but still can be of some help, since
there are very few more current directories in this field (see preceding two
entries). This directory lists 977 publications. Sixty-three ethnic groups are
covered, and the entries are arranged into fifty-one sections. The American
Indian press and Black American press are not covered. Entries include the

title of the publication (and translation if the title is not in English), sponsor, address, phone number, language(s), and a brief annotation. The usual directory-type information is also provided. A title index is provided as is a statistical analysis of ethnic publications.

Other Reference Works Containing Information on Periodicals

Writer's Market. Cincinnati, Ohio: Writer's Digest Books.

Many are familiar with this annual publication as the primary guide to American markets to which writers may sell their material. Although a portion of each year's volume is devoted to book publishers, the bulk of the work is comprised of descriptions of periodicals. Most of the entries are for United States publications, however some Canadian periodicals are also included.

The sections covering periodicals are grouped into two large categories, "Consumer Publications," and "Trade, Technical and Professional Journals." Each of these sections is further subdivided into more specific subject categories. The entries for periodicals include all of the expected directory-type data, plus a description of the editorial content. Extensive information is provided regarding editorial preferences and requirements for manuscript submissions. A title index is included.

Although this is not an exhaustive listing of currently published American periodicals, it is an extensive directory of those periodicals that accept manuscript submissions from freelance writers. As such it is an indispensable reference work. Since it is already part of the reference collection in most American libraries, *Writer's Market* can therefore be exploited as a readily available, albeit incomplete, American periodical directory.

Directory of Publishing Opportunities in Journals and Periodicals. Chicago: Marquis Academic Media.

This directory was first published in 1971 as the *Directory of Scholarly and Research Publishing Opportunities*, and the most recent revision was published in 1981. More than 3,900 specialized and professional journals are arranged into seventy-three specific fields of interest. International coverage is provided, but only publications that accept manuscripts in English are included. The individual entries include the addresses and phone numbers, along with the following:

Name of sponsoring group.

Description of contents or purposes of the periodical.

Description of intended audience.

Detailed information regarding manuscript requirements, submission, and disposition.

Four indexes are included listing titles, subjects, sponsoring organizations, and editorial staff.

The Europa Year Book. London: Europa Publications.

This standard reference work, published annually, is comprised mostly of surveys of the nations of the world. Each survey contains a section titled, "The Press." Within that section is a list of selected periodicals of that nation. The address of each publication is included along with a very brief description.

The World of Learning. London: Europa Publications.

This annual reference work is produced by the publishers of *The Europa Year Book* and is arranged in a similar manner. Major institutions such as academies, learned societies, research institutes, libraries, museums, universities, and colleges of each nation are listed. These listings include addresses, telephone numbers, and other information. The first section of this work surveys international organizations dealing with various aspects of learning.

Of importance to serials reference staff is that the publications of the various institutions are listed in their entries. Only the titles of the publications of the institutions are provided, with no indication of frequency or year first published. Periodicals that are available for exchange are marked as such. An index of institutions is provided. Although this is not an exhaustive listing of institutions or of their publications, the *World of Learning* can provide some answers to questions regarding the serials produced by these institutions.

Encyclopedia of Associations. Detroit: Gale Research.

This multi-volume annual publication is a standard reference work. The 1989 edition lists and describes over 25,000 national and international organizations. The individual entries include a list of the serial publications of the association being described. Frequency of publication for each serial is noted. A title and keyword index for the names of the associations is included. A geographic index and an executive index are also provided.

A companion publication to the *Encyclopedia of Associations* is the three volume *Encyclopedia of Associations. Association Periodicals* (see description earlier in this chapter).

National Trade and Professional Associations of the United States. Washington, D.C.: Columbia Books.

This annual directory, first published in 1966, lists approximately 6,250 national trade associations, labor unions, and professional, scientific, or technical societies. The main body of the work is an alphabetical listing of these organizations. Each entry contains a listing of the publications of the association, along with the frequency of those publications. Subject, geographic, and acronym indexes are included.

National Avocational Organizations. Washington, D.C.: Columbia Books.

This annual directory is a companion directory to *National Trade and Professional Organizations of the United States*. Listed are 2,500 national organizations serving the recreational and avocational interests of Americans. The individual organization entries include a list of the publications of the organization and their frequencies. Subject, geographic, and acronym indexes are included.

Yearbook of International Organizations. Edited by the Union of International Associations. Munich: K. G. Saur.

Originally published in 1908 as *Annuaire de la Vie Internationale*, this annual reference work has traveled a long history of changes to arrive at its current format of three volumes per edition. An attempt is made to cover all international organizations. For serials reference staff, the first volume, *Organization Descriptions and Index*, is of prime importance. In this volume are the entries for the individual associations. Listed in the entries are the publications of the associations, along with the frequencies of those publications. An extensive name and keyword index of the organizations is included in this volume.

Corpus Almanac & Canadian Sourcebook. Don Mills, Ont.: Corpus Information Services.

This is an annual almanac of information about Canada. One section is devoted to a listing of periodicals published in Canada. Although no total is provided, it appears that approximately 1,500 publications are included. They are arranged into six broad subject categories, and then subdivided into specific subjects. Entries include the publisher's name, address, and phone number.

Miscellaneous Sources of Periodical Information

Magazines for Libraries. By Bill Katz and Linda Sternberg Katz. New York: R. R. Bowker.

First published in 1969 and updated approximately every three to four years, *Magazines for Libraries* has become a standard reference work. The fifth edition, 1986, lists some 6,500 periodicals that have been chosen as the best and most useful publications for the average primary or secondary school library, public, academic, or special library. Over one hundred consultants were responsible for the selection of magazines they believed to be basic in their fields of subject expertise. Titles were selected to include:

General periodicals of interest to the layperson.

Major English language research journals sponsored by societies in the United States, Canada, and Great Britain.

Some high-quality commercial publications commonly found in research libraries.

Several other determining factors were also considered in making the selections.

The entries are arranged by broad subject categories and include the standard directory information such as address and phone number along with an indication of the type(s) of library for which the periodical is best suited. Each entry also provides a one-paragraph annotation, describing the periodical. An alphabetical title index is provided.

This work can be of great help to reference personnel. If, for instance, a reader would like to know what the recommended magazines about films and filmmaking are, then the "Films" section provides an answer. Over eighty such periodicals, complete with descriptions, are listed. The introduction to this section also mentions other guides to film periodicals. Two basic indexes to film literature are noted, and a brief title listing of basic periodicals in this field, divided by types of libraries to which they are suited, is also included.

Magazines for Libraries is the best overall source for lists of current recommended periodicals in various fields.

Magazines for School Libraries. By Bill Katz. New York: R. R. Bowker, 1987.

This directory, published for the first time in 1987, is a direct spin-off from *Magazines for Libraries* (see preceding entry). For this work, 1,300 periodicals were selected from the 6,500 periodicals contained in the original work. The titles listed here are suitable for the various levels of school libraries (elementary, junior high, and high school). The entries and format are virtually identical to *Magazines for Libraries* with the exception that the noted audiences will be either elementary/junior high, high school, or school professional. Listings are arranged into broad subject categories. An index of titles and an index of titles by audience are included.

Librarians' Handbook: A Guide to Periodicals/Serials. Birmingham, Ala.: EBSCO Subscription Services.

Of the catalogs available from the various subscription agencies, this guide from EBSCO is the most comprehensive and useful for reference work. Acquisitions librarians are familiar with this annual publication as a list of serials currently available through EBSCO. It is not stated how many titles are actually listed, but the main body of the work where the title entries are found in alphabetical order is about one thousand pages of fine print. The entries include title, nation of origin, frequency, ISSN, where indexed or abstracted, EBSCO title number, and price (when ordered through EBSCO). Notes indicating publishing characteristics (such as "Vol 43 published in 86," or, "Publ Mar Jun Sep Dec") are provided. Publications that have ceased, changed titles, or temporarily suspended publication are listed with such notations. A subject index is included. Other normal directory-type information such as addresses and phone numbers are *not* provided in this guide.

In using this guide, beware of the alphabetization of the title entries. Words such as "and," "of," and "for" (and their equivalents in other languages) are generally not considered in the alphabetizing of entries. As an example, the entry for the *Journal of Studies in Technical Careers* appears before the entry for the *Journal for the Study of The New Testament.*[15]

Although this work does not provide much information about the titles listed, it can be quite useful. In many cases, the *Librarians' Handbook* will be the only major serials reference source that will list a particular publication. When it is determined that a periodical is indeed being published in a certain nation, then a more in-depth search of other specialized sources can be undertaken in an attempt to discover more information.

The *Librarians' Handbook* is updated by the bimonthly *EBSCO Bulletin of Serials Changes.*

Other Formats and Unusual Sources
of Periodical Information

All of the sources of directory-type information for periodicals described thus far have been printed works. Just as in other areas of publishing, online and CD-ROM applications are making an impact here. Bowker has been the leader in offering its serials database in various non-print formats. The Bowker serials database is available in a microfiche set and is also available on CD-ROM under the title *Ulrich's Plus*. Finally, the database is available online through Dialog Information Services and through Bibliographic Retrieval Services. Both the CD-ROM and online versions open up a new vista of searching possibilities that have not been available in the printed directories. *The Serials Directory*, published by EBSCO, is also available in CD-ROM format.

The MARC serial records that are available in bibliographic databases, most notably OCLC, do provide a minimum of directory-type information. One can usually establish from the MARC record the publisher's name and address. See chapter 14 for a more complete explanation of the MARC serials record.

The most ubiquitous type of directory known, the telephone directory, can be used to locate periodical information. Often, a periodical cannot be located in any of the normal periodical directories, even though the publisher and city or country of publication are known. Searching through phone books in such cases often will yield an address and telephone number for the publisher.

Catalogs of micropublishers such as University Microfilms International will provide significant amounts of periodical directory-type data. More information about these publishers and their catalogs is provided in chapter 7.

Although the focus of this chapter has been on current periodical directories, it should be noted that a retrospective collection of periodical directories can be very valuable from a reference standpoint. Often, the information about periodical cessations, title changes, mergers, etc., never makes it to the cataloging record. In these cases, cessation notes, or other such notations, in retrospective editions of *Ulrich's* or another directory may be the only record of such a change. Indeed, a directory entry may be the only record that a periodical actually existed, especially when a cataloging record either does not exist or cannot be located. For these and other reasons, libraries should strive to maintain retrospective sets of periodical directories.

Identifying Other Sources of Periodical
Directory Information

The directories described in this chapter comprise a selected list, rather than an exhaustive list, of such publications. Other directories can be identified by using the previously mentioned *Guide to Reference Books*, tenth edition, by Eugene P. Sheehy (Chicago: American Library Association, 1986), and *Directories in Print* (Detroit: Gale Research). The following description is of a reference work that may also be of help.

Periodical Directories and Bibliographies. Edited by Gary C. Tarbert. Detroit: Gale Research, 1987.

The coverage of this work is described in its subtitle, *An Annotated Guide to Approximately 350 Directories, Bibliographies, and Other Sources of Information about English-Language Periodicals, from 1850 to the Present, including Newspapers, Journals, Magazines, Newsletters, Yearbooks, and Other Serial Publications.* The publisher or editor has chosen to use the word "periodical" to refer to various types of serials, even though the term "serial" is the generally accepted term.

This source can be used to identify some of the more obscure directories that are currently available or that may help in searching for information about older publications. The entries are listed in alphabetical order by title. A complete entry may contain the following data: publisher, address, telephone number, arrangement, pages, frequency, price, editor, publication date, and other information. However, the entries are extremely uneven, and key data elements are often missing. For instance, a publication date is usually provided for directories that were published once. For on-going publications such as *Ulrich's* or *The Standard Periodical Directory*, however, their current frequency of publication is provided. But there is no indication of when these directories were first published. Other entries are so brief as to be virtually useless. As an example, entry number 293 is for *Press Intelligence Directory*, and the only information given is that the publisher is, or was, Press Intelligence, Inc., of Washington, D.C. There is no indication of whether this is a current directory or if it was published seventy-five years ago. There is also no indication of this directory's coverage, or any other information. A subject index is included in this book.

Future editions, if published, will surely rectify some of its problems. Even with its flaws, a researcher or librarian may still want to consult this work to be certain that all pertinent sources have been checked. For the majority of current periodical information searches, however, the sources that have already been described in this chapter should be sufficient.

Notes

[1] *Ulrich's International Periodicals Directory, 1988-89*, 27th ed. (New York: R. R. Bowker, 1988), vii.

[2] Richard H. Oosterom, editor, Bowker International Serials Database, letter to the author, 4 November 1987.

[3] *The Serials Directory*, 2d ed. (Birmingham, Ala.: EBSCO Publishing, 1987), vii.

[4] *Benn's Media Directory. International*, 136th ed. (Tonbridge, U.K.: Benn Business Information Services, 1988), A9.

[5]*Gale Directory of Publications, 1987*, 119th ed. (Detroit: Gale Research, 1987), vii.

[6]U.S. Bureau of the Census, *Statistical Abstract of the United States, 1988*, 108th ed. (Washington, D.C.: Government Printing Office, 1987), 528.

[7]Kay Gill, senior editor, Gale Research Company, letter to the author, 12 November 1987.

[8]*The Standard Periodical Directory, 1988*, 11th ed. (New York: Oxbridge Communications, 1988), unnumbered page in the "Instructions for Use of the Directory" section.

[9]Ibid., 146.

[10]Ibid., preface.

[11]Matt Manning, editor, *The Standard Periodical Directory*, letter to the author, September 1987.

[12]*The National Directory of Magazines*, 1st ed. (New York: Oxbridge Communications, 1988), unnumbered prefatory page.

[13]*Newspaper Directory, 1989*, 39th ed., vol. 1 of *Working Press of the Nation*. (Chicago: National Research Bureau, 1989), unnumbered page in the prefatory section.

[14]*Gebbie Press All-In-One Directory*, 17th ed. (New Paltz, N.Y.: Gebbie Press, 1988), unnumbered page in the prefatory section.

[15]*Librarians' Handbook*, 1988-1989 ed. (Birmingham, Ala.: EBSCO Subscription Services, 1988), 611.

4

Union Lists of Periodicals

Hundreds of thousands of different periodicals have been published since the *Journal des Savants*, the first periodical, was founded in 1665. With the huge number of publications involved, no single library can ever hope to collect more than a fraction of the total number of periodicals that have existed. Indeed, most libraries can only aspire to collect a relatively small number of periodicals. Selective collection of periodical titles is necessitated by budget and space considerations.

Therefore, most libraries only have available a limited selection of the periodicals that have been published. Likewise, on a current basis, even the largest libraries can afford to receive and preserve just a selected number of the periodicals being published at any time. No library, regardless of size, can have a complete collection of periodicals.

Also, the fact that a library has decided to collect a current periodical is no guarantee that a complete set of that publication will be available in that library. The job of acquiring, preserving, and maintaining a complete, unmutilated, set of a current periodical is one of the most difficult endeavors in librarianship. Any number of common occurrences makes this an almost impossible task. Issues may never be sent by the publisher, or they may get lost in the mail. In such cases, prompt claiming may result in the eventual receipt of the missing issues, but this process is not always successful. Once received by a library, an issue may have pages ripped out, or it may be stolen. Some issues get lost or misplaced in the library, while others just fall apart from constant use. In all of these instances, the library's collection of the periodical is then incomplete.

As abstracting and indexing services have proliferated in the past few decades, increasing numbers of periodicals have been provided with coverage. This, in turn, has produced a demand for periodicals that might otherwise never have been requested. It is the norm for most libraries, especially research and academic libraries, to provide indexing and abstracting services that cover substantially more periodicals than are kept in the library's collection. Online searching is now offered by even the smallest libraries (and to users not in libraries at all), compounding this situation. The lack of immediate access to indexed periodicals can be extremely frustrating for the library user.

The patron may spend hours searching through indexes for a particular subject and finally locate citations to articles that appear to be exactly what is needed. Upon consulting the library's serials catalog or a librarian, it then becomes apparent that the library does not have the periodicals needed. In other cases, a library user may pay a relatively large sum of money and receive the results of an online search, only to discover that most of the articles cited are from certain esoteric or obscure periodicals that are not held by the library. An even more exasperating situation is when the library has holdings of the periodical needed, but the specific issue is missing or the article has been ripped out. The patron, unless a seasoned researcher, will probably be greatly disappointed in all of these instances.

In cases such as these, the serials reference staffer should first confirm that the library does not have the periodical or issue required. Never take the word of the patron that, "I checked the serials catalog, and it's not there," or, "You have all the other issues except for the one I need." Retracing the patron's steps may uncover a mistake or misunderstanding on the part of the patron and actually turn up the needed item in the library. If a periodical or an issue of a periodical is not in the library's collection, then a likely next step is to identify other libraries with holdings of the publication. This is most often accomplished through the use of a serials union list.

Serials Union Lists

The primary function of a serials union list is to record the libraries in which sets of serials may be found. Such a union catalog "is a single listing of the combined serial holdings of two or more (usually) independent libraries."[1] In most cases, many types of serials will be included in a single union list. Generally, such union lists are not limited to periodicals. Although many union lists of serials cover publications in a certain subject area, the most prominent union lists are those that list the serial holdings of specific libraries, regardless of subject. Usually, the libraries included in a particular union list are related geographically. Union lists of serial holdings in libraries within a metropolitan area or within a state or multi-state region are quite common. National union lists are less common, with the last such major comprehensive printed list in the United States being the third edition, 1965, of the *Union List of Serials in Libraries of the United States and Canada* (see description later in this chapter). Current national union listing activities are generally taking place online, particularly with the OCLC system.

As stated, the main purpose of a serials union list is to provide a record of serial holdings in whatever libraries are included in the list. These union lists are the basis for resource sharing of such items between libraries. If the libraries included in the list are located close to each other, then it is possible to refer a patron to the library with the needed periodical. If the libraries are far apart, the union list allows for accurate interlibrary loan requests. There are other uses for union lists of serials, too. Some libraries use them as a source of serials cataloging data, while they are also used as collection development tools in many institutions. Often, libraries participating in a union list or consortium arrangement will divide subject responsibilities so that all the member libraries are not collecting the same serials. Also, weeding of serials collections can be based on the knowledge of the holdings of the other participating libraries.[2]

Serials union lists are an integral component of the American interlibrary loan system. When a library does not have a periodical in its collection, usually the next step is to identify another library holding that periodical. The reader can then be referred to that library, or an interlibrary loan request can be transmitted. Since libraries often restrict the loan of periodicals, interlibrary loan requests for periodical items will normally specify the particular article needed and will result in a photocopy of the article being supplied. An alternative to this process is to order a copy of the article from a document delivery service such as the Article Clearinghouse, provided by University Microfilms International, or the Genuine Article, a subsidiary of the Institute for Scientific Information (see chapter 7 for more about these services).

So, serials union lists are essential for interlibrary loan work. This is especially true in the United States due to the fact that there is not a central periodicals center that can be depended upon to maintain a large collection of periodicals and to provide document delivery services on a gigantic scale. Such a center does exist in Great Britain at the British Library Lending Division (BLLD). A serials collection of 140,000 titles is kept there, with 54,000 current subscriptions in effect.[3] Nearly two million requests a year are received for serials items. Eighty-nine percent of these requests are satisfied by materials in the collection.[4] The system is designed for fast supply along with a high rate of success. If a request cannot be satisfied by the BLLD, it is then passed along to a library that can do so.

The United States has not developed a comparable institution to which any library in the country could send its requests for items from serials. Although there was a great amount of support in the 1970s for the establishment of the National Periodicals Center, the plan never came to fruition. It is thought that the Center will likely never be established.[5] The opposition of publishers and information entrepreneurs, combined with the desire to have the federal government fund this proposed center, spelled its doom. Thus, American librarians will continue to need serials union lists for referral of patrons and for interlibrary loan work.

Historically, serials union lists have been printed catalogs, often published in multiple volumes. Many union lists are still produced in that format. Increasingly, though, union lists are being compiled, updated, and accessed in an online environment. As a result of this, many of the current printed serials union lists are by-products of online cooperatives.

The rest of this chapter will be comprised of descriptions of essential serials union lists and other sources of serials holdings information.

Union List of Serials in Libraries of the United States and Canada. 3d ed. 5 vols. Edited by Edna Brown Titus. New York: H. W. Wilson, 1965.

Serials union lists have had a relatively brief history. A twenty-page pamphlet published in Milan in 1859 was the first such list.[6] The first American union list was published by Johns Hopkins University in 1876 and was titled, *Check List of Periodicals.* In 1927, after four years of work under the sponsorship of the American Library Association and the editorship of Winifred Gregory, the first edition of the *Union List of Serials in Libraries of the United States and Canada* was published. Included were 75,000 titles and holdings from 225 libraries throughout the United States and Canada. A second edition was published in 1943, containing 115,000 titles and holdings from 650 libraries. Finally, a third edition was published in 1965.

The third edition was the final revision of the *Union List of Serials*. The five volumes contain 4,649 pages. Over 156,000 serial titles are listed from 956 cooperating libraries. The following classes of serials were generally excluded from this work:

Government publications (except periodicals and monographic series).

Administrative reports of corporate publishing bodies.

Almanacs and gift books.

American newspapers.

English and other nonAmerican newspapers published after 1820.

Law reports and digests.

Publications of experimental stations.

Publications of local, religious, labor, and other specific types of organizations.

Publications of national and international congresses and conferences.

House organs.

Alumni, undergraduate, and intercollegiate fraternity publications.

Trench papers.

Titles with a highly limited value.

United Nations publications.

With these limitations in mind, a lot of useless searching can be avoided.

In general, serials are listed by title in this work and are arranged alphabetically. Serials published by societies and not having distinctive titles are listed under the names of the societies. So, for example, the *Bulletin* of the American Mosquito Control Association will be found listed under the name of that association. Colleges and universities having a geographical designation are entered under the name of the city, state, or country contained in the name. Thus, publications of the University of Tennessee are listed under the subheading "University" beneath the heading "Tennessee."

The serials are entered under the latest title, with notes indicating previous titles and dates. Cross references are provided in the list from the earlier titles to the latest title, which is where all of the holdings information will be found. The full serial entries provide a record of the history of the publication, including:

Place of publication.

Dates published along with volume numbering.

Notes of title changes.

Indication of the availability of indexes that are devoted solely to that serial.

Notations of any suspensions of publication or other publishing irregularities.

The libraries that have holdings of the publication are indicated with their appropriate library symbols and a holdings statement. In most instances, the holdings are shown in volume numbers only with the corresponding dates not given. Incomplete volumes in a library's collection are indicated by brackets around those holdings. In cases where a library's symbol is given and no holdings are shown, then that library is reporting that it has a complete set of the publication. There is a key to the library symbols in the front of each volume of this work.

Although now over two decades old, the *Union List of Serials* is still a vital serials reference tool. Of course, some of the holdings information reported in this work is no longer accurate. For the most part, though, it can be relied upon as a guide to retrospective serials holdings in the major libraries across the United States and Canada. Above and beyond its use as a union list, this set is extremely valuable because it lists over 150,000 serials and does provide brief bibliographic descriptions of those publications.

In using this set, one must remember that the information provided was current in the early 1960s. Do not assume in any instance that the holdings information is still correct. A serials reference librarian should warn patrons that all of the holdings information in this list should be confirmed by contacting the holdings library in question.

Another point to keep in mind is that the *Union List of Serials* is limited in that it covers serials holdings in less than one thousand libraries. This is just a small portion of the total number of libraries in the United States and Canada. If a serial title cannot be located in this source, then the search should be carried further into some of the other union lists and classes of union lists described later in this chapter. This applies to older serial titles as well as to the recent titles that may be too new to be listed in this work.

For older serials that are not listed in this work, the *National Union Catalog, Pre-1956 Imprints* (London: Mansell) is a secondary source to search. Some of the classes of publications excluded from the *Union List of Serials* are included there.

New Serial Titles. Washington, D.C.: Library of Congress.

New Serial Titles grew out of the publication *Serial Titles Newly Received*, which listed receipts in the Library of Congress only. The Joint Committee on the *Union List of Serials* recommended that *Serial Titles Newly Received* be expanded to become a new titles supplement to the *Union List of Serials*. Thus was created *New Serial Titles*, which lists titles first published after December 31, 1949, and received by the Library of Congress and other cooperating libraries.[7] It is published on a continuing basis by the Library of Congress with monthly and quarterly issues being cumulated annually. Annual editions are then cumulated every five years. The first twenty years of *New Serial Titles, 1950-1970*, are available in a four-volume cumulation. Subsequent volumes are cumulated quinquennially.

As of 1981, the titles listed in this work are those that meet the definition of "serial" as given in the *Anglo-American Cataloguing Rules, Second Edition* (see chapter 1). So, virtually all types of serials are included in *New Serial Titles*, with the exception of newspapers.

Each update issue or cumulation is arranged in alphabetical order by title or main entry. The entries are printed in the traditional "catalog card" format, and the cataloging data provided for each title can be quite detailed. Along with the name of the publisher, place of publication, and dates of publication, the following information may be found: ISSN, frequency, Library of Congress call number, Library of Congress control (or card) number, and Dewey Decimal classification number. Symbols of holdings libraries are listed. Since these are generally new titles, no indication of exact library holdings is given. Hundreds of libraries from the United States and Canada participate in *New Serial Titles*. Just as with the *Union List of Serials*, this is still a fraction of the total number of libraries in these two countries, and *New Serial Titles* should not be accepted as the final word on serials holdings.

A useful feature that was included in this work for many years was a section labeled, "Changes in Serials." This section included cessations and title changes, but it was discontinued after 1980. A companion publication, *New Serial Titles, Classed Subject Arrangement* was published from 1955 through 1980 and provides subject access to the entries included in the main publication.

Since 1950, *New Serial Titles* has, indeed, functioned as a supplement to the *Union List of Serials*. Hundreds of thousands of titles have been listed, with the 1950-1970 cumulation containing over 200,000 entries alone. This work is an indispensable serials tool which is handy not only for locating holdings libraries but also for tracking down new serials, which can often be quite elusive.

British Union-Catalogue of Periodicals. London: Butterworths.

The first set of four volumes of this work was published from 1955 through 1958. Its purpose was to record the periodicals of the world, regardless of language or subject, held permanently in British libraries. This first set contains over 140,000 titles held in approximately 440 libraries. The term "periodical" is interpreted in a broad sense so that this work includes magazines, journals, reviews, transactions, proceedings and annual publications. Some types of serials are not included, such as newspapers first published after 1799, annual and other reports of an administrative nature, and local and territorial directories.

The serial entries are arranged in alphabetical title order. Since this union list covers publications in all languages, transliterations have been provided where needed. Greek and Cyrillic alphabet titles are entered in their original characters first, followed by the transliteration. Publications issued by an organization are listed under the name of that organization if the publication lacks a distinctive title or if the name of the organization forms a direct or indirect part of the main title. As contrasted to the *Union List of Serials*, all publications are entered here under their earliest titles, with cross references from later titles. The individual entries give a brief publishing history of the serial, including all title changes. Holding libraries are represented by symbols along with an indication of the extent of their holdings. Generally these notations are given in volume numbers, rather than in dates. A library's symbol given without a notation of holdings indicates that the library has a complete set. Volume numbers within parentheses and marked with an asterisk indicate "imperfect" (incomplete) volumes.

In 1962, a one-volume supplement was issued to cover publications through 1960. After that, quarterlies were issued that were cumulated into annual volumes. These annuals were then cumulated into a larger cumulation covering 1960-1968. After 1968, the quarterly/annual publication schedule continued. In 1981, this publication was continued by *Serials in the British Library*, which lists holdings in the British Library only.

The value of the *British Union-Catalogue of Periodicals* to British librarians is obvious. However, this is a source that is often overlooked in American libraries. Since this work lists many titles not covered in the *Union List of Serials*, it should be used as a secondary source in any search to identify an older serial title.

World List of Scientific Periodicals. London: Butterworths.

The fourth, and most recent, edition of this union list, covering the years 1900 to 1960, was published in three volumes. Periodicals concerned with the natural sciences and technology are included. Such titles must have been published either entirely or partially in the period 1900 to 1960. Approximately sixty thousand publications are listed.

The title entries are arranged in alphabetical order of the important words in the title. Entries include title, place of publication, abbreviated title, and symbols of holding libraries along with an indication of their holdings. Over one hundred British libraries are represented in this list. Unlike a formal union list, this work also attempts to list titles that are not held by cooperating libraries but which meet the other requirements for inclusion. Thus, many titles are listed with no indication of holding libraries.

A 1960 to 1968 cumulation of new scientific periodical titles was published in 1970. This was followed by annual updates of new scientific periodicals selected from the *British Union-Catalogue of Periodicals*, which was published until 1980.

Other Printed Union Lists

In addition to the major serials union lists already described in this chapter and the online sources of holdings information (described later in this chapter), there are literally hundreds, if not thousands, of more limited union lists of serials. Most of these union lists represent holdings of libraries within a certain geographic area, ranging from multi-state cooperative lists to union lists of libraries in a single metropolitan area.

A prime example of a major, multi-state work of this sort is the third edition of *MULS: A Union List of Serials* (Minneapolis: MINITEX), which was published in 1980. This twelve-volume set is one of the largest regional union lists produced. It encompasses serials holdings from over three hundred libraries in the states of Minnesota, North Dakota, South Dakota, Wisconsin, and Iowa, and offers 120,000 entries. *MULS* is also available on OCLC.

Many union lists cover holdings within one state only. These lists are often produced or sponsored by the state library. Examples of these types of lists are the three-volume *California Union List of Periodicals* (Sacramento: California State Library, 1974) and the four-volume *Indiana Union List of Serials* (West Lafayette, Ind.: Purdue University Libraries, 1973).

Serials union lists of library holdings within a specific metropolitan area are also very common. Two such publications are *MAGS: Metropolitan Area Guide to Serials* (Washington, D.C.: Metropolitan Washington Library Council, 11th edition, 1986) and the *Union List of Serial Holdings* (Boston: Boston Chapter, Special Libraries Association, 1980). Many "local" union lists are published to provide a record of the serials holdings in the various branches of a single public library system or in the various libraries on a single university campus.

Serials union lists of another class contain entries for publications in a certain subject or special interest area. Examples are the *Union List of United Methodist Serials, 1773-1973*, compiled by John D. Batsel and Lyda K. Batsel (Evanston, Ill.: Garrett Theological Seminary, 1974), and the *Union List of Astronomy Serials*, compiled by Judith A. Lola (n.p.: Special Libraries Association, Physics-Astronomy-Mathematics Division, 1983). Often, subject union lists are limited to libraries in a certain geographic area, resulting in publications such as *Union List of Polish Serials in Canadian Libraries*, by Henryk Pawel Koylowski (Ottawa: National Library of Canada, Public Services Branch, Union Catalogue of Serials Division, 1977), and *Women's Periodicals and Newspapers from the 18th Century to 1981: A Union List of the Holdings of Madison, Wisconsin, Libraries*, edited by James P. Danky (Boston: G. K. Hall, 1982).

The examples provided here are just a few of the entire range of serials union lists. *Union Lists of Serials: A Bibliography*, compiled by Ruth S. Freitag and published by the General Reference and Bibliography Division of the Library of Congress in 1964, is the most comprehensive bibliography of serials union lists available. Recorded in this work are 1,218 publications. The entries are arranged geographically and are annotated. Three indexes are provided—a geographical index, an index of names (of authors, compilers, etc.), and a subject index. Virtually every type of serials union list is within the scope of this bibliography, including lists of newspapers, annuals, and proceedings. Although this work was published in the mid-1960s, it can still be put to good use by those providing serials reference service.

In 1983, the Resources and Technical Services Division of the American Library Association published the *Directory of Union Lists of Serials*, a fourteen-page work by Marjorie E. Bloss. A greatly-expanded second edition was printed in a 1988 issue (vol. 14, nos. 1-2) of the *Serials Review*. Entries for 137 union lists are arranged by state and include information regarding the number of member libraries, number of titles, and the name of the contact person and the address for the union list. Detailed information about each union list is provided in the "matrix section." Of particular interest to reference staff is the "output format" data. For each union list, one can determine in which format it is available, including print, computer output microform, and through online systems such as OCLC.

OCLC and Other Online Sources of Serials Holdings Information

Traditionally, printed union lists have been the format in which a number of libraries combine to indicate their holdings of serials. In the past two decades, however, online union listing capabilities have been developed and put to widespread use. Such systems have grown in importance to the point where they are often the first source consulted in searches for serials holding information. The most prominent such online system is OCLC (Online Computer Library Center).

Beginning in the late 1960s as a regional bibliographic database for academic libraries in Ohio, OCLC has grown into an international system with over nine thousand participating libraries. Although its primary purpose is to provide a cooperative online cataloging system, OCLC is extremely valuable as a source for locating libraries with holdings of particular items. OCLC is the online facility used by the CONSER project (see chapter 14) and thus contains many high-quality serial records. There are also many non-CONSER serial records in the OCLC database, and the quality of these records vary widely. There are over one million records for serials in the database,[8] and this far outnumbers any printed union list of serials ever produced. Since this is an online system, new records are being constantly added to the database. Thus, new serials theoretically could be listed online from the time of their inception and not months, or years, later, as they typically are, in *New Serial Titles* or in other printed union lists.

A record for a serial that is retrieved from the OCLC database is a MARC serial record, and it often gives full bibliographic information (see chapter 14 for a description of the MARC serial record). Many serial records in the database, though, are incomplete, and some are inaccurate.[9] Nevertheless, OCLC can be used effectively to locate libraries with holdings of particular serials. The 850 field of the MARC record will list the NUC (National Union Catalog) symbols of some of the libraries with holdings of that publication. A complete listing of holding libraries, however, can be requested, and the OCLC symbols of such libraries are then displayed in a state-by-state arrangement. By consulting an OCLC symbol directory, the searcher can identify the libraries that have holdings of the serial in question. The mere presence of a library's symbol, however, gives no indication as to the extent of that library's holdings. A complete set may be available at that library, or only one issue may be in the library's collection. Never assume that a library has a complete set based on the fact that its symbol is on the OCLC record.

Another assumption that should not be made involves the 040 field of the MARC record. This field lists the symbols of libraries that took part in the creation of the record. It should not be assumed that all of these libraries have holdings of the serial. Take holdings only from the 850 field or from the separate holding locations display.

OCLC has also made available a union listing capability, by which member institutions of particular union lists are able to display records of their holdings of serials and are also able to see records of holdings of other libraries. With this capability, there is no need to guess at the extent of another library's holdings of a particular publication. As of 1988, there were eighty union list groups participating in OCLC.[10] A member institution of a union list on OCLC can view holdings statements of others in the same union list. Such an institution may also see holdings from libraries in other union lists on OCLC, by calling up a specific serials record and then specifying the union list to be searched.[11]

Searching for the record of a particular serial in OCLC can be a frustrating experience. The OCLC system at present does not allow keyword or Boolean searching. If only the title of a serial to be searched is known, then the only possibility is to try a title search, which is in the form of 3,2,2,1 (first three letters of first word, first two letters of second word, etc.). A periodical search should almost always be limited to serials records ("/ser"), except when searching for serials in which each issue is cataloged as a separate monograph, or analyzed in full. With the hundreds of thousands of serials records in OCLC, merely limiting a search to serials records may not be enough. This is especially true for one-word serial titles. For instance, trying to retrieve an OCLC record for a periodical named *Insight* may be impossible or impractical due to the number of hits. A search can be further limited to a date, or range of dates, of first publication. This, however, is not a foolproof practice since a large percentage of OCLC records provide no date of first publication. The example of searching for *Insight* by title and limited to serials records ("Ins,,,/ser") produced over 450 serial records matching the search key, 121 of which showed no date of first publication, in a search conducted in November 1988. Reference staffers generally do not have the time to wade through all of these records.

There are other types of OCLC searches that may be more appropriate in cases where a straight title search results in an overwhelming number of hits. Foremost among these is the capability to search the database by International Standard Serial Number (ISSN), an eight character, unique number assigned to serials (see chapter 14). The ISSN is usually printed in issues of serials and can also be found in many periodical directories (see chapter 3). OCLC may also be searched by Library of Congress control (or card) number, or by CODEN (see chapter 14). Since serial records in OCLC are of an inconsistent quality, it is possible that a record for a particular serial exists in OCLC without an ISSN, CODEN, or Library of Congress control number. So, a negative response to any of these types of searches does not necessarily mean that there is no record for that publication in the database. Corporate name searching is another OCLC alternative that can be helpful in searching for serial records. It can also be applied in searching for proceedings of conferences and congresses (see chapter 8).

Another frustrating aspect of OCLC is that there may be several records for the same periodical in the database. These may be separate records for the original periodical itself, its microfilm edition, and its microfiche edition. There may even be a record that states not to use the record and refers the searcher to one of the other records. From a reference standpoint, it is important to realize that these various records for the same title will normally all have different holding libraries indicated. So, for a complete search of the system, carefully review each record.

OCLC is the most prominent online database for accessing serials holdings information. Other systems providing this same sort of service include:

Research Libraries Information Network (RLIN) — The network of the Research Libraries Group, a cooperative of a small number of very large United States research libraries.

Western Library Network (WLN) — Formerly the Washington Library Network, this network includes over 250 libraries in the Pacific Northwest.

University of Toronto Library Automation System (UTLAS) — A Canadian bibliographic network that has some library members in the United States.

Faxon, a serials subscription company, also offers online union listing capabilities. Its LINX system is an online serials check-in and maintenance package. Through this system, members of union lists are able to display their holdings to one another and to produce printed offline products.[12] Also, it is possible for a non-union list library using the LINX system to view union list holdings if a reciprocal agreement is made. In such a case, the library that is not a member of the union list agrees to open up its records also, so that mutual access is available.[13]

Despite the proliferation of online systems, serials reference staff must remember also to use the printed sources that are available. Particularly for older titles, there is no online system that quite compares to the *Union List of Serials* or to the *British Union-Catalogue of Periodicals*. If a periodical record is not located in an online system, or if only one or two holding libraries are indicated in an online system, then search in other likely sources, which in most cases will be printed sources. This is the only manner in which to do a complete job when searching for locations of holding libraries.

Words of Caution in the Use of
Serials Union Lists

It is important for those using serials union lists to realize that most of these publications are produced by different individuals or groups. There is nothing that can be depended upon as being standardized in this field, although certain standards do exist. Holdings statements are formatted in various ways from list to list. Some union lists enter publications that have changed titles under their earliest titles, some under their latest titles, and some under successive titles. Beware of idiosyncrasies in union lists of serials. Always read the introduction and preface when using a union list for the first time.

Also take care when referring a patron to another library based on the holdings shown in a union list. Often, a library will report its holdings based on its serial record, and no shelf check will be performed to confirm the holdings. Over the years, items disappear from collections or are incorrectly shelved and lost. So, instead of just telling your patron that another library has the year or issue of a periodical that is needed, tell your patron that the library *apparently* has the year or issue needed. Then, telephone that library or have the patron call them, to confirm their holdings.

A final point about searching for serial titles in union lists regards the hard-to-locate title. That a serial record cannot be found in OCLC or in the *Union List of Serials* does not mean that the publication is not available somewhere. A familiarity with various specific subject and geographic union lists will help in carrying difficult searches further. It should also be remembered that there are other means in which a needed article can be obtained. If the periodical is still being published, contact the publisher and ask if they will supply a back issue or a photocopy of the needed article. The publisher may also be able to state which libraries maintain backfiles of their publication. As mentioned earlier, document delivery services are also sources for obtaining copies of articles (see chapter 7).

Notes

[1]Marjorie E. Bloss, "The Serials Pastiche: Union Lists of Serials," *Drexel Library Quarterly* 21 (Winter 1985): 101.

[2]Ibid., 101-2.

[3]Maurice B. Line, "The British Library Lending Division," *Journal of Information Science* 2 (October 1980): 174.

[4]Stella Pilling and David Wood, "Serials at the British Library Lending Division," *The Serials Librarian* 10 (Fall 1985/Winter 1985-1986): 240.

[5]Mary Biggs, "The Proposed National Periodicals Center, 1973-1980: Study, Dissension, and Retreat," in *Library Lit. 15- , The Best of 1984* (Metuchen, N.J., and London: Scarecrow Press, 1985), 101.

[6]Andrew D. Osborn, *Serial Publications: Their Place and Treatment in Libraries*, 3d ed. (Chicago: American Library Association, 1980), 415.

[7]*New Serial Titles, 1950-1970 Cumulative.* (Washington, D.C.: Library of Congress; New York and London: R. R. Bowker, 1973), v.

[8]*OCLC Annual Report, 1987/88* (Dublin, Ohio.: OCLC Online Computer Library Center, 1988), 4.

[9]Michael Roughton, "OCLC Serials Records: Errors, Omissions, and Dependability," *The Journal of Academic Librarianship* 5 (January 1980): 316-21.

[10]*OCLC Annual Report, 1987/88*, 1.

[11]Terrence J. O'Malley, "Union Listing Via OCLC's Serials Control Subsystem," *Special Libraries* 75 (April 1984): 133.

[12]Ann C. Schaffner, "Implementation of the Faxon Union List System by the Boston Library Consortium," *The Serials Librarian* 9 (Spring 1985): 45-62.

[13]"Boston Library Consortium Offers Reciprocal Access to Serials Records," *FAX Letter* 1 (May/June 1985): 4.

5
Periodical Indexes and Abstracts

Many inexperienced researchers are not aware that periodical indexes and abstracts exist. These researchers arrive at the library knowing only that they need articles on a particular subject, and often the decision is made that the best way to accomplish this is to skim through issues of periodicals that might contain articles on the subject. Such a patron may approach a library staff member and ask where the periodicals on a particular subject are located. A poorly trained or uninformed staffer will direct the requester to the periodicals on the subject, where the patron may spend a lengthy amount of time in a fruitless search for relevant articles.

The scenario described here is all too common. Novice library users often have had no introduction to the concept of periodical indexing. If their request for help is poorly worded, or if it doesn't accurately state what is needed, and if the person responsible for serials reference has not been properly trained, then the patron can be sent off on the wrong track. What is required in these cases is a further questioning of the patron to determine what is really needed. This reference interview should take place whenever a library user asks to be directed to the periodicals or magazines in a particular subject area. Inquiring into the needs of the patron will normally uncover what is actually needed. However, if the patron only wants to browse through periodicals in a certain subject area, then it is appropriate to refer the patron to a serials catalog in which periodicals are classified under general subject headings. On the other hand, if the patron actually needs articles on a specific topic, then the first step is the use of a periodical indexing or abstracting service.

These services act as guides to the periodical literature in various subject areas. Most are produced by commercial companies and provide coverage of hundreds of periodicals. Some are produced by the publisher of a periodical itself. In such instances, an index to the articles of that periodical is produced (most commonly on an annual basis) and distributed to that periodical's subscribers. This type of index can be a separately-printed supplement or it may be printed within an issue of the periodical (most often within the last issue of a volume or year, or within the first issue of the subsequent volume or year).

It seems that only experienced researchers are aware of the vast array of periodical indexing and abstracting that is available. A great proportion of library users are familiar with only one index, the *Readers' Guide to Periodical Literature*, and assume that if a topic is not listed there, then it is not covered in any periodical. Other novice library users are not aware of periodical indexing at all. It is the responsibility of serials reference staff to serve as instructors and to introduce these library users to the various periodical indexing and abstracting services that are available.

Although they are linked together because of their similarities, indexing services and abstracting services are two different types of reference sources. A periodical index is a systematically arranged list of articles, or other printed items, that provides enough information to identify and trace the items. Indexes may be arranged by subjects, authors, or titles of articles. The entries normally provide only the bare bibliographical information such as subject, title of the article, author, periodical title, volume number and date of the periodical, and pages on which the article appeared.

An abstract of a periodical article differs in that it provides a summary of the information in the article along with sufficient bibliographical information to allow the item to be traced. There are two types of abstracts, the indicative and the informative. An indicative abstract is a short, descriptive summary, showing the scope and content of the article. An informative abstract goes beyond this by summarizing the principal arguments of the article and also provides its principal data. The indicative abstract, then, provides awareness of the information, while the informative abstract provides the essence of the information and can serve as a substitute for the original article.[1]

History of Periodical Indexes

Some of the earliest periodicals spawned the earliest periodical indexes. The first volume of the *Philosophical Transactions* of the Royal Society of London, which was the second printed periodical published, concluded with an index. In 1678, this periodical published a cumulative index to its first twelve volumes. The practice of publishing cumulative indexes soon became widespread.[2]

Eventually, indexes were developed that covered the articles in a number of different periodicals. In 1882, William Frederick Poole's *An Index to Periodical Literature* was published, in which 232 serials from 1802 to 1881 were indexed.[3] The late 1800s and early 1900s also saw the rise of major scientific indexing and abstracting services such as the *Zoological Record* (established in 1864), *Index Medicus* (est. 1879), *The Engineering Index* (est. 1884), and *Chemical Abstracts* (est. 1907).

An enormous growth in the number of indexing and abstracting services has taken place in the twentieth century. There are literally thousands of such services, and all major subject areas are covered. In 1975, it was estimated that there were two thousand abstracting and indexing services worldwide covering science and technology alone.[4] Osborn, in 1980, stated that a 1962 estimate of 3,500 abstracting and indexing services was still "reasonably reliable."[5]

These services are now available in several formats. In addition to the traditional print format, many can now be accessed through online databases. Some are published on compact discs as part of a CD-ROM file or in a microform format. Searching possibilities in the online and CD-ROM environments are much more varied and all-encompassing.

Despite the large number of abstracting and indexing services, there are just a few dozen core titles, or files, that are turned to most often. Descriptions of these services are given in the following sections.

Printed Indexing and Abstracting Services

Readers' Guide to Periodical Literature. New York: H. W. Wilson.

First published in 1901, the *Readers' Guide* has become the most widely-known index to articles in periodicals. Since it indexes general, popular periodicals, this work is well-suited for most types of libraries from public libraries to high school libraries and college libraries. Thus, a wide range of people learn to use this index and to rely on it.

The *Readers' Guide* offers indexing of 175 very popular periodicals such as *Time, Newsweek, Popular Photography*, and *Better Homes and Gardens*. Access to articles is through author and subject entries, which are interfiled in one alphabet. All entries give complete bibliographic information. Cross-references are found under virtually every subject heading to broaden or narrow a search. Since general interest magazines are indexed, articles on practically any topic can be found. This index is particularly good, though, for current events and news. A separate section provides citations to book reviews. Subscription information is also given for every periodical indexed.

The *Readers' Guide* is published in seventeen paperbound issues a year, four of which are quarterly cumulations. An annual clothbound edition cumulates a year's worth of issues. H. W. Wilson also publishes the *Abridged Readers' Guide*, which covers sixty periodicals and is more appropriate for small libraries. This edition is published in nine paperbound issues a year, plus a clothbound annual cumulation.

The *Readers' Guide* has had a tremendous impact in libraries. Many libraries, unfortunately, subscribe only to periodicals listed in this index.[6] Also, many users have become overly-dependent upon just this one source, simply because the *Readers' Guide* has served as the major access to articles in popular magazines for this entire century. It is hard to visualize any general interest library without it. Indexing information from this publication is also now available on microfiche, CD-ROM, and through an online database.

The aforementioned user who is overly-dependent on the *Readers' Guide* never progresses to other indexes. This type of patron automatically searches in this source when trying to locate periodical articles, regardless of the subject matter. Often this user does not know that other periodical indexes do exist. It is assumed that if a topic is not in the *Readers' Guide*, then there are no periodical articles on that topic. The related assumption is that all periodicals are indexed in this one work. Since there may well be over 100,000 periodicals currently in print and the *Readers' Guide* indexes 175 publications, this assumption is faulty. Whenever a reader asks specifically for this index by name, the person responsible for serials reference should attempt to perform a reference interview to ascertain that this is, indeed, the proper index to consult.

The *Readers' Guide* is the most commonly known periodical index, and its publisher, the H. W. Wilson Company, is the most widely-known name in periodical indexing. This company also publishes a number of other periodical indexes in various subject areas, all of which are noted for their quality. Listed below are some of H. W. Wilson's standard reference sources that librarians and researchers have come to rely upon.

Applied Science and Technology Index. New York: H. W. Wilson.

This publication first appeared in 1958, continuing the *Industrial Arts Index* (est. 1913), and currently indexes approximately 350 periodicals. A broad range of scientific and technical areas is covered. Articles are arranged by subject, with cross-references provided throughout. There is no author index. A separate index of book reviews is provided. It is published eleven times a year, plus an annual cumulation.

Art Index. New York: H. W. Wilson.

First published in 1929, this index now covers approximately 225 periodicals and other serials. Subjects covered include architecture, film, painting, sculpture, and video. The index is arranged by subject and author, in one interfiled alphabet. A separate index of book reviews is provided. It is published quarterly, plus an annual cumulation.

Bibliographic Index. New York: H. W. Wilson.

Although not exclusively a periodical index, this publication does list bibliographies by subject published in various sources, including the 2,600 periodicals that are regularly indexed by H. W. Wilson. This index first appeared in 1937 and is currently published twice a year, plus an annual cumulation.

Biography Index. New York: H. W. Wilson.

This publication lists sources of biographical material from the 2,600 periodicals indexed by H. W. Wilson, as well as from monographs and other publications. The index is arranged by the names of the biographees. A separate index, by profession, lists the names in that issue. First published in 1946, it is now issued quarterly, plus an annual cumulation.

Biological & Agricultural Index. New York: H. W. Wilson.

First published in 1964 as a continuation to the *Agricultural Index* (est. 1916), this work currently provides coverage of approximately two hundred periodicals in the field of life sciences. The index is arranged by subject, with cross-references. There is no author index. A separate index of book reviews is provided. It is published eleven times a year, plus an annual cumulation.

Book Review Digest. New York: H. W. Wilson.

Published since 1905, this work provides excerpts from, and citations to, reviews of nearly six thousand books each year. These citations and excerpts are taken from approximately eighty different periodicals. It is published ten times a year, plus an annual cumulation.

Business Periodicals Index. New York: H. W. Wilson.

All areas of business are covered in this publication, which first appeared in 1958. Approximately three hundred periodicals are currently indexed. The index is arranged by subject, with cross-references. There is no author index. A separate index of book reviews is provided. It is published eleven times a year, plus an annual cumulation.

Education Index. New York: H. W. Wilson.

Published since 1929, this work covers approximately 345 periodicals and other serials. The index is arranged by subject and author, interfiled in one alphabet. A separate index of book reviews is provided. It is published ten times a year, plus an annual cumulation.

General Science Index. New York: H. W. Wilson.

First published in 1978, this work covers approximately 110 scientific periodicals. The index is arranged by subject, with cross-references. There is no author index. A separate index of book reviews is provided. It is published ten times a year, plus an annual cumulation.

Humanities Index. New York: H. W. Wilson.

In 1974, the *Social Sciences & Humanities Index*, which could trace its history back to the establishment, in 1907, of the *Readers' Guide to Periodical Literature Supplement*, split into two separate indexes. Thus, the *Humanities Index* and the *Social Sciences Index* were formed. The *Humanities Index* now covers nearly three hundred periodicals. Broad subject areas covered include the arts, journalism, language, philosophy, and religion. The index is arranged by subject and author, interfiled in one alphabet. A separate index of book reviews is provided. It is published quarterly, plus an annual cumulation.

Index to Legal Periodicals. New York: H. W. Wilson.

This publication, which first appeared in 1908, provides coverage of over five hundred legal periodicals and other serials. Subject and author entries are interfiled in one alphabet. A "Table of Cases," and a "Table of Statutes" are included. A separate index of book reviews is provided. It is published eleven times a year, plus an annual cumulation.

Library Literature. New York: H. W. Wilson.

First published in 1921, this work now covers all aspects of librarianship in approximately two hundred periodicals and more than six hundred monographs per year. The index is arranged by subject and author, in one interfiled alphabet. A separate index of book reviews is provided. It is published six times a year, plus an annual cumulation.

Social Sciences Index. New York: H. W. Wilson.

This index was established, along with the *Humanities Index*, when the *Social Sciences & Humanities Index* split into two separate indexes in 1974. Over 350 periodicals are currently covered in this work. A wide range of topics is covered, including anthropology, ethnic studies, psychology, and sociology. This index is arranged by subject and author, in one interfiled alphabet. A separate index of book reviews is provided. It is published quarterly, plus an annual cumulation.

The following three periodical indexes are standard sources for coverage of general topics.

Access. Evanston, Ill.: John Gordon Burke.

Subtitled, *The Supplementary Index to Periodicals*, the purpose of this work is to complement other general periodical indexes. Basically, it indexes popular, general interest periodicals not covered in the *Readers' Guide. Access* was first published in 1975 and currently indexes approximately 130 periodicals. It provides good coverage of state and city magazines and also covers popular periodicals such as *Playboy* and *Village Voice*. This work is divided into an author index and a subject index. It is published three times a year, with the third issue being an annual cumulation.

British Humanities Index. London: Library Association.

This was first published in 1962 as the continuation of *The Subject Index to Periodicals* (est. 1915). It provides coverage of approximately three hundred periodicals, with a slant toward British publications. The index is arranged by subject, with an author index included in the annual cumulative volume. It is published quarterly, plus the annual cumulation.

PAIS Bulletin. New York: Public Affairs Information Service.

First published in 1915, this index is an excellent source for coverage of national and international political, economic, and social topics. In addition to articles from approximately 1,400 periodicals, selective coverage is provided of books and government documents. It is published eleven times a year in paperbound issues, plus an annual clothbound cumulation. The paperbound issues provide indexing by subject only, while the annual cumulation provides subject access and a separate author index. Since many books and government documents are covered in this index, it can be somewhat difficult for an inexperienced user to differentiate between the various types of citations. When introducing a patron to this index, point out the different types of entries to minimize this confusion.

The Institute for Scientific Information publishes a series of citation indexes. They are based on the idea that, within a current article or other work, an author's references to earlier works show a subject relationship between the earlier works and the current work. In effect, the earlier works are used as indexing terms and group together references to current works citing the earlier works. Thus, a researcher can locate current articles dealing with the same subject as the earlier works.

The *Arts & Humanities Citation Index* currently provides cover-to-cover indexing of approximately 1,400 periodicals and selective indexing from approximately 4,700 periodicals in the sciences and social sciences. Every item is indexed four ways—by author, author's organization, title word, and by citations. This index is published in two paperbound issues per year, each of which is in three physical parts, plus an annual hardbound cumulation. Coverage is available back to 1975.

The *Science Citation Index* currently covers over three thousand science periodicals with over 600,000 items indexed annually. This work also provides indexing by author, title word, author affiliation, and by citations. It is published in six paperbound issues per year, each of which is in several physical parts, plus an annual hardbound cumulation. Coverage is available back to 1955.

The *Social Sciences Citation Index* currently covers approximately 1,400 social science periodicals and selective relevant material from approximately 3,300 other periodicals. Once again, the author, title word, author's organization, and citation indexes are provided. It is published twice a year in paperbound issues, each of which is in several physical parts, plus an annual hardbound cumulation. Coverage is available back to 1966.

Since these works do not look like "normal" periodical indexes and since one must either be taught how to use them or take a fair amount of time to read the directions, many library staffers and library users do not use or recommend them. This is unfortunate because these indexes can be very powerful tools. Serials reference staffers with any of these indexes in their libraries should take the time to learn how to use them. It is then possible to teach patrons how to use them.

The Institute for Scientific Information also publishes a series of current awareness publications called *Current Contents*. Editions produced in this series are:

Agriculture, Biology & Environmental Sciences

Arts & Humanities

Clinical Medicine

Engineering, Technology & Applied Sciences

Life Sciences

Physical, Chemical & Earth Sciences

Social & Behavioral Sciences

Designed for scholars, researchers, and others who want to keep abreast of current developments, these publications reproduce the table of contents pages from current issues of the leading journals in the field. Each issue also contains a title index and an author index.

As mentioned earlier, there are literally thousands of abstracting and indexing services. Therefore, it has only been possible to describe some of the most important printed indexes here.

Some of the other standard printed services are:

Alternative Press Index

America History and Life

Biological Abstracts

Book Review Index

Chemical Abstracts

Consumers Index to Product Evaluations and Information Sources

Current Index to Journals in Education

Index Medicus

Index to Military Periodicals

Index to U.S. Government Periodicals (see chapter 6 for a full description)

Psychological Abstracts

Predicasts F & S Index

Other printed abstracting and indexing services can be identified by using Eugene P. Sheehy's *Guide to Reference Books*, tenth edition, 1986 (Chicago: American Library Association), and *Ulrich's International Periodicals Directory*. A separate section of *Ulrich's* lists abstracting and indexing services. Over a hundred major subject headings in the directory also have the subheading, "Abstracting, Bibliographies, Statistics," where such services are listed, too.

Microform Indexes

As alternatives to traditional printed indexes, the Information Access Company introduced the *Magazine Index* and the *Business Index* in the late 1970s. Each index is stored on one large reel of 16mm microfilm that is updated monthly and is housed inside a self-contained viewing machine. The user searches subjects and authors using the same types of search strategies as if the indexes were printed.

The *Magazine Index* covers over four hundred periodicals, with indexing for approximately the most recent four years. The *Business Index* covers over eight hundred periodicals, with the indexing extending back approximately two-and-a-half years. Citations for years that are too old to be on the current reel can be accessed on microfiche distributed by the company. Both of these indexes are easy to use and, since they cumulate a number of years at a time, they make for one-stop searching. These indexes also link up with two microfilm cartridge-based article retrieval systems called the Magazine Collection and the Business Collection (see chapter 7 for a full description).

A new product from the H. W. Wilson Company is the microfiche publication, *Readers' Guide Abstracts*, which combines the indexing of the *Readers' Guide* with abstracts of the items indexed. It is issued in cumulated sets every six weeks and includes the most recent two years of coverage. A printed version of this publication titled, *Readers' Guide Abstracts Print Edition* has also been introduced.

Online Abstracting and Indexing Services

In the past few decades, the online availability of databases that contain the contents of abstracting and indexing services has opened up new searching possibilities for librarians and library patrons alike. Libraries have had to face the thorny question of whether to charge for such searching, and if so, how much. Reference librarians have had to become familiar with the vast number of databases that are available online. A great many librarians have become expert online searchers.

The process by which a patron has a database searched for periodical article citations or abstracts is quite different than the process used for searching in traditional printed sources. With printed indexes, the reference staffer suggests the most appropriate index for a particular search and then provides some brief instruction on how the index can most effectively be used. In most cases, the patron then performs the search. When pertinent citations are found, the patron can write them down, or the index page(s) can be photocopied.

For database searching, the burden is put on the librarian, in most cases. First, a patron's exact needs are determined through an interview. This is an extremely important type of reference interview, since dollars hang in the balance. Once the needs of the patron are determined, the librarian must decide which database or databases would be most appropriate to search. Next, a search strategy must be formulated. Finally, the librarian signs on to the database desired and performs the search. The resulting citations, abstracts, or full-text items can be printed out online, with the results immediately available. The printing can also be done offline, with the printout mailed to the library. For long lists of citations, offline printing is frequently chosen since it is more economical. Once the printout is available, it is given to the patron who usually must pay for the service, based on the fee schedule of that particular library.

There are hundreds of abstracting and indexing databases available online for searching. They range from International Pharmaceutical Abstracts to Coffeeline to the Religion Index. These databases are produced and maintained by various private companies, government agencies, and organizations. Access to these databases is available through companies that act as vendors and offer a more or less standardized approach to the databases. The three major vendors are DIALOG Information Services, BRS Information Technologies, and ORBIT Search Service. DIALOG is the largest of these, providing access to over three hundred databases.

In general, online searching offers many possibilities that are not available with printed indexes. Boolean logic can be employed. Sets of citations can be combined. Multiple access searching points are available for bibliographic records. Some databases offer full-text retrieval of entire articles (for example, the Harvard Business Review Database). This enables keyword searching of words within an article, which is certainly a very powerful tool.

The H. W. Wilson Company offers an online retrieval system called WILSONLINE. It is not available through vendors and must be accessed directly. Over twenty-five H. W. Wilson databases can be accessed, including all of their major periodical indexes described earlier in this chapter. Most of the databases cover from 1983 or 1984 to the present. The system offers forty-three different access points for bibliographic records, and multifile searching can be performed.

As mentioned, there are online systems that provide full-text online access to publications. These systems, such as NEXIS, VU/TEXT, and DataTimes, make available full-text versions of newspapers and wire services (see chapter 12). In addition, some magazines and newsletters are available on these systems. Such publications are usually of a business nature.

Periodicals that are available in full-text or abstracted or indexed online can be identified by using *Ulrich's International Periodicals Directory* (see chapter 3 for a full description of this directory). One section lists these periodicals by title, and another lists them by online vendor. The *Directory of Periodicals Online: Indexed, Abstracted & Full-Text, News, Law & Business* (Washington, D.C.: Federal Document Retrieval) is another publication that provides this type of information. This directory, first published in 1985, lists periodicals and the online systems in which they are indexed or abstracted and where they are available in full-text. The third edition, 1987, contains listings for over 7,700 periodicals. Another similar directory is *Books and Periodicals Online: A Guide to Publication Contents of Business and Legal Databases* (Oxford: Learned Information), which was first published in 1987. Over 6,800 serial titles are listed, giving the database(s) in which each is available, including those that provide full-text retrieval and those that provide indexing or abstracting data.

In addition to catalogs that are available from the major vendors such as DIALOG, BRS, and ORBIT, there are directories that can be used to identify databases that are available for searching. Some of these directories are:

Directory of Online Databases. Santa Monica, Calif.: Cuadra Associates. Quarterly.

Database Directory. White Plains, N.Y.: Knowledge Industry Publications. Annual.

Encyclopedia of Information Systems and Services. Detroit: Gale Research. Annual.

Computer-Readable Databases: A Directory and Data Sourcebook. Chicago: American Library Association. Irregular.

CD-ROM and Laser Disc Indexes

In 1985, Information Access Corporation, the company that produces the *Magazine Index* and the *Business Index*, introduced InfoTrac. The InfoTrac system combines laser disc and microcomputer technologies to produce an easy-to-use index. Users search the index on a personal computer and print out references at the workstation. Updated laser discs containing references to nearly nine hundred periodicals for the most recent four years are sent to subscribers once a month.

InfoTrac is the ultimate in user friendliness. No training is required, and the searching is not complicated. Basically, users key in a topic and push the search key. If there is an exact match, the relevant citations will appear on the screen and can be printed. If there is not a subject match, then the closest entry in the subject guide is displayed. In essence, searching on InfoTrac is the same as searching in a printed index but with the advantages that citations can be printed out and that several years at a time are searched. Boolean searching and other complex types of searching are not a possibility with this system.

InfoTrac has been enthusiastically accepted by users and by most librarians. Users love the system because it is very easy and quick to use, and because citations can be conveniently printed out. Patrons soon become hooked on the system, with reports of waiting lines forming to use InfoTrac.[7] One library reported that some of its users drove thirty miles out of their way to use InfoTrac at another library when the system in their own library was temporarily unavailable.[8] Surveys at libraries with InfoTrac have shown that an overwhelming majority of users prefer it over other reference tools[9] and that a majority would even be willing to pay a small fee in order to use it.[10]

On one level, librarians have embraced this system, too. First, it means less work for them. Since InfoTrac is so self explanatory, it is not necessary to take the time to instruct the user on how to use it. Second, InfoTrac has produced many satisfied patrons who are pleased with the results of their searches. Third, even former non-users of libraries have been attracted into the library by InfoTrac.[11]

On another level, though, librarians have become alarmed by the library users who foresake all other periodical indexes and use InfoTrac only. Although InfoTrac is a good source for popular and business materials, it is not at all appropriate for scholarly or scientific research. Yet, patrons use InfoTrac for all types of inappropriate searches, assuming that the computer coverage is comprehensive. When very little is found on a subject, the assumption is made that there are no periodical articles on that topic. This is the *Readers' Guide* syndrome modernized and transferred to InfoTrac. In libraries with InfoTrac, those responsible for serials reference must be aware that patrons, especially those who are novices at research, may be using InfoTrac inappropriately. In some cases, libraries have posted warning signs at InfoTrac workstations.[12] Wherever InfoTrac is available, serials reference personnel must realize that even though the system is very user friendly, the unsophisticated user deserves some instruction and an explanation of the limitations of the system.

In 1987, the Information Access Corporation stepped beyond the world of laser disc into the realm of CD-ROM (compact disc — read-only memory) when it introduced Magazine Index/Plus on InfoTrac II. The InfoTrac II workstation also consists of a PC and a printer, but the indexing information is stored on a compact disc, which is much smaller than a laser disc. While the name InfoTrac refers to the workstation, retrieval software, and to the database that can be searched by that software, the name InfoTrac II refers only to the CD-ROM workstation and retrieval software. There is not a database called InfoTrac II. Magazine Index/Plus was the first database produced for the InfoTrac II system, and it provides coverage of approximately four hundred periodicals. Perhaps in answer to the criticism of InfoTrac being non-scholarly, Information Access Corporation has also introduced the Academic Index on InfoTrac II. As an InfoTrac II application, this index also employs CD-ROM technology. Three hundred seventy-five scholarly and general interest periodicals are covered in this source, which seems to be slanted toward the humanities and the social sciences.

It appears that CD-ROM technology is destined to have an immense impact in libraries. As such, several publishers in addition to Information Access Corporation have begun to produce CD-ROM indexes. In particular, H. W. Wilson has marketed a system called WILSONDISC. As part of this system, nineteen different databases are available on separate compact discs. This includes the *Readers' Guide* starting with January 1983 and many of the other H. W. Wilson indexes described earlier in this chapter. These discs are updated and cumulated quarterly. Searching possibilities range from simple browse capabilities to Boolean searching, incorporating the same searches and commands used with WILSONLINE (see earlier in this chapter). WILSON-DISC offers the attractive feature that a CD-ROM search can be updated online so that one is certain to retrieve all of the most recent citations.

The number of periodical indexing or abstracting services available on CD-ROM systems is constantly growing. As of late 1988, some of the major services available in this format include ABI/Inform, MEDLINE, PAIS, Periodical Abstracts (from University Microfilms International), and the Science Citation Index.

Reference Work with Periodical Indexes and Abstracts

Often, a library user is in search of an article that is known to have appeared in a certain periodical, but for which no other information is available. In other cases, patrons search for all of the articles that a particular periodical has printed on a certain subject. To handle these types of requests, first determine if a cumulative index for that periodical is available. In the absence of such an index specifically printed for that periodical, determine which indexing or abstracting service covers the periodical in question. If a copy of the periodical is nearby, check the publishing statement, where this information may be provided. Otherwise, the first place to search for this information regarding current periodicals is in *Ulrich's International Period-icals Directory*. The entries for individual periodicals do provide notations of what services cover them. Other periodical directories provide this information, too (see chapter 3). For retrospective indexing information, a good source to consult is *Indexed Periodicals: A Guide to 170 Years of Coverage in 33 Indexing Services,* by Joseph V. Marconi (Ann Arbor, Mich.: Pierian Press, 1976). Another source of indexing information is the MARC CONSER cataloging record for a serial (see chapter 14). The 510 field(s) of such a record will indicate the abstracting and indexing service(s) that cover the periodical.

Librarians have a respect for the standard indexing services and rarely question if the index actually covers all of the material in a particular periodical. Yet, the depth of indexing is often something less than comprehensive. A recent survey of book review indexing in standard sources showed that omissions occur due to carelessness and unpublicized policies of limitation.[13] Another factor to be aware of is that incorrect citations do find their way into abstracting and indexing services, often resulting in researchers and librarians embarking on fruitless searches. Also, all such services suffer from a time lag in indexing. In the online, full-text environment, the time lag may be as short as twenty-four hours. However, the delays are much more evident in the printed services. Users who are accustomed to a world of instant access must be made aware that the printed services are often several months behind in indexing.

As described earlier, one of the most common mistakes committed by novice library users in searching for periodical articles is to request periodicals on a certain subject and then browse through them looking for appropriate articles. Whenever a patron inquires about periodicals in a certain subject area, a reference interview should ensue to determine if the patron is actually looking for articles on a specific topic. If that is the case, then the patron should be shown appropriate indexes in which to search for citations to such articles.

A second major mistake made by unsophisticated library users is to rely on just one indexing service to the exclusion of all others. Traditionally, this has happened with the *Readers' Guide* and more recently with InfoTrac. Serials reference staff should be aware that when patrons ask specifically for either of these sources, they may not know about other, possibly more appropriate, indexes. Once again, it is the duty of the library staffer to inquire into the needs of the patron and to refer the user to other indexes, if appropriate.

The responsibility of the serials reference staffer does not end after the correct index has been selected, and the patron has been shown where it is. For the novice researcher, staff assistance will be needed at every step of the process. First, the purpose, scope, and arrangement of the index should be explained to the patron. A few sample searches should be demonstrated. The patron should be advised to search under the most specific heading first and then, if unsuccessful, look under more general headings. The tendency for many first-time users is to search under a general heading, assuming that a specific heading will not be included in the index. The concept of cross-referencing should be explained, and the patron should be encouraged to follow through on any appropriate cross-references.

There are certain common mistakes that occur repeatedly in the use of abstracting and indexing services. The major area of confusion regards interpretation of the article citation itself. Inexperienced users will not be able to differentiate between the article title and the periodical title. Since the periodical title will usually be abbreviated, the user will not know what the abbreviation stands for. Of course, the abbreviations are spelled out in the front of most indexes, and a sample citation is dissected there. These sections should be shown to the user, also, to avoid later problems.

The periodical abbreviation can lead to significant problems. Often, a user will make up a title based on the abbreviation. For instance, the patron will assume that the *Social Sciences Index* abbreviation "Cent Mag" stands for *Century Magazine*. The user then approaches the periodical information desk and asks, "Does the library have *Century Magazine*?" The staffer finds an entry for *Century* in the serials list and sends the patron off to the stacks. Ten minutes later, the patron returns and says, "I'm looking for a September-October 1984 issue, and that stops in the year 1930. Don't you subscribe to it anymore?" After checking the serials list and determining that *Century* did, indeed, cease publication in 1930, the patron is questioned by the staffer as to the origin of his citation. A few more questions reveal that the citation was found in abbreviated form in a recent volume of the *Social Sciences Index*, and the patron assumed that it was *Century Magazine*, "What else could it be?" he asks ingenuously. The staffer replies that his answer is in the key to abbreviations in the index. The patron disappears to the reference collection and then reappears with a sheepish look on his face. "I guess I made a mistake. It's *Center Magazine* that I need."

Other common problems include the fact that novice researchers will take any abbreviated part of the citation and try to make it part of the periodical title. For instance, the "il" that indicates illustrations accompany the article will be added to the title so that patrons will ask for *Illustrated Newsweek* or *Plays and Players Illustrated*. Another common misunderstanding involves the dating of indexes and their coverage. A cumulative index for a single periodical dated "January-March 1989" will cover all of the issues of that periodical in that time period. On the other hand, an abstracting and indexing service that covers hundreds of periodicals and is dated "January 1989" will not cover the January 1989 issues of the periodicals. Instead, there will most likely be coverage of late 1988 periodical issues. This can be a confusing distinction for novice index users.

Finally, it must be noted that there is a significant body of periodical literature that is not indexed at all. Many newsletters, limited interest periodicals, and other obscure publications can fall into this category. Short of calling or writing to the publisher and asking them if they have published articles on a particular subject, one can only search issue-by-issue and page-by-page to locate items.

Notes

[1]Bernard Houghton, *Scientific Periodicals: Their Historical Development, Characteristics and Control* (London: Clive Bingley, 1975), 68-69.

[2]Verner W. Clapp, "Indexing and Abstracting Services for Serial Literature," *Library Trends* 2 (April 1954): 509-10.

[3]Ibid., 512.

[4]Houghton, *Scientific Periodicals*, 85-86.

[5]Andrew D. Osborn, *Serial Publications: Their Place and Treatment in Libraries*, 3d ed. (Chicago: American Library Association, 1980), 420.

[6]Brian Aveney and Rod Slade, "Indexing of Popular Periodicals: The State of the Art," *Library Journal* 103 (1 October 1978): 1917.

[7]Carol Tenopir, "Infotrac: A Laser Disc System," *Library Journal* 111 (1 September 1986): 168.

[8]Douglas J. Ernest and Jennifer Monath, "User Reaction to a Computerized Periodical Index," *College & Research Libraries News* 47 (May 1986): 317.

[9]Ann Bristow Beltran, "Use of InfoTrac in a University Library," *Database* 9 (June 1986): 66.

[10]Mary Ann Walker and Helen Westneat, "Using InfoTrac in an Academic Library," *Reference Services Review* 13 (Winter 1985): 18.

[11]Cynthia Hall and Harriet Talan, "InfoTrac in Academic Libraries: What's Missing in the New Technology?" *Database* 10 (February 1987): 53.

[12]Tenopir, "Infotrac," 168.

[13]Michael D. G. Spencer, "Thoroughness of Book Review Indexing: A First Appraisal," *RQ* 27 (Winter 1986): 188-99.

6

Serials of the United States Government and of International Governmental Organizations

The United States federal government produces tens of thousands of publications each year. According to a survey compiled in the late 1970s, over 100,000 publications were issued during an eighteen month period in 1977 and 1978. Of these, approximately one-third were never properly cataloged as mandated by the law.[1] The United States government, as a publishing entity, thus, is huge and not well controlled in a bibliographic sense.

In 1981, the Reagan administration, as part of its "War on Waste," ordered a temporary moratorium on new government-produced periodicals, pamphlets, and audio-visual products. Departments and agencies also were ordered to eliminate publications that were useless and wasteful.[2] Between 1982 and 1986, the *Serials Supplement* (later titled the *Periodicals Supplement*) of the *Monthly Catalog of United States Government Publications* listed 263 discontinued periodicals.[3] Some of the more established and respected periodicals that have ceased publication include the *Pesticides Monitoring Journal, Reclamation Era, American Education,* and *Psychopharmacology Abstracts.*[4] Other periodicals have been forced to merge, while others have had subscription prices raised or initiated, where previously they had been distributed free of charge.

Despite these cutbacks, the United States government still produces a colossal number of periodicals, ranging from the weekly *Daily Weather Maps* to the quarterly *Military Law Review* and practically everything in between. The 1988 *Periodicals Supplement* has 1,545 entries, and this does not account for all federal government periodicals. Joe Morehead, the leading writer in the field of government documents, has stated that "there are no reliable figures on the total number of periodicals issued by the entities of the federal establishment."[5] So, just as in the world of privately-printed periodicals, there exists a well-established, well-documented group and an undocumented group of United States government periodicals. The established group is comprised of periodicals under bibliographic control, while the undocumented group is comprised of those not under standard bibliographic control. For publications not under bibliographic control, the best approach to tracking them down is to directly contact the issuing agency (department, division, bureau, or unit) or that agency's library.

Identifying United States Government Periodicals

For periodicals under bibliographic control, there are standard sources in which to search. The best source for identifying current United States government periodicals is the *Periodicals Supplement* of the *Monthly Catalog of United States Government Publications* (Washington, D.C.: Government Printing Office). This supplement, formerly known as the *Serials Supplement*, is published annually at the beginning of the calendar year. As was mentioned earlier, the 1988 edition has entries for 1,545 periodicals arranged by their issuing agencies. Each entry contains a full cataloging record, including subscription price and notes on which abstracting and indexing services cover the periodical. Several indexes are provided, the most important being those that are arranged by author, title, subject, and title keyword. Detailed information is also given regarding how to order these periodicals. The *Monthly Catalog* is also available in various formats other than print, including reel microfilm, CD-ROM, and as an online database.

A second source for identifying United States government periodicals is *Ulrich's International Periodicals Directory*. A separate index of such periodicals is not actually provided. However, if one knows the title of the periodical being searched for, the regular title index can be used. Also, many of the United States government periodicals listed in this directory can be found in the title index under the heading, "U.S.," followed by the name of the issuing government agency. The entries for individual periodicals give the address and phone number of the agency that produces the publication and an address to which orders should be sent. Indexing and abstracting information is also given, along with notations as to availability in formats other than print. Other periodical directories with coverage of the United States such as *The Serials Directory, The Standard Periodical Directory*, and the *Gale Directory of Publications* also include United States government periodicals (see chapter 3).

A third major source is the annual *Guide to U.S. Government Publications*, edited by John L. Andriot (McLean, Va.: Documents Index). Formerly titled, *Guide to U.S. Government Serials and Periodicals*, this work is a detailed breakdown, arranged by agency and Superintendent of Documents classification number, of publications of the United States government. Both current and retrospective serials are listed. Short statements of purpose are given for many of the serials, along with other salient information. An agency index and a title index are provided.

Another source for identifying these periodicals is the *Publications Reference File*, also known as the *GPO Sales Publications Reference File*, which is published on microfiche, by the Government Printing Office. This is a frequently updated catalog of government publications currently available for sale by the Government Printing Office. It also lists forthcoming titles and recently out-of-stock publications. The main section of this catalog arranges the entries in an interfiled index of titles, keywords and phrases, subjects, and personal authors. Entries include brief bibliographic information and a physical description, as well as the price and the Superintendent of Documents classification number. This file is also available as an online database.

Two other specialized guides are available to assist in the use of government serials. *Government Reference Serials*, compiled by LeRoy C. Schwarzkopf (Englewood, Colo.: Libraries Unlimited), was first published in 1988 and is a companion and supplement to *Government Reference Books: A Biennial Guide to U.S. Government Publications*, which began publication with an edition dated 1968/69. This supplemental work contains listings of approximately 580 federal government serial publications. They are arranged in four main sections ("General Library Reference," "Social Sciences," "Science and Technology," and "Humanities") and are subdivided into various topics and subtopics. The entries for individual serials provide a wealth of information including issuing agency, Superintendent of Documents number, Library of Congress control (or card) number, ISSN, OCLC record number, and the *Monthly Catalog* entry number. A detailed publishing history is given for many of the titles. A descriptive annotation of approximately one paragraph in length is provided for each publication. There are four separate indexes included in this work; one each for titles, authors, subjects, and Superintendent of Documents numbers. Presumably, this guide will be published on a continuing basis. For more recent information in this area, see *U.S. Government Documents: A Practical Guide for Non-Professionals in Academic and Public Libraries* (Englewood, Colo.: Libraries Unlimited).

Business Serials of the U.S. Government, 2d edition, 1988, edited by Priscilla C. Geahigan and Robert F. Rose (Chicago: American Library Association) is an eighty-six page work intended primarily for the use of librarians in small and medium-sized public and academic libraries that do not subscribe to the *American Statistics Index*. Serials included in this bibliography are those that have been determined to be chiefly business or business-related in nature. Included are 183 publications arranged under broad subject headings such as "International Business" or "Taxation." The individual entries give date of first publication, frequency, previous title(s), special features, and Superintendent of Documents number. An evaluative and descriptive annotation of approximately one paragraph is included in each entry. Sources of indexing for the serial are also noted. A subject index and a title index are provided.

Indexing and Abstracting of United States Government Periodicals

Major United States government periodicals are covered in abstracting and indexing services just as other major periodicals are covered. For instance, the *Monthly Labor Review*, produced by the Bureau of Labor Statistics in the Department of Labor, is indexed in at least ten services, including the *Readers' Guide to Periodical Literature*, the *Business Periodicals Index*, and the *PAIS Bulletin*. Likewise, the *Department of State Bulletin* is covered in nearly a dozen different services. Even a more obscure government periodical such as *Tree Planters' Notes*, produced by the U.S. Forest Service in the Department of Agriculture, is covered in five services, including *Biological Abstracts* and *Weed Abstracts*. In order to determine where a government periodical is indexed or abstracted, one should first consult *Ulrich's International Periodicals Directory*, which provides this type of information. Another place to check is the *Periodicals Supplement* of the *Monthly Catalog* (see earlier in this chapter). Other sources for obtaining abstracting and indexing information are described in chapter 5.

The *Index to U.S. Government Periodicals* (Chicago: Infordata International) is, as the title indicates, devoted solely to indexing periodicals published by the United States government. Approximately 175 such publications from all subject areas are covered. First issued in 1970, this index provides article-level access through interfiled author and subject entries. Each entry is assigned a number so a microfiche copy of the article or periodical issue can be obtained from Infordata International. This index is published quarterly, with the last issue of the year being an annual cumulation.

Another source that provides extensive indexing of United States government periodicals is the *American Statistics Index* (Bethesda, Md.: Congressional Information Service). The stated goal of this work is to be the master guide and index to all the statistical publications, including periodicals, of the United States government. It provides coverage of six hundred periodicals. In some instances, each issue of a periodical will be abstracted in detail, such as the *Survey of Current Business*, a monthly produced by the Bureau of Economic Analysis of the Department of Commerce. In other cases, a general description of the periodical will be provided without full indexing of each issue. An example of a publication receiving this type of treatment is *Eggs, Chickens, and Turkeys*, a monthly produced by the Agricultural Statistics Board of the Department of Agriculture.

The *American Statistics Index* is issued monthly, with annual cumulations. It began publication in 1973, and its 1974 edition included selective retrospective indexing back into the early 1960s. Each issue or cumulation is published in two separate parts, "Index" and "Abstracts." The major "Index" sections are arranged by subjects and names, categories, and titles. The brief "Index" entries provide access to the expanded "Abstracts" entries where the publications are described in full. Virtually every document described in this source can be purchased, on microfiche, from the Congressional Information Service. The *American Statistics Index* is also available as an online database.

Locating United States Government Periodicals

United States government periodicals are acquired, or not acquired, by most libraries based on the same criteria applied to all periodicals. Thus, patrons searching for specific government periodicals will run into the same access problems common to any other type of serial publication. No one library can have all periodicals. However, in searching for holding locations of United States government periodicals, one can take advantage of the Federal Depository Library Program. This program is comprised of over 1,300 selective depositories and approximately fifty regional depositories throughout the nation. As one could infer, the selective depository libraries choose from the thousands of items that are available. Regional depositories, on the other hand, receive a copy of every depository item that is distributed. Thus, if a United States government periodical listed in the *Periodicals Supplement* of the *Monthly Catalog of United States Government Publications* is designated as being a depository item, then a regional depository should have it (assuming that the library was a regional depository at the time the publication was distributed). Each issue of the *Monthly Catalog* contains a list of the nation's regional depository libraries, with addresses and telephone numbers. An address is also given where one can write to obtain a complete list of depository libraries.

In searching for other libraries with holdings of United States government periodicals, one can also search through various union lists, as described in chapter 4.

Major United States Government Periodicals

Although not usually thought of as periodicals, a number of standard United States government publications do fall into that category. Foremost is the *Congressional Record*, which is issued for every day that Congress is in session and is relied upon to give an official account of Congressional debate. This is not a verbatim transcript of the proceedings of the Senate and the House of Representatives, since members may revise and extend spoken remarks and may submit unspoken material for insertion. The ability to insert unspoken remarks has been a controversial issue in Congress for years, with some members strongly supporting it and others adamantly opposing it.[6] Those who oppose it point to the *Congressional Record* of October 18, 1972, in which Representative Hale Boggs was quoted as giving a speech regarding legislation that had been enacted during the session. Unfortunately, he had died in a plane crash two days earlier.[7] In the past decade, insertions into the *Congressional Record*, where no part was spoken, supposedly have been preceded and followed by a "bullet" symbol. However, there are means in which the placement of the symbol can be avoided. So, it is not a foolproof system.[8] Though not a verbatim transcript, the *Congressional Record* does serve to document the progress of legislation. It also serves as a means of communication among members of Congress.

The *Federal Register* is another periodical that is of great importance. Published Monday through Friday, it contains executive orders, new rules and regulations, proposed rules, and announcements from government agencies. The rules and regulations printed in the *Federal Register* are codified in the *Code of Federal Regulations.*

The *Weekly Compilation of Presidential Documents* is published every Monday and is comprised of statements, messages, and other Presidential materials released during the preceding week. A companion to this publication is the *Public Papers of the Presidents* series which annually cumulates such materials.

The *Department of State Bulletin*, which was established in 1939, is the "Official Monthly Record of United States Foreign Policy." As such, its purpose is to provide information on developments in the foreign relations of the United States and on the work of the Department of State. Included are the texts of speeches and news conferences of the President and of the Secretary of State, selected official statements and press releases, and information on current actions regarding treaties.

The *Commerce Business Daily* is published by the Government Printing Office for the Department of Commerce. It is a list of government "procurement invitations, contract awards, subcontracting leads, sales of surplus property and foreign business opportunities."

The following is a list of some other important United States Government periodicals.

Air University Review

Business America

Business Conditions Digest

Children Today

Employment and Earnings

Energy and Technology Review

FDA Consumer

Federal Reserve Bulletin

MMWR: Morbidity and Mortality Weekly Report

Monthly Labor Review

Naval War College Review

Problems of Communism

Survey of Current Business

Another class of United States government periodicals is composed of the valuable publications of the Foreign Broadcast Information Service (FBIS), and of the Joint Publications Research Service (JPRS), which is administratively part of FBIS. The Central Intelligence Agency now has jurisdiction over FBIS. Therefore, much information about the operations of JPRS and FBIS is not known.[9] The FBIS *Daily Report* series covers nine regions of the world (for example, the Soviet Union or East Asia). Each issue is a compilation of translated texts of radio broadcasts. The JPRS *Report* series covers twelve regions of the world, many of which are then broken down into specific continuing reports on particular aspects of that region (for example, "China Reports: Science and Technology"). The JPRS *Report* series primarily provides translations of newspaper, periodical, and book articles. The FBIS and JPRS series are published in hardcopy and on microfiche.

Access to FBIS translations is through a series of indexes produced by NewsBank titled, *Index to the Foreign Broadcast Information Service Daily Reports*. These indexes are available for the various editions of the *Daily Report* and are arranged in an interfiled subject, geographic, and personal name index. Monthly cumulations of title pages of specific FBIS *Daily Report* editions are available with the microfiche edition, thus providing another means of accessing articles. Access to the JPRS translations is through the *Transdex Index*, published by University Microfilms International. The main section provides indexing by keywords, descriptors and identifiers. A personal name index is included for the authors and personal subjects of articles. A serials reference staffer should become familiar with both of these series, even if they are not received in one's own library. Translated items cover scientific and technical subjects as well as political and social subjects. JPRS alone produces approximately 300,000 pages of translations per year,[10] and "is undoubtedly the most comprehensive source of translations available to librarians."[11]

Periodicals of International Governmental Organizations

It has been written that "the publications of intergovernmental organizations ... are perhaps the least understood and least utilized of all government documents."[12] Intergovernmental, or international governmental, organizations are bodies created by the action of two or more governments. The most well known, and probably the largest, intergovernmental organization is the United Nations, with its 159 member nations. A number of specialized agencies operate within the United Nations system, including the United Nations Educational, Scientific and Cultural Organization (UNESCO), and the World Health Organization (WHO).

There are also many other intergovernmental organizations that are not part of the United Nations. In this group are the European Communities, the North Atlantic Treaty Organization (NATO), the Organization for Economic Cooperation and Development (OECD), the Organization of American States (OAS), and the Organization of the Petroleum Exporting Countries (OPEC). The 1988/89 edition of the *Yearbook of International Organizations* states that there are over 1,700 intergovernmental organizations.[13] There is a wide and varied assortment of such organizations. As one might expect, it can often be difficult to identify or access the periodicals of these organizations.

Identifying Periodicals of Intergovernmental Organizations

As with all other searches to identify current periodicals, those of international governmental organizations can be searched first in *Ulrich's International Periodicals Directory* (see chapter 3 for complete description). This directory is of particular value in this type of searching, since it provides three indexes specifically for these types of periodicals. These indexes list separately the periodicals of the United Nations, the European Communities, and international organizations.

The *Directory of United Nations Serial Publications*, compiled by the Advisory Committee for the Co-ordination of Information Systems (New York: United Nations), was first published in 1982 under the title, *Register of United Nations Serial Publications*. The 1988 edition of this work is five hundred pages in length and provides bibliographic and ordering information on approximately four thousand serial titles published by thirty-eight United Nations organizations. In addition to currently published serials, this work lists approximately nine hundred non-current publications. This directory has been compiled from the data in the official files of the organizations covered. Individual entries provide the standard bibliographic data elements such as publisher, place of publication, years of publication, ISSN, frequency, language, former and successor titles, other language editions, and subject descriptors. The entries are in an alphabetical title listing. Three indexes are included to allow access by organization, subject, and ISSN. Addresses of United Nations Headquarters Publications Offices and of selected United Nations libraries are given.

International Bibliography: Publications of Intergovernmental Organizations (New York: UNIPUB), a quarterly that was formerly titled, *International Bibliography, Information, Documentation*, was first published in 1972. Each issue contains a "Periodicals Record" section in which a few hundred periodicals of intergovernmental organizations are listed alphabetically by title. In some cases, general descriptions of the periodicals are provided, while in other instances, the articles within individual issues of periodicals are listed. Subscription information is provided for all listed periodicals.

There are a number of reference sources that provide information about intergovernmental organizations, and, in so doing, note the publications of the organizations. The first source in which to find this type of information is the previously mentioned *Yearbook of International Organizations* (Munich: K. G. Saur). Entries for individual organizations in this work provide a list of the publications of the organization, with their frequency of publication. A separate volume of the annual *Encyclopedia of Associations* (Detroit: Gale Research) also covers international organizations including some intergovernmental organizations. United Nations-related organizations and multilateral treaty organizations in particular are covered. The entries for individual organizations include a list of publications with their frequencies. Similar information can also be found in *The Europa Year Book* (London: Europa Publications). *The World of Learning* (London: Europa Publications), an annual, provides this type of information for intergovernmental organizations concerned with education.

Indexing and Abstracting of Periodicals of International Governmental Organizations

Major intergovernmental organization periodicals can be found covered in some of the standard abstracting and indexing services. For instance, the *UN Chronicle* is covered in the *Readers' Guide to Periodical Literature* as well as in several other services. *Ulrich's International Periodicals Directory* is the first source to check to determine if such a periodical is covered in one of the standard sources. The *PAIS Bulletin*, in particular, indexes many of these periodicals. The fall 1982 issue (volume 8, no. 3) of *Serials Review* includes an article that lists indexed international government organization periodicals.[14] Over 130 periodicals are listed, with many shown to be indexed in several sources.

As mentioned earlier in this chapter, the quarterly publication, *International Bibliography: Publications of Intergovernmental Organizations*, lists individual issues of these periodicals. In many cases, the contents of specific issues are enumerated. There is also limited subject indexing.

For indexing of statistical information in these periodicals, the *Index to International Statistics* (Bethesda, Md.: Congressional Information Service) is an excellent source. It is published by the same company that produces the *American Statistics Index* and is arranged in much the same manner. This work is published monthly, with quarterly and annual cumulations. It is arranged in two sections for each issue or volume: "Index," and "Abstracts." This service covers monographs and serials. For most of the periodicals covered, each specific issue is described briefly. Other periodicals are described in general terms and not by specific topics in particular issues.

Major Periodicals of Intergovernmental Organizations

There are a number of periodicals of international governmental organizations that can be considered to be standard titles in any academic periodical collection. Foremost among these are (with publishing body in parenthesis):

Americas (Organization of American States)

Courier (UNESCO)

Finance and Development (International Monetary Fund)

International Labour Review (International Labour Office)

International Review of Education (UNESCO)

International Social Science Journal (UNESCO)

NATO Review (North Atlantic Treaty Organization)

The OECD Observer (Organization for Economic Cooperation and Development)

UN Chronicle (United Nations)

WHO Chronicle (World Health Organization)

World Health (World Health Organization)

Notes

[1]Joe Morehead, *Introduction to United States Public Documents*, 3d ed. (Littleton, Colo.: Libraries Unlimited, 1983), 28-29.

[2]Ronald Reagan, *Public Papers of the Presidents of the United States, Ronald Reagan, 1981* (Washington, D.C.: Government Printing Office, 1982), 364-65.

[3]Joe Morehead, "Lost and Gone Forever: The Demise of Selected Federal Serials," *The Serials Librarian* 12, nos. 3-4 (1987): 6-7.

[4]Ibid., 10-16.

[5]Ibid., 7.

[6]Michelle M. Springer, "The *Congressional Record:* 'Substantially a Verbatim Report?' " *Government Publications Review* 13 (May/June 1986): 371-72.

[7]Joe Morehead, "The Forlorn Passion of William Steiger," *Technical Services Quarterly* 3 (Spring/Summer 1986): 120-21.

[8]Springer, "The *Congressional Record*," 375.

[9]David Y. Allen, "Buried Treasure: The Translations of the Joint Publications Research Service," *Government Publications Review* 9 (March/April 1982): 91-92.

[10]Ibid., 92.

[11]Bruce Morton, "JPRS and FBIS Translations: Polycentrism at the Reference Desk," *Reference Services Review* 11 (Spring 1983): 101.

[12]Diane K. Harvey, "Periodicals of International Organizations: An Untapped Resource," *Serials Review* 8 (Fall 1982): 11.

[13]Union of International Associations, *Yearbook of International Organizations, 1988/89*, 25th ed. vol. 1 (Munich: K. G. Saur, 1988), Appendix 7, Table 1.

[14]Steven D. Zink, "International Government Periodicals," *Serials Review* 8 (Fall 1982): 51-59.

7
Other Aspects of Reference Work with Periodicals

Periodicals on Microform

Backfiles of periodicals in libraries have traditionally been preserved in bound volumes. In the most common situation, these backfiles are steadily accumulated through the years as a result of a library's current subscriptions to periodicals. The issues of periodicals are normally received by a library one at a time as they are published, and these current, paperbound issues are stored and made available as individual issues. Once a substantial amount of issues has accumulated, they are pulled off the shelves and collated; that is, arranged in order based on dates or volume and issue numbers. This bundle of issues is then sent to a commercial bindery, or in some cases, to an in-house bindery, to be bound into a single, hardback volume. The amount of issues and the date coverage of any bound volume is largely determined by the frequency of publication of the periodical and the thickness of the issues. Thus a bound volume of a weekly periodical may contain only three months of issues, while a bound volume of a quarterly may contain a year, or more, of issues. From the time that the unbound issues are removed from the shelf until the bound volume returns from the bindery, these issues are not available to the patrons of a library. The binding process can take weeks or months to complete.

Although this process of receiving paperbound issues and later binding them for permanent retention is still prevalent, many libraries have begun to acquire backfiles of periodicals on microfilm or on microfiche. Microfilm is defined as a length of photographic film bearing a number of microimages, while microfiche is a flat sheet of photographic film bearing a number of microimages. Microfilm has been used in libraries for over half a century as a storage and preservation medium for newspapers (see chapter 13).[1] More recently, microfilm and microfiche have begun to be accepted as formats in which to retain periodicals. Those who favor retaining periodicals on microform have noted several advantages. Space savings is one, with microform periodicals requiring approximately one-tenth of the storage space of bound volumes, according to University Microfilms International (UMI), a large microform publisher.[2] The cost of purchasing microform sets is also stated as being less than the cost of binding volumes. There is also no need to replace lost, stolen, or mutilated issues prior to binding.[3] After binding, volumes are often defaced or mutilated. This does not usually happen to microforms. When backfiles are retained on microform, there is no period when the periodical is "at the bindery" and not available. This is a prime consideration since most libraries send issues to be bound within a year or two of their publication. This is also the time when an issue of a periodical is receiving its heaviest usage due to its coverage in abstracting and indexing services.[4] In purchasing complete retrospective backfiles of periodicals on microform, libraries are able to obtain publications that would be unavailable in hardcopy or prohibitively expensive in that format. Periodicals published on newsprint, such as *Computerworld* and *The Chronicle of Higher Education*, are preserved better on microform. Another advantage of periodicals on microform is that photocopying from microfilm can sometimes be easier than photocopying from bound volumes. This is especially true when a volume is bound so tightly that the print continues deep into the gutter, making it almost impossible to obtain a good photocopy without ruining the binding.

There are disadvantages to keeping periodicals on microform, one of these being considerable user resistance to microforms. Most patrons would prefer to read the hardcopy version of a publication. One of the primary reasons for user resistance is that one must rely on microform reading equipment to read the publication. If the reading equipment is not of high quality, or if the equipment is not properly maintained, a patron can become very frustrated in using microforms. Another major disadvantage to using microforms is that they are very difficult to browse. Such an attempt can even result in motion sickness for the reader. Although there has been some question as to the validity of the stated advantages of periodicals on microform,[5] it seems apparent that the trend toward the permanent retention of periodical backfiles on microform will continue to grow.

To determine if a periodical is available in a microform edition, first consult *Ulrich's International Periodicals Directory*. The individual entries in this directory indicate whether the periodical is available on microform and, if so, which company produces it. Information from over thirty micropublishers is included in *Ulrich's*. The addresses and telephone numbers of these companies are given. Other periodical directories also provide information about the availability of microform editions (see chapter 3).

In addition, micropublishing companies publish their own catalogs, which list the periodical titles they film. University Microfilms International is one of the most prominent publishers of periodicals on microform, offering sixteen thousand different periodical publications, more than ten thousand of which are currently published.[6] Their massive catalog, *Serials in Microform*, is published annually. The periodical entries are arranged alphabetically and give complete information regarding the price and extent of a periodical's microform editions. Most of the publications are available in 35mm microfilm, 16mm microfilm, and on microfiche. Also provided is the publication's ISSN and an indication of what abstracting and indexing services cover the periodical. It is also noted if copies of articles or entire issues of the periodical can be provided through UMI's Article Clearinghouse (see later in this chapter). A subject index of the serials in the catalog is included. Another huge microform catalog, titled *Microforms Annual*, is published by Microforms International and Oxford Microforms Publications. It lists microform collections and periodicals micropublished or distributed by Microforms International and its affiliates, including Oxford Microforms Publications. Over twenty thousand items are listed in its seventh edition, dated 1986/87.

The *Guide to Microforms in Print, Author, Title* (Westport, Conn.: Meckler) is an annual directory of microform titles comprising books, periodicals, collections and other materials currently available. Micropublishers from throughout the world are included. A companion publication is the annual, *Guide to Microforms in Print, Subject*, which arranges the materials by subject.

The *National Register of Microform Masters* was published annually by the Library of Congress from 1965 through 1983, with a cumulated set covering 1965 to 1975. The purpose of this work was to serve as a catalog of master microforms produced to preserve printed materials on film. The listings are arranged by main entry and provide bibliographic information about the work and an indication of the institution or company that owns the master microform. Both monographs and serials are listed in one interfiled alphabet. Although the primary purpose of this work was to prevent the needless duplication of microforms, it can also be put to reference use when some of the previously mentioned sources do not list the title that is needed.

One can also identify microform editions by searching for records in the bibliographic databases, such as OCLC. The 533 field of a MARC record is known as the "photoreproduction note." If the record is for a microform edition, this field will list the type of microform, the name of the micropublisher, and the publisher's location. (See chapter 14 for a fuller description of the MARC serial record.)

In providing periodicals reference service in a library with a collection of periodicals on microform, one must be prepared to handle the various situations and problems that can arise with such a collection. In dealing with patrons who have never used microforms before, the library staffer should be patient and take the time to instruct the patron on the use of microforms. A demonstration of the reading equipment should be provided. Even if the equipment displays directions for its use, it is best to show the first-time user how to operate it. In conjunction with this, some reluctant patrons need to be encouraged to use the microforms. Many such readers resist using microforms simply because they have had no experience with them. A positive attitude on the part of the staff member, along with a demonstration of how to use the equipment, will help to put many reluctant users at ease. Also, at the outset, the inexperienced user should be told that it is possible to make photocopies from microforms. This is necessary since many patrons are unwilling to use microforms because they think that photocopies cannot be made from them.

Reference staff working with a microform collection should become very familiar with all of the microform reading and photocopying equipment that is available for users of the collection. Such staff should know how each type of machine operates and be able to correct minor problems with the equipment (changing bulbs, adjusting exposure for photocopies, etc.). Also, staff must become experienced at handling the problems of film that has been wound backwards on a reel and that of microfilm that has been improperly threaded on a reading machine and will not rewind.

There are two specific reference problems in relation to periodicals on microform that should be noted. First, occasionally a reel of microfilm will be inexplicably missing an issue or a supplement of a periodical.[7] In these cases, the micropublisher has inadvertently left out the issue when filming or knowingly filmed the run of issues without the issue that was missing. Since most libraries discard their paper issues of a periodical once the microform of those issues is received, there is usually no recourse except to find another library, or other source, for the item needed. Be careful not to refer a patron to a library with microform of the publication, since that microform will also have the issue missing.

Another common problem regards indexes that are issued for specific periodicals. These indexes are often issued as separate supplements. In libraries where such periodicals are bound, the indexes are bound with the volume that it covers. Even if the index arrives after the issues that it covers have been bound, it is still possible to "tip in" the index to the proper volume. With microfilm editions of periodicals the handling of indexes is inconsistent. Sometimes they will be found at the beginning of a reel or sometimes at the end of a reel. Often, if they are received late, such indexes are filmed along with whatever volume of the periodical is currently being filmed.[8] The labels on microfilm boxes will frequently provide some indication of the indexes on the enclosed reel of microfilm.

Special Microform Sets of Periodicals

The Information Access Company, the producer of numerous nonprint indexing services (see chapter 5) such as the *Magazine Index* and InfoTrac, also produces two innovative microform sets. The Magazine Collection was introduced in 1983, and the Business Collection in 1984. Both of these collections reproduce issues of hundreds of periodicals on 16mm microfilm cartridges. These cartridges can be used on reader-printer machines that are designed to accept them. An individual cartridge will contain various issues of different periodicals. The issues are apparently filmed as they are received and indexed by the company. A constantly-updated guide to the periodicals is available for each collection. Using this guide, a patron can locate the appropriate cartridge and frame number to find a specific issue of a periodical.

The Magazine Collection provides microform editions of approximately 250 periodicals, with coverage of most going back to 1980. The Business Collection covers approximately 450 periodicals, with many being available back to 1982. A number of the periodicals are included for local and regional business coverage, and only selected issues and articles are available. Both of these collections contain many very popular publications and some relatively obscure titles. Among others, the Magazine Collection provides a microform edition of *Time* and *Newsweek*, and the Business Collection has *Forbes* and *Fortune*.

These two collections are enhanced and transformed into a unique type of product. Citations to articles in the Information Access Company indexes such as the *Business Index, Magazine Index,* and InfoTrac give a cartridge number and frame number if the article is available in the Magazine Collection or

Business Collection. Taken in tandem, searching on the indexes and the quick retrieval on microfilm cartridges is an innovation that is very popular with users. It is quite possible to search a subject and print out a few cited articles literally within minutes. The searching and retrieval process could not be easier or quicker.

Its ease of use and simplicity, may, in some cases, be one of this system's drawbacks. The Information Access Company indexes do not allow any type of advanced searching techniques. Also, the types of periodicals available in these two collections are usually business oriented or of general interest. Thus, a patron can retrieve articles rapidly, but these articles may not be the best on the topic. So, even users who are seemingly progressing nicely, copying articles and enthused about a system that allows such rapid research, might be falling into a trap. Whenever possible, the librarian responsible for serials reference service should intervene to explain the limitations of the system and to perhaps suggest other indexes or abstracting services that might be more appropriate.

A major disadvantage of owning a microform edition of a periodical in either of these collections is that browsing of a number of issues is practically impossible. Since the issues are not filmed consecutively, they each must be accessed separately. For instance, the twelve monthly issues of *Road & Track* for 1987 are located on twelve separate cartridges in the magazine collection. Although it is possible to eventually access all twelve issues, it would not be the same as browsing through a bound volume of the same issues or even in searching through a "traditional" microfilm reel with the same twelve issues in consecutive order.

In addition to offering for sale microform editions of particular periodical publications, microfilming companies also package together collections that contain runs of many periodicals. These periodicals are usually related to one another by subject or by place of publication. Normally, the focus of such collections is on periodicals and other materials that are either old, rare, or not generally available in libraries. Collections such as these are quite important since they do make available a body of materials that most libraries could never amass in hardcopy format.

There are many collections of this type. One of these is published by University Microfilms International and is known as the American Periodical Series. Actually, this series is in three separate collections, and they are:

American Periodicals, 18th century

American Periodicals, 1800-1850

American Periodicals, 1850-1900, Civil War and Reconstruction

In total, these three sets include more than 1,100 periodicals, with publishing dates ranging from 1741 to 1900.[9] Periodicals in all types of subject areas are covered, from religion to surgery to satire. A 341-page printed guide to the collection, titled *American Periodicals 1741-1900: An Index to the Microfilm Collections* (Ann Arbor, Mich.: University Microfilms International, 1979), provides title, subject, and editor indexes for the periodicals in the collections. Descriptions of the periodicals are given.

At over 2,700 microfilm reels, the American Periodical Series is one of the larger and more prominent such microform collections. However, there are many other microform collections in general and specific subject areas. Some others are also quite huge, while some are relatively small. An example of a small collection is the sixteen-reel *Little Magazine Series: Selected Short-Run Cinema Periodicals, 1889-1972*, published by World Microfilm Publications in association with the British Film Institute.[10] This collection also has a printed guide, as do virtually all of these microform collections. The *Guide to Microforms in Print*, can be used to identify microform collections. Also, the individual catalogs of the various micropublishers will also list the collections they have available.

From the serials reference standpoint, it is essential that staff members be aware of the special microform collections that are owned by their respective libraries. They should have enough knowledge about these collections so that when an inquiry is received in a subject area that relates to one of these collections, the staffer remembers to suggest the microform collection as a possible source. It is also important to realize that some libraries do not annotate their central serials record or serials catalog to show the periodicals and holdings that are owned as parts of these collections. In this situation, serials reference service providers must be even more familiar with these collections.

Periodicals in Other Formats

In addition to hardcopy and microform formats, periodicals are becoming increasingly more available in other formats, particularly through online systems. The full-text retrieval of publications online has focused predominantly on newspapers. However, many periodicals are available, in full-text, through online databases. These periodicals can be identified by using *Ulrich's International Periodicals Directory* (see chapter 3). Other sources for this type of information are the *Directory of Periodicals Online: Indexed, Abstracted & Full-Text, News, Law & Business* and *Books and Periodicals Online: A Guide to Publication Contents of Business and Legal Databases* (see chapter 5).

A few journals are "published" only online, with no print equivalent. It is possible that this may become a more widespread practice in the future (see chapter 16). Currently, a few periodicals are published on disks that must be used on personal computers for viewing. At present, CD-ROM technology has been embraced by abstracting and indexing services and by libraries. It is possible that other periodicals may be soon published in that format.

Abbreviations

One of the most consistent and difficult problems that arises in reference work with periodicals is the abbreviated periodical title in a citation. Such abbreviations come to the attention of reference staff when a patron is in need of a cited item but is unfamiliar with the abbreviation given for the periodical. When a patron does not know what an abbreviation stands for, it is preferable that the question be taken to a library staff member immediately. Often, though, readers will create a non-existent title based on an abbreviation or will assume, incorrectly, that it stands for a different title. This results in wasted effort for the patron and added confusion for the reference staffer.

When a patron asks for help in identifying the full title for which an abbreviation stands, the library staffer should ask to see the citation and inquire as to its source. In many cases, the citation will have come from an abstracting or indexing service. If that service is available in the library, the patron should be referred back to it and told that the full title should be listed in that service's key to abbreviated titles. If the service is not available in the library, then the standard periodical abbreviations reference works (described later in this section) should be consulted.

A more difficult problem is posed when the citation with the abbreviated title is from an article, book, report, or other type of document. In these cases, the first step is to check the actual citation to be certain that the patron has interpreted it correctly. Often, within an article or report, only the first citation to an item will provide full bibliographic information, while subsequent citations to the same item will provide only the barest information. It is therefore worthwhile to determine if there is a more complete citation to the item earlier in the work or in a bibliography at the end of the work. If that procedure is of no help then the abbreviation must be deciphered.

Although there are standards for abbreviations and different style manuals to prescribe correct citation format, many writers still devise their own citation format and their own periodical title abbreviations. First, search for the abbreviation in the standard abbreviation reference works. The sixth edition of *Periodical Title Abbreviations: By Abbreviation* (Detroit: Gale Research, 1988) lists 103,000 abbreviations and the titles that they stand for in alphabetical order by abbreviation. A companion publication is *Periodical Title Abbreviations: By Title*, which lists the publications alphabetically by title. These two volumes are published in updated editions every few years, and are supplemented, between editions, by *New Periodical Title Abbreviations*. Another standard periodical abbreviation reference tool is Otto Leistner's *Internationale Titelabkürzungen von Zeitschriften, Zeitungen, wichtigen Handbuchern, Wörterbuchern, Gesetzen usw.* (Osnabruck, West Germany: Biblio Verlag). The third edition, published in 1981, lists approximately 60,000 periodical abbreviations.

A problem that might crop up at this point is that one of these works will show that several publications share the same abbreviation. For instance, the standard abbreviation "JRS" is known to stand for at least five publications, these being the *Journal* of the Market Research Society, the *Journal of Regional Studies*, the *Journal of Research in Singing*, the *Journal of Roman Studies*, and the *Journal of Russian Studies*.[11] It is usually possible to make an educated guess, based on the subject matter of the cited item, as to which periodical title is most likely the appropriate one.

Another approach in attempting to decipher an abbreviation is to search in an appropriate abstracting or indexing service to locate a full citation to the article. This is a possibility since one usually knows the name of the author of the article and what subject it concerns.

Should all other approaches fail, an experienced serials reference staffer should be able to deduce a possible full title based on the abbreviation. For instance, an abbreviation given as "JAWWA" could be easily deciphered, even if it is not listed in any of the periodical abbreviations works. A "J" will often stand for "Journal," while an "A" might stand for "Association" or "America," or "American." The "WW" is the hardest part to decipher. But it could be deduced that the abbreviation "JAWWA" refers to the *Journal* of the American Water Works Association. This guessing process is much easier for those familiar with the thousands of different periodical titles commonly referred to within the various subject disciplines. Even without this knowledge, it is often possible to decide on the most likely beginning of the title by simply looking at an abbreviation. With an educated guess at the first word, a scan of the title index of *Ulrich's International Periodicals Directory* or *The Serials Directory* can be performed in an attempt to identify a current title. The subject sections of one of these directories may also reveal an appropriate match. For citations to older publications, employ the technique of scanning for titles in conjunction with the *Union List of Serials in Libraries of the United States and Canada* or in other older periodical title compilations.

Another problem similar to the abbreviated title is the situation in which an initialism is part of the periodical title or a part of the logo or design of the publication. Examples of this type of title are *JAMA, The Journal of the American Medical Association; WWD, Women's Wear Daily;* and, *FN, Footwear News.* These types of publications cause problems in that it is often not clear whether the initialism is part of the official title of the publication or if it is just part of a logo or design. Many users, when encountering an initialism as a title, such as *JAMA*, will assume that it is an abbreviation and will try to expand the initialism into something that it isn't. (Initialisms are also covered in chapter 14.)

Translations

A large body of periodical literature is published in languages other than English. A researcher can become frustrated when confronted with an article written in a language that cannot be understood. It is equally as frustrating for a library patron to do in-depth research on a particular region of the world if the most valuable source materials are in a language that the patron cannot comprehend. So, there is a constant demand for periodical materials that have been translated into English.

Cover-to-cover translations of foreign language periodicals into English do exist. Most such translations are of journals from the Soviet Union. In fact, there are a few American publishers who publish numerous Soviet journals in English translations. The Allerton Press and Plenum Press (Consultants Bureau), both located in New York City, each publish dozens of journals translated from Russian.

The third edition of *Journals in Translation* (Boston Spa, U.K.: British Library Lending Division; Delft, The Netherlands: International Translations Centre), published in 1982, lists over one thousand current and retrospective cover-to-cover translations and journals containing selected translated articles. The publisher and/or distributor of each translation is noted. A separate section gives the addresses of these publishers and distributors. The fourth edition of this work was published in 1987. Another source for translations information is the *World Translations Index*, which is published ten times a year, plus an annual index, by the International Translations Centre (Delft, The Netherlands) in conjunction with the National Translations Center (John Crerar Library, University of Chicago, and, as of 1989, at the Library of Congress). It is the continuation of two former publications, *World Transindex* and *Translations Register-Index*. This periodical announces translations of literature relating to science and technology from all languages into Western languages. Most of the items listed are individual translations of particular articles. A list of journals translated cover-to-cover is printed in the annual index.

In the realm of translations also falls the category of periodicals that provide compilations of English language translations of articles that have appeared in various sources. One such publication is *The Current Digest of the Soviet Press*, which is limited to translations of Soviet publications. A very popular periodical of translations is the *World Press Review* (with former titles, *Atlas World Press Review* and *Atlas*), which provides articles from worldwide sources. Also, any patron interested in translated works should be made aware of the publications of the Foreign Broadcast Information Service and of the Joint Publications Research Service (see chapter 6).

When a patron has located an article in a foreign language for which no translation can be identified, it is possible for a freelance researcher to be hired to perform a translation. Such individuals may be listed in a local telephone directory under "Translators" or "Translators & Interpreters."

Document Delivery Services

Commercial document delivery services have been developed to provide libraries and researchers with fast and convenient access to copies of articles from a wide range of publications. No one library can possibly have a "complete" collection of periodicals. In fact, most libraries subscribe to just a small percentage of the total number of currently published periodicals. On the other hand, most libraries, especially those of an academic or research nature, have available various specialized abstracting and indexing services and provide access to online databases. These services provide coverage of many more periodicals than are actually in the collections of most libraries. In addition, researchers find citations to articles in bibliographies or in citations in articles, reports, books, and other documents. Many of these cited items are also not in the collections of a library. Thus, a constant demand surfaces for articles from periodicals that are not in the collection of a library.

Some of these demands can be met by referring the patron to another local library that has the publication in question. If the patron can travel to the other library and has the time to do so, this can be an efficient manner in which to handle the situation. Demands of this type are also often handled through interlibrary loan requests. The interlibrary loan process, though, can be very inefficient and time-consuming. Some patrons don't have the time or the patience to travel to another library or to wait for a response to an interlibrary loan request. This can be especially true in research libraries and in special libraries.

Commercial document delivery services have been established in response to these demands. For a fee, such a service will quickly provide a copy of an article. The larger companies in this field promise a one- to two-day turnaround on requests. In "rush" situations, these services can also provide same-day service by employing telefacsimile technology. For libraries and individuals who can afford it, such services can alleviate much of the problem caused by the fact that no library can "have it all."

University Microfilms International operates one such service called the UMI Article Clearinghouse. Over ten thousand periodical titles are offered in a variety of subject areas, including those that are general, popular periodicals. The Institute for Scientific Information has a service known as The Genuine Article, which provides articles from over eight thousand journals. Most of the publications available through this service are scientific or technical in nature. The CAS Document Delivery Service provides copies of articles from the nearly ten thousand serials that are currently received at the Chemical Abstracts Service (CAS). Virtually anything that has been abstracted or cited in CAS publications and services is obtainable. In cases where CAS does not have right-to-copy arrangements, clients of this service can receive loan copies of the documents. Other abstracting and indexing services also offer document delivery of items cited in their publications. The Congressional Information Service, publisher of the *American Statistics Index* and other works (see chapter 6), provides this service as does Infordata International, the publisher of the *Index to U.S. Government Periodicals* (see chapter 6). Other document delivery services can be identified in *Document Retrieval: Sources & Services* (San Francisco: Information Store, 4th ed., 1987), which lists sources for all types of documents, including periodical articles.

Regional and Variant Editions of Magazines

A rather common, though not widely-known, practice is for publishers of popular American magazines to print variant editions of the same issue of a periodical. In general there are three types of variant editions: international, regional within the United States, and special interest.[12] Variant editions are printed to allow magazine advertisers to reach a more defined market. Thus, variant editions of the same issue of a periodical will carry different advertisements. In addition, editorial content may vary between editions. Since most periodical publishers do not note on the cover or in the publishing statement that there are variant editions, considerable problems can arise for the patron and librarian.

Most libraries receive only one edition of any magazine. Most abstracting and indexing services index only one edition of a magazine. If the edition in a library is not the same as the edition covered in an abstracting or indexing service, then the patron is often left searching for a "phantom" article. In these cases, look carefully through the entire issue, since the same article may have appeared on different pages in different editions. Also, examine the index to determine if it states what edition is indexed. For instance, the *Readers' Guide to Periodical Literature* states that it indexes the Central (U.S.) edition of *Sunset*.[13] Not all indexes will state this information, and the problems caused by variant editions can sometimes only be solved by contacting the abstracting or indexing service or by contacting the periodical publisher.[14]

Special Issues and Supplements

Special issues and supplements are two types of publications that are produced by periodical publishers. A special issue, also known as a special number, is a single issue of a periodical devoted to a particular subject. These issues may, or may not, bear the numbering scheme that the periodical carries. A supplement, on the other hand, is an extra issue or extra publication that is published to accompany a regular issue or volume of a periodical. Supplements most often do not bear the numbering scheme of the periodical, and supplements are often monographic in nature.

Special issues are usually published on a continuing basis, and readers and subscribers come to expect them. As such, library patrons begin to request these issues by name or by subject. For instance, a reader may ask for the automobile issue of *Consumer Reports*, which is the April issue every year. Another reader might ask for the *Survey of Buying Power* special issues of the periodical *Sales & Marketing Management*, which are published each year in July and October. Of course, it is impossible to remember all of the special issues of periodicals. Also, a special issue will usually be checked in, or accessioned, in a serial record as if it was just another issue, especially if the special issue carries the same volume and issue numbering of the periodical. So, it is often necessary to consult a reference work to determine when such special issues appear.

Bacon's Media Alerts (Chicago: Bacon's Publishing) is an annual directory of editorial calendars from the major magazines and top daily newspapers in the United States. Its purpose is to provide advance notice of special issues and special sections to the public relations and advertising industry. The 1988 edition lists over 1,800 magazines in a subject arrangement, for each title indicating special issues or issues with a special editorial focus to be published. A title index is included. Other reference works that can be consulted for special issues information include the *Special Issues Index*, compiled by Robert Sicignano and Doris Prichard (Westport, Conn.: Greenwood Press, 1982), and the *Guide to Special Issues and Indexes of Periodicals*, edited by Miriam Uhlan (Washington, D.C.: Special Libraries Association, 3d ed., 1985). Each of these publications covers over 1,300 periodicals.

Supplements, unlike special issues, cannot be systematically tracked, listed, and predicted. By their nature, supplements are usually one-time only publications. There are supplements to journals and other periodicals, however, that are published on a continuing basis and often have a separate serial numbering scheme such as, "Supplement No. 1," "Supplement No. 2," etc. These publications would then constitute a new series (or subseries) and would no longer be the hard-to-handle supplement that is being referred to here. Since supplements are often published on a one-time only basis or on an irregular basis, their arrivals cannot be predicted, and the searching for those that have been published can often be difficult.

The serials record can often give some clue in this type of search, since most supplements have unusual numbering, if any at all. A check-in clerk will often make a note of a supplement being received, whereas a special issue does not usually receive this treatment. Sometimes a supplement will be bound together with the volume that it accompanies, particularly in cases where it is printed on the cover of the supplement that it is a supplement to a specific issue of the periodical. As mentioned earlier, many supplements are monographic in nature and may be cataloged as separate publications. Even though cataloged as a monograph, most cataloging systems, manual and automated, will provide added entries or access points to allow retrieval under the name of the periodical that the supplement accompanied.

The Publishing Statement

Most periodicals provide a publishing statement in each issue. At the very least, such a statement usually gives the name and address of the publisher along with subscription price and frequency of publication information. Some periodicals, though, have very detailed statements that may provide any or all of the following:

Description of the periodical.

Description of publishing company or association.

ISSN and/or CODEN.

Names of those on the staff of the periodical.

Telephone numbers of staff members.

Names of those on the editorial board.

Listing of which abstracting and indexing services cover the periodical.

Information regarding other formats in which the periodical is available.

Availability of back issues.

Information about copyright and restrictions regarding copying from the periodical.

Information regarding submission of manuscripts.

Subscription and advertising rates along with appropriate mailing addresses and telephone numbers.

Readers often ask questions that can quickly be answered by the information in the publishing statement.

The Confused Patron

When inexperienced researchers become confused or are uncertain about how to proceed in a search, they usually choose one of two alternatives. The first, and preferable, alternative is to seek help from the library staff. In that manner, the staffer can provide explanations, guidance, and advice to the patron. The second alternative that a confused patron is likely to choose is not to seek help at first but to guess at the answers to questions. This often leads to much more complicated problems. There are some basic areas that cause confusion for inexperienced researchers. One of the foremost such areas concerns abbreviations of periodical titles. Patrons who do not ask for assistance in identifying the correct, complete title for which an abbreviation stands will often guess at the title. Such deductions are, in many cases, incorrect. Novice researchers will also incorrectly interpret citations in any number of ways. Often, a citation to a book will be searched as if it was a periodical, and vice versa. Other patrons will assume that the volume number given in a citation is the page number. Inexperienced library users may also look for a periodical title in the library's serials catalog and not find the entry, due to their own unfamiliarity with library cataloging and filing rules, even though the library does have the publication.

In many of these cases, the researcher will turn for help to the library staff as a last resort. At that point, the researcher will not detail the entire search but will just state an incorrect conclusion. These conclusions are reported in words such as, "The article isn't on the page that the index says it is," or, "The library doesn't have the journal I need." When these types of statements are made, library staff should never assume that they are correct. The first step for serials reference staff is to retrace the patron's search from the very beginning. This will often uncover an error on the part of the patron. The library staffer can then take this opportunity to provide on-the-spot bibliographic instruction. If the patron has not made a mistake and the conclusion is correct, then the library staffer can proceed from that point knowing that the foundation for further searching is accurate.

Special Problems in Periodicals Reference Work

Inaccurate citations to articles are quite frustrating both for the library user who is trying to locate the cited item and for the library staffer trying to assist the user. These incorrect references show up not only in footnotes and bibliographies of published books, articles, and reports, but also in the abstracting and indexing services. Once it has been established that a citation is inaccurate, then the person responsible for serials reference must be resourceful and attempt to find a reference to the same article in another source. Often this can be accomplished by searching in a likely abstracting or indexing service for the author, title, or subject of the article needed. Also, search the index, if such an index exists, of the periodical in which the article supposedly appeared.

Citations to periodical articles sometimes refer to articles on pages with unusual numbers such as "E3" or "SP92." This can often be confusing to a patron who cannot locate the article even though the appropriate issue is in hand. Normally, such numbers refer to pages within a separately-paged section of a periodical issue or in the supplement to a particular issue. In many of these cases, a careful search through the issue will locate a special section that has its own pagination. If no such section is located, then attempt to determine if a supplement was published to accompany that issue.

Another common problem in periodicals reference work is that many different publications have the same title. The most obvious examples of this are generic titles such as *Bulletin* or *Journal*. Even nongeneric titles can be found duplicated by different publications. For instance, there are two different current business periodicals with the titles, *Mergers & Acquisitions* and *Mergers and Acquisitions*. The only difference is the ampersand instead of the word "and" in one of the titles. *Mergers & Acquisitions* is published in Philadelphia, while *Mergers and Acquisitions* is published in London. Normally, periodicals with the same title are differentiated by place of publication. Also, such publications can usually be differentiated by their volume numbering schemes in relation to dates. For instance, the London *Mergers and Acquisitions* carries no volume numbering, just dates, while the Philadelphia *Mergers & Acquisitions* carries volume and issue numbers such as volume 22, no. 3, November/December 1987. Such publications can also be identified by the unique numbers or designations that may be assigned to them such as ISSN or CODEN (see chapter 14).

Notes

[1]Louis H. Fox, "Films for Folios," *Library Journal* 62 (1 May 1937): 361.

[2]*Serials in Microform*, 1987 ed. (Ann Arbor, Mich.: University Microfilms International, 1987), 4.

[3]Lynn S. Smith, *A Practical Approach to Serials Cataloging* (Greenwich, Conn.: JAI Press, 1978), 216.

[4]James S. Healey and Carolyn M. Cox, "Research and the *Readers' Guide:* An Investigation into the Research Use of Periodicals Indexed in the *Readers' Guide to Periodical Literature,*" *The Serials Librarian* 3 (Winter 1978): 185.

[5]Ann Niles, "Conversion of Serials from Paper to Microform," *Microform Review* 9 (Spring 1980): 90-95.

[6]*Serials in Microform*, 1989 ed. (Ann Arbor, Mich.: University Microfilms International, 1989), 8.

[7]Jean B. Johns, "The Mailbag," *Serials Review* 8 (Fall 1982): 3; Karen G. Roughton and Michael D. Roughton, "Serials on Microfilm," *The Serials Librarian* 5 (Summer 1981): 42.

[8]Roughton and Roughton, 42-43.

[9]Jean Hoornstra and Trudy Heath, eds., *American Periodicals 1741-1900: An Index to the Microfilm Collections* (Ann Arbor, Mich.: University Microfilms International, 1979), xiii.

[10]Anna Keller and Eugene Ferguson, eds., *Microform Collections and Selected Titles in Microform in the Microform Reading Room* ([Washington, D.C.]: General Reading Rooms Division, Library of Congress, 1987), 31.

[11]Leland G. Alkire, Jr., comp. and ed., *Periodical Title Abbreviations: By Abbreviation*, 6th ed. (Detroit: Gale Research, 1988), 414.

[12]Elin B. Christianson, "Variation of Editorial Material in Periodicals Indexed in *Readers' Guide,*" *ALA Bulletin* 62 (February 1968): 173.

[13]*Readers' Guide to Periodical Literature.* (New York: H. W. Wilson, 1986), Vol. 46, x.

[14]Kent Stephens, "Laserdisc Technology Enters Mainstream," *American Libraries* 17 (April 1986): 252.

8

Annuals, Irregular Serials, and Conference Publications

Thus far, the focus of this book has been on periodicals or serials (other than newspapers) that are published more frequently than once a year. Serials that are published on an annual, or less frequent, basis are the focus of this chapter. Also included are irregular serials which do not have a defined frequency of publication, but which usually appear less frequently than once a year.

The generic term for any serial that is published once a year is "annual." This class of serial is very common. Some of the most popular types of annuals are almanacs, yearbooks, directories, reports of corporations and other organizations, college catalogs, and all kinds of reference works. Almanacs are compendiums of facts and statistics, both retrospective and current, and are valued as ready-reference sources. The prime examples of this type of annual publication are *The World Almanac and Book of Facts* (New York: World Almanac) and *Whitaker's Almanac* (London: Whitaker). Yearbooks are also compendiums of facts and statistics, but they are normally limited to information regarding the current or preceding year only. Some examples of general yearbooks are the annual updates printed by encyclopedia publishers. Many yearbooks are limited to certain subject areas; an example of this being *The Europa Year Book* (London: Europa Publications), which provides basic, current information about the nations of the world and about many international organizations. There are also certain annual statistical publications that possess some of the characteristics of both almanacs and yearbooks. One of the most popular in this category is the *Statistical Abstract of the United States* (Washington, D.C.: Government Printing Office).

Numerous types of directories are published on an annual basis. A directory is a list of persons, organizations, or other entities that is usually arranged in alphabetical or subject order, giving addresses, telephone numbers and other information. Examples of popular annual directories include the *American Library Directory* (New York: R. R. Bowker), *Who's Who in America* (Chicago: Marquis Who's Who), and the *Encyclopedia of Associations* (Detroit: Gale Research). Another type of annual is the publication known simply as "annual report." These annual reports are issued in the thousands by corporations, associations, organizations, and governments, including governments' ministries, agencies, departments, divisions, sections, bureaus, etc. Such annual reports normally provide an official description of the events in that organization during the preceding year. Often, these reports are buttressed with pages of statistics, charts, and tables.

Other types of serials published annually include proceedings, transactions, reports, and other publications of conferences, congresses, symposia, and meetings of organizations (discussed in detail later in this chapter). College catalogs and telephone directories are important annuals. "Annual reviews" are published in many subject fields to provide a survey of the previous year's publications and research.

Directories of Annuals and Irregular Serials

Irregular Serials & Annuals (New York: R. R. Bowker) began publication in 1967 and served as a companion volume to *Ulrich's International Periodicals Directory*. The thirteenth edition, 1987-88, was the last separately published edition of *Irregular Serials & Annuals*. It provided information on approximately 35,900 annuals, conference proceedings, and other publications issued irregularly or less frequently than twice a year. Effective with the twenty-seventh edition, 1988-89, of *Ulrich's*, the information formerly provided in *Irregular Serials & Annuals* has been incorporated into *Ulrich's*. Thus, all serials, regardless of frequency of publication, are included in this one directory, which is now produced in three physical volumes. The 1988-89 edition contains 108,590 titles arranged under 554 subject headings. A typical entry for a serial in this directory will provide the following: publisher, address, phone number, frequency of publication, price, date first published, ISSN, circulation, and an indication of where the publication is indexed. In some instances, a brief description will be included. A title index and an ISSN index are provided along with separate indexes for international organizations, international congress proceedings, the European Communities, and the United Nations. Two other separate sections list publications that are available online. One section arranges these publications by title, and the other arranges them by online vendor. Serials that have recently ceased publication are listed in yet another section. (See chapter 3 for a complete description of this directory.)

The information in this directory can be searched online through the Bowker International Serials Database, or by searching Ulrich's PLUS, a CD-ROM file. Finally, this database is also available on microfiche, which is updated quarterly.

The Serials Directory (Birmingham, Ala.: EBSCO Publishing) lists all types of serials, including periodicals, annuals, irregulars, and serials published less frequently than once a year. Apparently, this directory will be published annually, with updates issued between the main editions. This reference work was introduced in 1986 as an alternative to the two R. R. Bowker directories, *Ulrich's International Periodicals Directory* and *Irregular Serials & Annuals*, which have now merged under the *Ulrich's* title. There are 118,000 serial entries, arranged under subject headings, in the third edition, 1988-89, of *The Serials Directory*. All classes of serials are interfiled. Thus, there is not a separate section for annuals and irregular serials. Serial entries provide the following: publisher, address, telephone number, frequency of publication, price, date first published, ISSN, an indication of where it is indexed, and a brief description of the publication. A title index and an ISSN index are included as well as an index of publications that have ceased (see chapter 3 for a complete description).

Willings Press Guide (East Grinstead, U.K.: British Media Publications) is an annual directory that lists newspapers and serials from throughout the world, although it is most useful for its coverage of the United Kingdom. This directory includes annual publications. *Benn's Media Directory. United Kingdom* (Tonbridge, U.K.: Benn Business Information Services) is an annual directory of the British media, including newspapers and other serials. A separate section titled, "Directories and other Reference Serials," lists over two thousand such British publications alphabetically by title. Most of the works covered in this section are annuals. A subject index of these titles precedes this section. (See chapters 3 and 10 for more complete descriptions of *Willings Press Guide* and of *Benn's Media Directory. United Kingdom*.)

In 1977, the *Directory Information Service* began publication as a periodical issued three times a year. Three years later, it was transformed into *The Directory of Directories*, a reference work that has been published every few years since then and has recently started publishing on an annual basis. Beginning with the sixth edition, 1989, the title changed again to *Directories in Print* (Detroit: Gale Research). The 1989 edition lists over ten thousand directories, published in the United States, in all fields. Membership directories of professional organizations and societies are also included. Most of the publications listed are issued annually or irregularly. The entries are arranged alphabetically under a few very broad subjects and include the following information: publisher, editor, address, telephone number, description of the coverage of the directory, frequency, and price. Additional information may also be provided such as availability in other formats, including online and computer readable formats. A title and keyword index and a subject index are included.

Directories in Print is supplemented by the *Publishers Volume*, which was first published in 1987 to accompany the fourth edition of the main work. This volume covers approximately seven thousand directory publishers and arranges them alphabetically and geographically. In the alphabetical arrangement, the titles of the directories of each publisher are listed with references to the entries for those publications in the main work. An updating service is issued between publication of the main editions of *Directories in Print*. This supplement was formerly titled, *Directory Information Service*, and effective with 1989 will apparently be titled simply, *Directories in Print Supplement*.

Gale Research has also introduced *International Directories in Print*, which covers directories mostly published outside the United States. The first edition of this work is dated 1989-90 and lists approximately five thousand titles.

Serials for Libraries: An Annotated Guide to Continuations, Annuals, Yearbooks, Almanacs, Transactions, Proceedings, Directories, Services (New York: Neal-Schuman) was first published in 1980, with a second edition in 1985. This work is comprised of a selective listing of publications, with nearly two thousand items covered. The major purpose of this guide is to aid in the selection and acquisition of these types of serials by libraries. However, it can also be used by reference staff as an annotated guide to these publications.

Generally, the serial publications included are English language titles that are available in the United States, published on an annual or less frequent basis, and appropriate for a public, school, academic, or special library collection.

The title entries are arranged under five broad categories and are broken down further into specific subjects. Entries contain the following information: year first published, frequency, publisher, address, editor, and an indication of where it is indexed. "Audience levels" are assigned for each title, showing the most appropriate types of libraries for the publication. Also included for each title is an annotation of approximately one paragraph in length in which the publication is described. These annotations allow librarians and patrons to select serials suitable to their needs, which makes this work an important reference tool.

Also provided in this directory is a title index and a subject index. A separate section lists publications that are available online. Another section is titled, "When to Buy What," and lists the announced publication schedule of over eight hundred serials. The month or season in which a serial is to be published is given. This section was designed for acquisitions librarians, and its purpose is to provide data on when these publications should be ordered. However, reference staff can refer to this list to determine when a new edition of a serial is likely to be available.

The term "continuations" used in the subtitle of this work refers simply to any publication that is ordered on a continuing basis by a library. A "continuation" can be defined as "a part issued in continuance of a monograph, a serial, or a series."[1] Generally, this term is not applied to periodicals, and is more often used in reference to the types of serials that are covered in this chapter.

Union Lists

Normally, union lists are not created to report holdings just of annuals, irregular serials, and other serials published less frequently than once a year. Usually these types of holdings are integrated into union lists that also contain periodical listings (see chapter 4). There are exceptions to this, though, with some specialized union lists of conference publications (see later in this chapter).

Conference Publications

The publications of conferences, congresses, meetings, and symposia are some of the most difficult items for librarians to handle. Not only do they pose cataloging problems, but they also are a source of continuing challenges for reference staff. The following describes the conference publications of one well-known organization.

> Conference publications of the Institute of Electrical and Electronics Engineers are simultaneously a blessing and a curse for research libraries. They are a blessing in that they provide a staggering amount of authoritative information on electrical engineering and computer science at a reasonable cost.... Controlling this formidable mass of royal-blue volumes is the attendant curse.[2]

In general, most conference publications present the advantage of authoritative information and the disadvantage of difficulty in cataloging. To take it one step further, any class of works that is difficult to catalog will also cause difficulties for staff attempting to provide reference service for such works.

A conference is defined as "a meeting of individuals or representatives of various bodies for the purpose of discussing and acting on topics of common interest."[3] Such meetings are usually held for the members of one or more associations, organizations, or societies, and/or are sponsored by such a group or groups. At such meetings, discussions are held, talks are given, and papers may be presented. The published record of this type of meeting is its proceedings. The transactions are the published papers and abstracts of papers presented at such a gathering.[4]

Because meetings such as these are often held on a regular, continuing basis, the resulting publications are then published and distributed on the same continuing basis. It is this characteristic that allows conference publications to be considered serials. Such publications may retain the same title from one conference to another and may be numbered serially. For example, the *International Conference on Software Engineering, Proceedings* carries numbering such as, "2nd International Conference on Software Engineering, 13-15 October 1976," and, "3rd International Conference on Software Engineering, May 10-12, 1978." In other cases, conference publications are considered monographs. Often, such publications exhibit both serial and monographic characteristics, thus making it difficult for catalogers to decide what sort of bibliographic treatment to impose. Catalogers have argued for the serial treatment of such publications and for the monographic treatment of these publications.[5] The arguments against treating conference publications as serials raise three main problem areas. First, titles of such publications frequently change from one conference to another, based upon the theme of the conference. Second, the names of the conferences themselves often change from one meeting to another. Finally, other important bibliographic data such as publisher, place of conference, place of publication, and editor frequently change.[6]

Recently, the *Cataloging Service Bulletin*, published by the Library of Congress, provided the following guidelines for the handling of conference and exhibition publications.

> Even though items of this class often give evidence that the event is held repeatedly (e.g., the name of the event includes numbering or frequency as part of its name or title), there is much unpredictability as to the stability of the name of a conference or exhibit or of the title under which its publications are issued. In addition, if cataloged as a serial, much of the necessary and desired detail in access

points is lost, or the record will need to be updated frequently and *ad infinitum* to be of maximum use. International meetings especially tend to be published in different countries and thus, even if the language of the title page remains the same, the sponsoring bodies, editors, and the availability of the publication tend to vary from meeting to meeting.[7]

Such publications are then to be cataloged as serials only if both of the following conditions are met:

(1) the name of the meeting or exhibition remains constant and this constancy is documentable for five consecutive issues within no wider than a 15-year period.... (2) the title remains constant and in the same language, and this constancy is documentable for five consecutive issues within no wider than a 15-year period.[8]

With these strict guidelines in place, it is thus apparent that fewer conference publications are now being handled as serials, and this trend should continue. Regardless of this cataloging reality, reference problems regarding conference publications will probably continue to be seen as "serial" problems. Those responsible for serials reference must then be prepared to deal with questions regarding these publications.

As mentioned, conference publications are subject to various changes from one issue, or edition, to the next. Titles, sponsoring organizations, publishers, and editors often change. This results in difficulties for researchers and for reference staff alike. To cope with these problems, reference works exist that aid in the identification of conferences and their publications. All of the previously described directories of annual publications, irregular serials, and other serials published less frequently than once a year, also list conference publications such as proceedings and transactions. Conference publications are very susceptible to change, however, and directory entries may contain outdated information. Of course, all information provided in any directory of serials, whether it covers periodicals, newspapers, or other serials, should be viewed in this manner. In the case of conference publications, however, it is more likely that key elements will change from one issue, or edition, of a conference publication to another.

In using the general directories that cover annuals and irregular serials to locate conference publications, it is necessary to check under several headings to perform a complete search. If the conference publication has retained a title for a number of years, or seems to have such a title, search under that title. If it is not found under title, try searching under the name of the conference or under the name of the sponsoring body.

Since most conference publications are now considered monographs, they will not be listed in directories of serials. However, the following specialized sources can be used to identify conference publications regardless of whether they are monographs or serials.

The *Index to Scientific & Technical Proceedings* (Philadelphia: Institute for Scientific Information) is published monthly, with an annual cumulation. This source indexes published scientific proceedings from throughout the world and the papers printed within those proceedings. Both monographic publications and proceedings published within journals are covered. For 1987, this resulted in coverage of 4,329 proceedings and 146,854 papers.[9] According to the publisher, this accounts for nearly half of all published scientific proceedings.[10] Each item is indexed in a number of ways including the words in the titles of books, conferences, and individual papers. Other indexes provide coverage by conference topic, authors and editors, conference sponsors, the city in which the conference was held, and the organizational affiliations of the authors.

This index also provides the information necessary for ordering copies of any of the proceedings published as monographs. For individual papers, the name and address of the first author are listed as a possible source of reprints. Also, some of the papers are available through the publisher's Genuine Article document delivery service (see chapter 7). Annual cumulations of this work are available back to 1978.

The *Index to Social Sciences & Humanities Proceedings*, also published by the Institute for Scientific Information, is practically identical in format to the *Index to Scientific & Technical Proceedings*. However, this index is published quarterly, with an annual cumulation, and covers significantly fewer publications. Covered in 1987 were 3,016 proceedings and 22,353 papers from throughout the world.[11] Annual cumulations are available back to 1979.

The *Conference Papers Index* (Bethesda, Md.: Cambridge Scientific Abstracts) is currently published seven times a year and was established in 1973 under the title *Current Programs*. It annually provides coverage of approximately 48,000 conference papers in the fields of life sciences, physical sciences, and engineering. The scope is international. Publication of a paper is not a prerequisite for inclusion in this index. So, all papers that are presented at included conferences are indexed here. Conferences and their papers are arranged into broad subject areas. Ordering information is provided for proceedings or papers. An author index and a keyword subject index are included.

The *Bibliographic Guide to Conference Publications* (Boston: G. K. Hall) is an annual guide that was first issued in 1976. It lists publications cataloged during the preceding twelve months by the Research Libraries of the New York Public Library and by the Library of Congress. Proceedings, reports, and summaries of meetings in all fields are included. The guide is international in scope and covers all languages.

The entries provide full cataloging information for each publication, as well as an indication if the title is in the holdings of the New York Public Library. Access is by main entry, added entries, titles, series titles, and subject headings in one interfiled alphabetic sequence. This work lists publications cataloged within a specific twelve-month period and not necessarily those published during that period. So, publications that were issued in earlier years but that were not cataloged until the preceding year will also be included.

The *Directory of Published Proceedings: Series SEMT—Science/ Engineering/Medicine/Technology* (Harrison, N.Y.: InterDok) was first published in 1965 and is currently issued ten times a year, with an annual cumulation. The citations to published proceedings are arranged by year and month of the conference. Proceedings from throughout the world are included. Entries provide information about the conference, the title of the publication, editor, publisher, and subject descriptors. Individual papers are not listed. The following indexes are included: editor, location of conference, acronym, and subject/sponsor.

InterDok also publishes two other directories of proceedings that have the same arrangement and indexes as those described above. The *Directory of Published Proceedings: Series SSH—Social Sciences/Humanities* began in 1968 and is currently published quarterly, with cumulations issued every four years. The *Directory of Published Proceedings: Series PCE—Pollution Control/Ecology* is currently published annually and was established in 1974. The information in *Series PCE* is abstracted from the other two publications, *Series SEMT* and *Series SSH*.

Proceedings in Print (Halifax, Mass.: Proceedings in Print) is an index of the proceedings of conferences, congresses, symposia, and other meetings, in all subject areas and in all languages. This work is international in scope. First published in 1964, this guide is now issued six times a year, plus an annual cumulative index. Proceedings that have been published both in book form and in journals are included. The entries are arranged alphabetically by the conference names. A single index in each issue provides access by personal and corporate authors, sponsoring bodies, editors, and subjects. Some of the entries provide information needed for ordering copies of the proceedings. Approximately three thousand proceedings are covered each year.

A few union lists that cover only conference publications have been published. *International Congresses and Conferences, 1840-1937*, edited by Winifred Gregory (New York: H. W. Wilson, 1938), is a union list of the publications of these meetings. The holdings of over one hundred libraries are represented in this work. Entries are arranged alphabetically by the name of the conference or of the sponsoring body, in most cases. A subject index is included.

Another union list that can be helpful in identifying conference publications is the German publication, *Gesamtverzeichnis der Kongress-Schriften in Bibliotheken der Bundesrepublik Deutschland einschliesslich Berlin (West)* (Munich: Verlag Dokumentation). The English title is the *Union List of Conference Proceedings in Libraries of the Federal Republic of Germany Including Berlin (West)*, and the original edition of this work, published in 1976, lists publications from conferences held before 1971. Subsequent supplements were issued in 1980 and 1982. This union list acts as a complementary publication to *Gesamtverzeichnis Ausländischer Zeitschriften und Serien, 1939-1958* (GAZS), the German union list of foreign serials.

As an adjunct to reference work with conference publications, it is sometimes desirable, or necessary, to know when and where a conference took place, or when and where future conferences are scheduled to take place.

There are reference works that provide this type of information. The *International Congress Calendar* (Munich: K. G. Saur) is prepared by the Union of International Associations and was first published in an edition dated 1960-1961. It is currently issued on a quarterly basis. Each issue is comprised of an updated list of international meetings due to take place in the current year and in subsequent years. The publication is arranged into three different sections to list these meetings geographically, chronologically, and analytically (by title and subject). In 1987, this source listed more than nine thousand announcements of future international meetings.

The *Directory of Conventions* (New York: Bill Communications) is an annual guide to conventions to be held in the United States and Canada during the next two years. First published in 1952, this work lists events by date under the cities in which they are to meet. Two indexes are included, one listing the conventions by name and the other by industry or profession. A supplement is published at mid-year to update the main edition.

Another source for this type of information is the annual *Encyclopedia of Associations* (Detroit: Gale Research). Future conventions and meetings are listed in the individual association entries, giving dates and locations.

There are additional sources that can be used in searching for publications of conferences and congresses, two of which are *The National Union Catalog: Pre-1956 Imprints* (London: Mansell) and *The National Union Catalog* (Washington, D.C.: Library of Congress). The online bibliographic databases, such as OCLC, can also be used. Often a corporate author search under the name of a conference or a sponsoring body will result in success.

Notes

[1]Michael Gorman and Paul W. Winkler, eds., *Anglo-American Cataloguing Rules, Second Edition.* (Chicago: American Library Association, 1978; Ottawa: Canadian Library Association, 1978), 565.

[2]Michael E. Unsworth, "Treating IEEE Conference Publications as Serials," *Library Resources & Technical Services* 27 (April/June 1983): 221.

[3]Gorman and Winkler, *AACR2*, 565.

[4]Heartsill Young, ed., *The ALA Glossary of Library and Information Science* (Chicago: American Library Association, 1983), 178, 231.

[5]Unsworth, "IEEE Conference Publications," 221-24; Jim E. Cole, "Conference Publications: Serials or Monographs?" *Library Resources & Technical Services* 22 (Spring 1978): 168-73.

[6]Cole, "Conference Publications," 171-72.

[7]"Special Problems," *Cataloging Service Bulletin*, no. 20 (Spring 1983): 9.

[8]Ibid., 9-10.

[9]*Index to Scientific & Technical Proceedings*, no. 10 (October 1988): xviii.

[10]Ibid., v.

[11]*Index to Social Sciences & Humanities Proceedings*, no. 2 (April/June 1988): xviii.

9

Newspapers and Their Place in the Library

Humankind has an unquenchable thirst for news, which can be defined as "the report or account of recent events or occurrences, brought or coming to one as new information."[1] "News" has also been described as "the same thing happening every day to different people."[2] People seek out and receive their news through various channels. Perhaps the most pervasive, traditional, and least dependable source of news is word-of-mouth. As society has developed, methods to formally gather news and dispense it to the people have been established. Today, news is distributed in many of the mass media, including radio, television, and print. The most widespread application of the print medium for the distribution of news is, of course, the newspaper.

A newspaper can be defined as,

> A serial issued at stated frequent intervals (usually daily, weekly, or semiweekly), containing news, opinions, advertisements, and other items of current, often local, interest.[3]

It is important to note that a newspaper, from the library point of view and by definition, is a publication such as *The New York Times* or the *Chicago Tribune* that reports all types of news. Any publication that reports news in a specific subject area is considered to be a periodical, regardless of whether it "looks" like a newspaper. This is a significant distinction since many library patrons will refer to anything published on newsprint as a "newspaper."

Newspapers are omnipresent in our society. The 1988 edition of the *Gale Directory of Publications* lists 10,088 currently published newspapers from the United States and 985 currently published newspapers from Canada.[4] *Willings Press Guide*, in its 1988 edition, has entries for 1,746 currently published newspapers from the United Kingdom.[5] According to UNESCO, there are 8,230 daily newspapers published worldwide with an estimated daily circulation of 502,000,000.[6] In addition, UNESCO statistics show 46,332 non-daily, general interest newspapers published worldwide for a world total of 54,562 newspapers currently in print.[7] Apparently, the actual worldwide total of newspapers exceeds this figure since UNESCO's statistics regarding non-daily newspapers do not cover every nation of the world. In the United States, over 60 percent of those over eighteen years of age read daily newspapers, and Sunday newspapers are read by over 63 percent of that population.[8]

Brief History of Newspapers

The earliest precursor of today's newspaper is generally thought to have been the *Acta Diurna*, which was a daily manuscript publication that reported the proceedings of the Roman senate and other official information. Another early forerunner of the newspaper was the Chinese handwritten publication *Ti-pao*, which existed for hundreds of years and was a type of court report distributed to officials. As the age of printing approached, manuscript newsletters came into prominence. These handwritten publications were produced by the large mercantile houses of Europe to convey business information. The extensive networks of correspondents that produced these newsletters were the predecessors of the correspondent networks later to be organized by newspapers.

The first printed newspaper to be published on a regular basis is considered to be the German *Avisa Relation oder Zeitung*, which appeared in 1609. Due to censorship restrictions, newspaper publishing did not become firmly established in England until the 1640s. In 1665, *The Oxford Gazette* was founded and became *The London Gazette* the next year. It was the "first English news publication regularly issued in what is now recognized as newspaper format."[9] Files of this newspaper were available even in the American colonies, and at least two issues of it were reprinted there.[10]

The first American newspaper was *Publick Occurrences Both Forreign and Domestick*, which appeared in Boston on September 25, 1690. It was suppressed after that single issue. The next American newspaper, the Boston *News-Letter*, did not appear until nearly fourteen years later, on April 24, 1704. It became the first continuously published American newspaper and was in operation until it ceased publication in 1776.

The Daily Universal Register was established in London during 1785. Three years later, its name changed to *The Times*. Today, over two hundred years later, *The Times* is still being published and is regarded as one of the most influential newspapers in the world.

The nineteenth century saw many developments involving newspapers. Great advances were made in printing technology throughout the century. This, accompanied by the availability of inexpensive paper made from wood pulp, allowed newspapers to be produced in large quantities.[11] The telegraph was also introduced in this century, thus enabling newspapers to receive news in a much more efficient and timely manner. This invention led to the establishment of cooperative news-gathering organizations. The first such American organization, the Harbor News Association, was founded in New York in 1849 and later became known as the Associated Press.[12] News gathering organizations were also formed in Europe at mid-century, including the Reuters organization.

Several extremely popular newspapers were established during the 1800s. Founded in 1860, *The World*, of New York, become the largest newspaper operation in the United States. In March 1897, the combined circulation of its morning and evening editions reached one million.[13] Other important American newspapers founded during the nineteenth century were the *New York Herald* (est. 1835), the *New York Tribune* (est. 1841), and *The New York Times* (est. 1851).

By the turn of the century, the newspaper had become established as a medium to reach the masses. In 1914, there were more than thirty newspapers in the United States with a circulation greater than 100,000.[14] In the twentieth century, trends developed toward the consolidation of newspapers and the building of newspaper chains. The tabloid newspaper was introduced early in the century and first became popular in England. This type of newpaper was characterized by a page size approximately half that of a standard newspaper page and by a reduced amount of text within the newspaper. *The Illustrated Daily News*, of New York, (later titled, the *Daily News*), founded in 1919, was the first American tabloid. It became extremely popular, reaching a circulation of one million by December 1925.[15]

Although syndicated materials had been used in American newspapers since the Colonial period, the feature syndicates became a significant factor in newspaper publishing after World War I. Columns, commentaries, and other special features were made available to newspapers across the country.

Recently, the most interesting trend in United States newspaper publishing has been the attempt by a few different publishers to create a national, general interest newspaper. In 1980, *The New York Times* began printing a national edition, and *The Wall Street Journal* also enhanced its publication, which is aimed at a national audience.[16] On September 15, 1982, the Gannett chain introduced *USA Today*, a Monday through Friday daily that bills itself as "The Nation's Newspaper." It employs a concise, fact-filled writing style and makes heavy use of color and graphics. Nationwide distribution is made possible via satellite technology and printing plants located across the country. *USA Today* has been very popular with readers, and has become the second-highest circulating daily newspaper in the United States, behind only *The Wall Street Journal*.[17] Many other newspapers have been influenced by *USA Today*. This has resulted in more colorful newspapers with more widespread use of graphics.

This section has provided a very brief history of newspapers and has touched only on the most important events and trends in that history. For more detailed coverage of newspaper history, consult:

The Newspaper: An International History. By Anthony Smith. London: Thames and Hudson, 1979.

American Journalism, A History: 1690-1960. 3d ed. By Frank Luther Mott. New York: Macmillan, 1962.

The Press and America: An Interpretive History of the Mass Media. 6th ed. By Michael Emery and Edwin Emery. Englewood Cliffs, N.J.: Prentice-Hall, 1988.

Current State of Newspaper Publishing

That there are over 54,000 currently published newspapers worldwide would attest to the fact that this form of publishing is basically healthy and prevalent. Despite competition from radio and television, the newspaper is viewed by many as an irreplaceable source of news. From 1950 to 1985, the total circulation of daily newspapers in the United States rose from 53.8 million per day to 62.8 million per day.[18] Another indication of the popularity of newspapers is the amount of dollars spent for newspaper advertising. By 1984, 26.8 percent of the nation's advertising expenditures were for newspaper advertisements. This far exceeds any other advertising medium, including television, which accounted for 22.4 percent of advertising dollars.[19]

In 1981, cable television magnate Ted Turner told those in attendance at the American Newspaper Publishers Association convention, "Newspapers as we know them today will be gone within the next ten years or certainly [will be] serving a very reduced role."[20] Although the number of daily American newspapers has dropped in the years following that statement from 1,730 in 1982 to 1,645 in 1988,[21] there seems to be no great movement by readers away from newspapers nor any indication of the impending end of newspapers. In fact, the newspaper industry appears to be quite vibrant and thriving. A study of thirty-four newspaper companies during the period of 1982 through 1986 showed that they were very profitable, with five percentage points added to their profit margins in those years.[22] Newspapers have been published for the better part of four centuries and are likely to exist well into the foreseeable future.

Newspapers in Libraries

Newspaper collections in libraries are used by patrons with a number of purposes in mind. These purposes can generally be classified either in the realm of current awareness or in the realm of historical research. For most of society, newspapers are to be read today and thrown away tomorrow. For a library and its patrons, though, noncurrent newspapers hold as much value as the recent issues.

A library subscribes to newspapers in order to provide its users with the most up-to-date printed information regarding international, national, and local current events. Of particular importance is the local news component of any newspaper. Although daily newspapers are all likely to give coverage to the same major national and international news stories, most local stories will be covered only by the newspaper(s) of that area. Thus, if one wishes to remain current on the local news of a particular area other than one's own, a reading of the newspaper(s) from that area is usually the easiest way in which to accomplish that goal. Current newspapers also allow the reader to see local coverage and commentary on national and international topics.

A survey at the University of Notre Dame showed that library patrons there read newspapers for the following reasons (in descending order of response):

To keep up with national and international news.

For news from my hometown.

For news from home (outside the U.S.).

To learn about the culture and current events of another country.

To improve knowledge of a language.

To locate a piece of information.

To read classified ads.

As a class assignment.

As part of a research project.[23]

In other libraries, out-of-town newspapers may be used for purposes other than those listed in the survey above, such as obtaining information about local individuals of importance, or to follow local elections or trials. Many patrons read newspapers from cities where they once lived to stay current with local happenings. Other patrons read out-of-town newspapers for pure recreation.

Another purpose served by having the current issues of the library's local newspaper(s) is to make them available to those who cannot afford even the relatively small amount that a newspaper issue costs. When combined with a selection of out-of-town newspapers, the library may find that such a collection attracts large numbers of homeless people and vagrants. This is a concern particularly for public libraries, and it is not a new situation. In 1956, a guide to the organization and administration of academic libraries stated that a separate newspaper room "is more of a public library feature for the primary purpose of attracting transients away from the other rooms of the library."[24]

Indeed, this type of situation seems to have existed for at least a hundred years. At the 1894 American Library Association conference, Dr. Albert W. Whelpley, the librarian of the Public Library of Cincinnati, presented his views on the supplying of current newspapers in public libraries. Regarding the question of whether those who read the newspapers in the library were of a "vagrant" class who repelled others from the reading room, Dr. Whelpley stated that if "the masses (sometimes, in political language, called 'the great unwashed'), mal-odorous though they may be, take the advantages provided in the newspaper reading-rooms, and are contented, nay eager to read, it shows there is hope for them, and that they may still rise to heights of cleanliness."[25]

Newspaper collections in libraries are also used for historical research. Such research ranges from the frivolous to the scholarly. An example of the former is the common request of library patrons to see a newspaper from the day they were born. Old newspapers are also used by some for recreational reading. For serious historical research, though, newspapers are of great value. For a genealogical researcher, they hold the marriage notices and obituaries of past generations. For a historian, they hold the contemporary feel of a time and place. Also, they can provide the details that can enable a historical account to come to life.

The Use of Newspapers in Historical Research

In the introduction to his classic union list, *History and Bibliography of American Newspapers, 1690-1820*, published in 1947, Clarence S. Brigham wrote,

> I doubt whether any contemporary expression of printed opinion and fact, both for national and local history, measures up to the newspaper. No history of a town or city can be written without recourse to its newspapers. In the eighteenth and early nineteenth centuries even the advertisements have unique value in social and economic study. In the wider fields of history, whether state or national, the whole trend of events is reported at regular intervals, in the printing of documents and letters, in the arguments of partisan communications, and in editorial opinion. The newspaper is omnivorous. Not only political history, but religious, educational and social history, find places in its pages. Literature, especially essays and poetry, was constantly supplied to its readers. If all the printed sources of history for a certain century or decade had to be destroyed save one, that which could be chosen with the greatest value to posterity would be a file of an important newspaper.[26]

By the time that Brigham had written those words, historians had begun to accept newspapers as sources for scholarly research. This had not always been the case, though. Historians believed for a long period that newspapers were unacceptable as historical sources. This attitude had its basis in that scholars were men of the book who disdained the newspaper because of "its gossip large and small, its sensational news and its sensational advertising."[27] It was also seen as an unreliable type of publication that was designed to be thrown away the day after it was read.

John Bach McMaster went against the prevailing sentiment of the day with the publication in 1883 of the first volume of his eight-volume set, *History of the People of the United States from the Revolution to the Civil War* (New York: D. Appleton, 1883-1913). Historians were surprised by this work.

> The surprise was in large measure to be ascribed to the material on which the work was apparently based, -- an examination of the foot-notes showed references, not to the conventional authorities, but to newspapers, pamphlets, dodgers, and every variety of ephemeral material. That old newspapers were interesting reading had always been appreciated, but no historian had hitherto ventured to use them as a main authority for his work.[28]

In the century that has followed, newspapers have come to be looked upon as valuable sources in historical research. With their news, editorial columns, and advertisements, newspapers can present a contemporary "graphic picture of society."[29] By reading through a file of newspapers, a researcher can obtain a feel for the daily life and prevailing attitudes in a particular community at a certain time. Newspapers, with their reporting of relatively insignificant local stories, can also add the small details that can make a historical account come to life. For instance, a researcher looking into the local situation in Hawaii after the attack on Pearl Harbor could gain much insight from reading the newspapers of that area. Numerous short articles and announcements convey a feeling of fear, uncertainty, and near hysteria that followed the attack. One story that epitomized the local conditions ran in the *Honolulu Star-Bulletin* and reported the beating death of an "oriental" Hawaiian a day after the attack. At the time of his beating, the man was acting as a fire warden and was wearing a helmet. His assailants, one of whom was his friend and neighbor, mistook him for an "enemy parachutist," according to the newspaper accounts.[30] It is this type of detailed local story that can infuse a historical recounting with realism.

As a part of historical research, caution must be exercised in using any of the "facts" discovered in newspaper articles or columns. The time-honored adage of, "Don't believe everything you read," should be strictly employed in regard to newspaper research. At times, newspaper reporting may be slanted, or the information reported may be inaccurate. It must be remembered that a newspaper is "a hasty gatherer of the facts, a hurried commentator on the same," and inaccuracies do abound.[31]

This remains true today, and can be exemplified by the reporting of a news event of international importance. On April 6, 1988, a young Jewish girl and two Arabs were killed during a clash in the West Bank between Arab villagers and a group of Jewish settlers and their Israeli guards. In a front page article the next day, *The Washington Post* led its report with "Arab villagers today stoned to death a 15-year-old Jewish girl...."[32] The source of the information for the article is not given until the tenth paragraph on the continuation page (page A35), where it is noted that details were provided by Israeli Army officials. In a front page article the following day, it was noted that the responsibility for the killing of the girl "was uncertain" since "a preliminary investigation indicated she had been shot in the head as well as hit with a stone." This time, the source, Israel television, was attributed in the lead sentence.[33] On April 9, an article printed on page A26 stated, "Military sources were quoted by Israeli radio as saying the bullet was fired from one of the weapons used by the guards...."[34] Finally, on April 28, a front page article began, "A long-delayed Israeli Army report on the killing of a teen-aged Jewish settler in the West Bank village of Beita earlier this month concluded that she was shot dead accidentally by one of her armed Israeli escorts during a clash with Arab villagers."[35]

It is thus necessary to verify facts that are found in newspaper accounts. An assistant editor of the editorial page of *The New York Times*, one of the most influential newspapers in the United States, wrote in 1967 that he constantly received complaints from prominent individuals. Such complaints were "always in virtually identical terms, 'Whenever I read a story about something in which I really know what's going on, I'm astonished at how little of what's important gets into the papers—and how often even that little is wrong.' "[36] A well-informed historical researcher, however, can learn much about the spirit of a time or the contemporary attitudes toward a topic from the inaccuracies in a newspaper account, as long as the true facts are separated from the inaccuracies. Since a historian is involved in the narration of events and the interpretation of what those events mean in terms of the time and place, both accurate and inaccurate reporting are of value.[37]

In countries with freedom of the press, most newspaper reporting is reliable. Where there is such freedom, newspapers are allowed to present the news truthfully. Libel laws, on the other hand, help to guarantee that known falsehoods are not published as the truth. Another guarantee of reliability is that the writers of most newspaper articles and other items are identified. Thus an individual, as well as the newspaper itself, takes responsibility for the accuracy of the printed item. For the historical researcher, an important guarantee of reliability is that newspaper accounts are contemporary and are written without the knowledge of the ultimate outcome of an event or a series of events. So, the writing cannot be biased by the knowledge of what eventually occurs or results from the news event.

Of course, guarantees of reliability and accuracy do not exist among newspapers published without the cloak of freedom of the press. Newspapers in countries that tightly control the press are likely to be no more than vehicles of propaganda for the regime in power. Each and every "fact" presented in these newspapers must be viewed skeptically. The careful researcher should be well aware that what is printed in these newspapers is not necessarily the news but may just be propaganda with little or no basis in fact. Obviously, a researcher cannot make the same use of newspapers from controlled societies as with newspapers from free societies.

As the scholarly regard for newspapers has grown so have the efforts by libraries to make them available and to preserve them. Newspapers have only recently come to be accepted unquestionably by libraries. The previously mentioned 1894 American Library Association conference symposium on the supplying of daily newspapers in public libraries showed that it was still a debatable topic at that time. There were questions as to whether newspapers should be made available in public libraries and whether files of out-of-town newspapers should be collected.[38] Since then, scholars have accepted newspapers as historical sources, and the microfilming of newspapers has become standard practice. The latter development has enabled libraries to store large newspaper collections in a fraction of the space that a collection of bound original issues would consume and has also allowed libraries to purchase files of historical newspapers that otherwise would have been unavailable or prohibitively expensive to purchase in original issues.

In 1955, a librarian writing on the topic of the place of the newspaper in the library stated that there were indications of "a definite trend towards acceptance of the principle of collecting newspapers on a universal and at the same time cooperative basis."[39] Today, there seems to be total acceptance of newspapers as part of the permanent collections of libraries. This acceptance is symbolized by the ongoing United States Newspaper Program, a project sponsored by the National Endowment for the Humanities. The purpose of this program is to identify, catalog, preserve, and provide access to the estimated 300,000 newspapers that have been published in the nation (see chapter 11).

Elements of Reference Work with Newspapers

As with periodicals, there are three major areas of newspaper reference work. The first involves identifying currently published newspapers and locating information about them. This can be the easiest area of newspaper reference since there are several directories to provide such information. A second area of newspaper reference involves identifying the libraries or other repositories with collections of particular current or retrospective newspapers. These searches are done through union lists, which are available in various formats. The final major area of newspaper reference service involves identifying, or locating, particular articles or other items within newspapers. This can be the most difficult element of newspaper reference service since traditionally there has been very little indexing of newspapers as compared to the indexing of periodicals.

The following three chapters cover newspaper directories, newspaper union lists, and newspaper indexing and abstracting. Chapter 13 includes additional aspects of newspaper reference service not covered in the other chapters.

Notes

[1]*The Compact Edition of the Oxford English Dictionary* (Oxford: Oxford University Press, 1971), 1920.

[2]Eugene E. Brussell, ed., *Dictionary of Quotable Definitions* (Englewood Cliffs, N.J.: Prentice-Hall, 1970), 398.

[3]Heartsill Young, ed., *The ALA Glossary of Library and Information Science* (Chicago: American Library Association, 1983), 153.

[4]*Gale Directory of Publications*, 120th ed. (Detroit: Gale Research, 1988), viii.

[5]*Willings Press Guide*, 114th ed. (East Grinstead, U.K.: British Media Publications, 1988), unnumbered page in the preliminary section.

[6]*UNESCO Statistical Yearbook*, 1987 ed. (Paris: United Nations Educational, Scientific and Cultural Organization, 1987), 6-13.

[7]Ibid., 7-156 — 7-158; *UNESCO Statistical Yearbook*, 1985 ed., vii-141 — vii-143.

[8]U.S. Bureau of the Census, *Statistical Abstract of the United States, 1988*, 108th ed. (Washington, D.C.: Government Printing Office, 1987), 523.

[9]Frank Luther Mott, *American Journalism, A History: 1690-1960*, 3d ed. (New York: Macmillan, 1962), 8.

[10]Ibid.

[11]Ibid., 498.

[12]Michael Emery and Edwin Emery, *The Press and America: An Interpretive History of the Mass Media*, 6th ed. (Englewood Cliffs, N.J.: Prentice-Hall, 1988), 136-37.

[13]Mott, *American Journalism*, 546.

[14]Ibid., 547.

[15]John Tebbel, *The Compact History of the American Newspaper*, new and rev. ed. (New York: Hawthorn Books, 1969), 224.

[16]Peter Prichard, *The Making of McPaper: The Inside Story of USA Today* (Kansas City: Andrews, McMeel & Parker, 1987), 93.

[17]Mark Fitzgerald, "Circulation Report," *Editor & Publisher* 121 (5 November 1988): 12.

[18]U.S. Bureau of the Census, *Statistical Abstract of the United States, 1987*, 107th ed. (Washington, D.C.: Government Printing Office, 1986), 536.

[19]Ibid., 538.

[20]Prichard, *The Making of McPaper*, 138.

[21]*Editor & Publisher International Year Book*, 1982 and 1988 eds. (New York: Editor & Publisher), unnumbered pages in preliminary section.

[22]Andrew Radolf, "Newspapers Showed Outstanding Profitability in '86," *Editor & Publisher* 120 (7 November 1987): 13.

[23]Stanley P. Hodge and Marilyn Ivins, "Current International Newspapers: Some Collection Management Implications," *College & Research Libraries* 48 (January 1987): 56.

[24]Louis Round Wilson and Maurice F. Tauber, *The University Library*, 2d ed. (New York: Columbia University Press, 1956), 503.

[25]Albert W. Whelpley, "Supplying of Current Daily Newspapers in Free Library Reading Rooms," in *The Library Within the Walls* (New York: H. W. Wilson, 1929), 257-58.

[26]Clarence S. Brigham, *History and Bibliography of American Newspapers, 1690-1820* (Worcester, Mass.: American Antiquarian Society, 1947; repr., Hamden, Conn.: Archon Books, 1962), xvii.

[27]Icko Iben, "The Place of the Newspaper," *Library Trends* 4 (October 1955): 140.

[28]Lucy Maynard Salmon, *The Newspaper and the Historian* (New York: Oxford University Press, 1923; repr., New York: Octagon Books, 1976), xxxvii.

[29]James Ford Rhodes, "Newspapers as Historical Sources," in *The Library Within the Walls* (New York: H. W. Wilson, 1929), 239.

[30]"Bootblack Is Hurt; Civilian Watchers Think He's Suspect," *Honolulu Star-Bulletin*, 9 December 1941, 1; "Bootblack Dies from Injuries," *Honolulu Star-Bulletin*, 10 December 1941, 1.

[31]Rhodes, "Newspapers As Historical Sources," 240.

[32]Glenn Frankel, "Israeli Girl Is Stoned to Death; 2 Arabs Killed," *The Washington Post*, 7 April 1988, A1, A35.

[33]Glenn Frankel, "Report Says Israeli Girl Hit by Bullet from Guard's Gun," *The Washington Post*, 8 April 1988, A1, A26.

[34]"Israeli Cites 'Misunderstanding' in Killing," *The Washington Post*, 9 April 1988, A26.

[35]Glenn Frankel, "Army Says Israeli Shot Jewish Girl," *The Washington Post*, 28 April 1988, A1, A36.

[36]A. H. Raskin, "What's Wrong with American Newspapers?" *The New York Times Magazine*, 11 June 1967, 77.

[37]Salmon, *The Newspaper and the Historian*, xlii-xliii.

[38]Whelpley, "Supplying Daily Newspapers," 257-59.

[39]Iben, "The Place of the Newspaper," 142.

10

Newspaper Directories and Other Sources of Current Newspaper Information

There are numerous types of factual questions regarding current newspapers that constantly arise for those providing reference service. Examples of such inquiries are:

What is the name and address of the newspaper in Pine Bluff, Arkansas?

Who is the Fashion Editor of *The Gazette*, of Montreal?

Where can there be found a list of the newspapers published in the Soviet Union?

Which Los Angeles newspaper has the largest circulation?

How much would it cost to place an advertisement in *The Washington Post*?

What newspapers in Minnesota carry United Press International articles?

Accurate, reliable, and up-to-date information must be obtained in order to correctly answer the types of questions listed above. There are any number of newspaper directories that attempt to provide this service. Some are devoted to only one nation or region, while others are international in scope. In general, newspaper directories fulfill two major purposes. First, they list newspapers geographically, by country, state, province, city, or town. A second major function is to provide publishing information about specific newspapers. The basic data elements given in directories for newspapers include:

Address and telephone number.

Editor, publisher, and/or other key staff members.

Subscription price.

Advertising rates.

Circulation.

Each major directory that covers newspapers also offers special features or in-depth coverage of a certain region or country. Just as with periodical directories, no one newspaper directory gives complete, exhaustive coverage of the entire field. It is therefore necessary for a library to own a number of directories in order to attain the most complete coverage. Although superficially similar, these directories all have specific characteristics, and it is important for library staff dealing with them to be aware of their strengths, weaknesses, peculiarities, and limitations.

The balance of this chapter is comprised of descriptions of the most useful newspaper directories and of other sources that include current directory-type information about newspapers. These works fall into three major categories:

Directories with international coverage.

Directories with coverage of a single region or country.

Reference works that are not newspaper directories but that do contain such information.

Directories Providing International Coverage

Editor & Publisher International Year Book. New York: Editor & Publisher.
   Editor & Publisher is a weekly independent magazine devoted to the world of "newspapering." From 1921 to 1958, the *International Year Book Number* was issued annually in January as a regular number of the weekly. Since 1959, it has been issued every year as a separate publication. Whereas most of the other directories to be described in this chapter cover newspapers and periodicals, the *Editor & Publisher International Year Book* covers only newspapers. With its international coverage, this publication provides a thorough directory-type survey of the newspaper industry worldwide.

This publication is arranged into seven different sections. The first section covers daily newspapers published in the United States, arranged geographically by state and city. The individual newspaper entries contain very detailed information, including:

Title.

Publication frequency and schedule of publication (for example, morning or evening).

Address and telephone number.

Circulation.

Subscription prices.

Advertising rates.

Advertising representatives.

News or wire services subscribed to.

Political affiliation.

Year established.

Special editions and sections published.

Supplements published.

Corporate officers and other key employees in management, advertising, circulation, and production.

Various editors and news executives.

Extensive information on printing and other specialized equipment used.

The second section lists, by state and city, United States newspapers that are published from one to three times a week. Much less information is given for these newspapers, but entries do include title, address, day(s) of publication, circulation, advertising rate, publisher, editor, and telephone number. The third section of this directory lists Canadian daily newspapers and provides much the same type of information given for United States dailies. Also listed in this section are weekly newspapers and foreign language newspapers published in Canada.

Section four lists newspapers published in countries other than the United States and Canada, arranged by general regions and then subdivided by country and city. Only the very basic information is provided in the individual newspaper entries, including title, year established, address, circulation, advertising rates, editor, proprietor or publisher, and advertising manager and/or managing director. Although the international coverage presented here is quite extensive, be cautioned that this directory is not exhaustive. When needed, more detailed regional or national directories should be employed (many are described later in this chapter). Nevertheless, as a general international survey, this work is quite adequate. It should be the first source to consult for information regarding international newspapers.

The last three sections of this directory cover news and feature syndicates, wire services, mechanical equipment, and various newspaper organizations and industry services.

Many special features add to the value of this publication. There are a number of pages containing all types of newspaper industry statistics. House organs and other periodicals from the newspaper industry are also listed. Other segments cover:

Groups of newspapers under common ownership (known as newspaper chains).

Weekly Black newspapers published in the United States.

Foreign language newspapers published in the United States.

College and university newspapers published in the United States.

In addition, the advertisements carried in this publication also provide directory-type information. An index to the advertisers is included.

There is no title index provided in this directory. The general index in the rear of this work is, to a great extent, a geographic index of regions covered. Particularly when searching for newspapers from a country other than the United States or Canada, it is much easier to use this index than to use the table of contents in the front of the volume or the listings at the beginning of the foreign section. The index shows exactly what section and pages cover any particular country. It is cumbersome to use the table of contents or the section listing since exact page numbers are given only for the regions and not for particular countries. Using this approach, a page-by-page search to locate the listings of a particular country is still necessary, and this can be a difficult exercise, especially at a busy reference desk. So, use the index at the rear of the volume and don't bother with the table of contents or section listings.

The *Editor & Publisher International Year Book* is extremely useful for obtaining addresses and other information regarding newspapers from around the world. Due to its simpler arrangement, though, many may find the *Gale Directory of Publications* (described later in this chapter) to be easier to use for locating an address or telephone number of a newspaper from the United States or Canada. However, the *Editor & Publisher International Year Book* provides much more technical information about the newspapers listed and also gives more data about the newspaper industry in general.

Benn's Media Directory: International. Tonbridge, U.K.: Benn Business
    Information Services.

In the "here today, gone tomorrow" world of publishing, it is truly amazing to note the longevity of many of the newspaper directories described in this chapter. *Benn's* has been published since 1846, originally as *The Newspaper Press Directory*. The title of this directory was changed in 1986 from *Benn's Press Directory* to *Benn's Media Directory*. The current two volume format was instituted in 1978, with one annual volume covering the United Kingdom (described later in this chapter) and another annual volume to serve as a worldwide directory.

From a newspaper standpoint, the *International* volume covers much of the same ground as does the *Editor & Publisher International Year Book*. However, *Benn's* takes a slightly different approach. In its prefatory material, it is noted that "the whole volume has been planned with the outward-looking British businessman especially in mind."[1] As such, more is included than just newspapers. The segment for each nation contains information regarding various nationwide broadcasting and publicity sources. British-located sources of information for each nation are also given. The major newspapers and periodicals of the country are then listed in separate sections. (See chapter 3 for the periodical aspects.) Within a country's listings, the newspaper entries are arranged by state (or province) and city. The amount of information provided for individual newspaper titles varies. At the least, one will find listed the title, frequency, and address. More important newspapers will also have listed a telephone number, telex number, British office address, and circulation.

There is no title index in this volume. A geographic index is provided, and it is useful since the various country listings are not arranged alphabetically in one list but are divided into broad geographic areas such as "Africa/Middle East" and "The Americas."

Although *Benn's* does publish a separate United Kingdom volume, a section is included in the *International* volume that lists British newspapers, periodicals and other information sources.

Willings Press Guide. East Grinstead, U.K.: British Media Publications.

This annual directory, published since 1874, lists newspapers and periodicals printed throughout the world. (See chapter 3 for the periodical aspects.) With its 1988 edition, listings of the African press are included for the first time, thus giving this directory almost complete international coverage. The glaring omission is the press of the Soviet Union.

Perhaps the greatest value of this directory lies in its coverage of the United Kingdom. In the 1988 edition, over 1,700 newspapers are listed in the first section, which is an alphabetical, interfiled title list of newspapers and periodicals published in the United Kingdom. The individual entries include year established, political affiliation, frequency, subscription and/or per copy price, circulation, editor, advertising director, circulation manager, address, and telephone number. Since the listings for the United Kingdom press are alphabetical by title, a separate geographic newspaper index is included in the rear of the volume. Another section, "Publishers & Their Titles," lists publishers who have more than three publications listed in the section of United Kingdom newspapers and periodicals. So, groups of British newspapers published by single companies are listed there.

The second major section lists periodicals and newspapers published "overseas." This section is arranged geographically, first in large regions ("Europe," "The Americas," etc.) and then by individual countries. A table of contents at the beginning of the section lists each nation and the page on which its coverage begins. As with the entries in the United Kingdom section, the individual newspaper and periodical entries for a country are interfiled by title in one alphabetical list. However, there is not a separate geographic newspaper index included for the overseas section. So, rapid access to newspaper entries by city is not possible. Also, the listings cover just the "major" periodicals and newspapers published worldwide, resulting in a very selective list. For instance, "The Americas" section, which covers the United States, Canada, and over forty other nations, gives listings of less than four hundred newspapers.[2] The overseas newspaper entries contain the same type of information included for the United Kingdom entries. In addition, if there is a British address for advertising or subscriptions, that information is given.

Willings Press Guide should be used primarily for information regarding British newspapers and periodicals. For "overseas" newspapers, consult the *Editor & Publisher International Year Book* or *Benn's Media Directory: International* first.

Gale International Directory of Publications. Detroit: Gale Research.

The first edition of this directory has recently been published and is dated 1989-90. It is intended to serve as an international companion volume to the *Gale Directory of Publications* (described later in this chapter) and thus contains selective listings of both newspapers and periodicals circulating primarily outside the United States and Canada. Entries for 2,098 newspapers from 132 countries are included in the first edition.

The arrangement of this directory is by country, then subdivided by cities and towns. Under each city or town is an alphabetical title list of the publications produced in that locale. Individual entries may include some, or all, of the following data elements: address, telephone and telex numbers, date established, frequency, language, format, advertising rates and closing deadline, contacts, United States source, subscription price, and circulation. Three indexes are provided, one each for newspaper titles and periodical titles, and one combined alphabetical title and keyword index.

As a companion volume to the *Gale Directory of Publications*, this international directory will undoubtedly be purchased by many libraries. The ultimate value of this work as a newspaper directory has yet to be established, however, and can only be determined through repeated usage in reference situations over an extended period of time.

Directories Providing Coverage of a Single Region or Country

Gale Directory of Publications. Detroit: Gale Research.

One of the most familiar and most heavily used directories is the *Gale Directory of Publications*, which until fairly recently was known as the *Ayer Directory of Publications*. It was established in 1869 as the *American Newspaper Directory* and has been published annually since then. In the 1980s, this directory has changed titles several times, from the *Ayer Directory of Publications* to *The IMS Ayer Directory of Publications* and then to *The IMS Directory of Publications*. Finally, it became the *Gale Directory of Publications* effective with the 119th edition for 1987.

Regardless of title, this directory has continued to provide accurate, in-depth information about newspapers and periodicals published in the United States and Canada. (See chapter 3 for the periodical aspects.) Beginning with the 120th edition, 1988, a two-volume format was adopted, whereas previously it had been published in a single volume. The first volume, titled, *Catalog of Publications*, is comprised of the entries for publications, arranged geographically by state (or province) and city. A page of general descriptive and statistical information is included before the listings of each state or province. Volume 2 is titled *Indexes and Maps*, and contains maps and various indexes to the publications listed in volume 1. Another enhancement initiated with the 120th edition, is the assignment of entry numbers to each publication's listing, thus making access to individual entries from the various indexes much easier.

The 1988 edition of the *Gale Directory of Publications* includes listings for 10,088 United States newspapers and 985 Canadian newspapers. A typical entry for a newspaper includes the following: title, address, telephone number, year established, frequency, format, contacts (usually editor, publisher, and/or advertising manager), subscription price, advertising rates, and circulation. As mentioned, the publication entries in volume 1 are arranged geographically. All newspapers and periodicals for a specific town or city are then filed alphabetically. For most cities and towns, it is generally not a problem to pick out the newspaper entries. However, for larger publishing centers such as New York or Washington, D.C., it can be a problem. In these cases, it may be more efficient to consult the "Daily Newspapers" and "Weekly, Semiweekly, and Triweekly Newspapers" segments in the cross-reference indexes section in the second volume.

Since the *Catalog of Publications* volume is in a geographic arrangement with publications listed alphabetically under each city or town, it is possible to use this volume independently of the index volume. The most frequent such use would be in situations when a patron needs to know the newspaper(s) from a particular locale. For most other uses of this directory it is necessary to employ the indexes provided in volume 2. This enables efficient use of this directory. There are separate "cross-reference indexes" to cover the following:

College publications.

Foreign language publications (arranged by language and then broken down geographically).

Jewish publications.

Black publications.

Hispanic publications (new with the 1988 edition).

Daily newspapers.

Weekly, semiweekly, and triweekly newspapers.

Free newspapers.

Most of these cross-reference indexes interfile listings of periodicals and newspapers. In many cases, it is impossible to differentiate the type of publication within the indexes. The only manner in which this can be done is to examine the actual publication entries in the first volume.

The "Alphabetical Title and Keyword Index" is the most extensive index in this directory. It lists all publications found in the directory by title and by keywords in the titles. Notices of recent cessations and of former titles are given in this index, and this is the only place in this directory where such information can be found. Be aware that this index employs the confusing filing arrangement that totally disregards words such as "and" or "of" in its alphabetization. For example, *Science Books and Films* is listed before *Science and Children*.

The second volume also includes a valuable section titled, "Newspaper Feature Editors," which provides the names, addresses, and telephone numbers of the editors of the most popular features in daily newspapers with a circulation of at least fifty thousand. For instance, the individual editors of twenty-seven different features in *The Orlando Sentinel* are listed in the 1988 edition of the *Gale Directory*. Some of the features sections included are automotive, editorials, fashion, medical, and travel. This section can be very helpful to patrons who are trying to identify feature editors, usually with the purpose of trying to sell a piece of writing or to carry out some type of public relations or promotional campaign.

One other special feature endears this directory to librarians and to researchers. This publication can double as an atlas of the United States and Canada. A one hundred page section of maps is located at the beginning of volume 2. The entry for each city or town listed in volume 1 provides coordinates to locate that place on the appropriate state or province map.

Traditionally, the *Ayer Directory of Publications* has been the primary source to consult for basic information regarding newspapers of the United States and Canada. Now, as the *Gale Directory of Publications*, this work is expanding its coverage and adding new enhancements, including an annual supplement and an annual updating service, that serve to enforce its standing as the first source to check for this type of information.

The Working Press of the Nation, Volume 1, *Newspaper Directory*. Chicago: National Research Bureau.

The Working Press of the Nation is an annual directory published in five volumes. The entire set is "designed for persons needing information for contacting media personnel or for mailing list compilation, media selection or market analysis."[3] Volume 2 is a magazine directory, and volume 5 is a directory of internal publications of companies and other groups. (See chapter 3 for descriptions of both.) Volume 4 is a directory of feature writers and photographers, and volume 3 is a radio and television directory.

The *Newspaper Directory*, volume 1, lists newspapers published in the United States. The first section covers daily newspapers, arranged geographically by state and city. The individual entries include information such as title, address, telephone number, owner(s), year established, circulation, frequency and schedule of publication, wire services subscribed to, deadlines, types of publicity materials accepted, management and editorial personnel, supplements published, and bureau office information.

The second section lists weekly newspapers of the United States. Individual entries in this section contain most of the same data elements that are included in the entries in the first section. This is in contrast to the *Gale Directory of Publications*, which provides far less information about the weeklies. In *The Working Press*, the editorial personnel listed for both daily and weekly newspapers include extensive lists of feature editors. This is another enhancement that goes beyond that which is provided in the *Gale Directory*, which lists feature editors only for newspapers with a circulation of fifty thousand or more.

Other separate sections cover the following:

Special interest newspapers, arranged by topic

Religious newspapers

Black newspapers

Foreign language newspapers

The listings in all of these sections include the same type of detailed information found in the first two sections.

Separate indexes list editorial personnel by subject and newspapers by metro area. Other sections list news and photo services, feature syndicates, national newspapers, and newspaper-distributed magazines.

Bacon's Publicity Checker, Volume 2, *Newspapers*. Chicago: Bacon's Publishing.

This annual directory is intended for the public relations market and provides information suited to that audience. The first volume of this directory covers magazines (see chapter 3). Volume 2, *Newspapers*, covers daily and weekly newspapers of the United States and daily newspapers of Canada. In the first section of the 1987 edition, 1,683 United States dailies and nearly a hundred Canadian dailies are covered. The entries are arranged geographically and include title, address, telephone number, circulation, and the names of various editors or writers assigned to twenty-two news departments, such as sports and travel.

The second section lists over 7,500 United States weekly, semiweekly, and triweekly newspapers, arranged geographically. Each entry contains title, address, editor's name, telephone number, day(s) of issue, and circulation. A separate section at the end of each state's entries lists the Black press weeklies for that state. Other special features in the directory include a list of news services and syndicates. There is also included a list of newspaper-distributed magazines and Sunday supplements.

Although this type of directory is of most use to those in the public relations field, others can use it as a quick source of basic information.

Gebbie Press All-in-One Directory. Edited by Amalia Gebbie. New Paltz, N.Y.: Gebbie Press.

This is another annual directory intended for the use of public relations personnel. It was first published in 1972 and covers in detail ten major fields of media in the United States available to the public relations practitioner. These include television and radio stations, newspapers, general magazines, business and trade periodicals, and farm publications (see chapter 3 for the periodical aspects). Daily and weekly newspapers are listed geographically, and in separate segments, in the last section (or "Yellow Pages") of the directory. Only the most basic information is provided, including title, address, telephone number, and circulation. There are separate listings of news syndicates and Black newspapers.

As with *Bacon's Publicity Checker*, this can be used as a quick source for obtaining basic newspaper information. Neither of these sources, however, provide the in-depth information that can be found in either the *Gale Directory of Publications*, the *Editor & Publisher International Year Book*, or volume 1 of *The Working Press of the Nation*.

Directory of the College Student Press in America. New York: Oxbridge Communications.

This directory, first published to cover 1967/68, is updated irregularly. It covers over 6,000 newspapers, periodicals, and other serials published at 3,600 institutions of higher learning in the United States. The directory is arranged geographically by state, with the entries for individual institutions within a state arranged alphabetically. General information about the college or university, such as address, telephone number, and enrollment, is given. The publications and other media available on each campus are listed. Entries for newspapers include title, year established, frequency, circulation, subscription rate, advertising cost, and format.

Benn's Media Directory: United Kingdom. Tonbridge, U.K.: Benn Business Information Services.

Benn's Media Directory: United Kingdom is the companion volume to *Benn's Media Directory: International* (described earlier in this chapter). Both are published annually and cover newspapers, periodicals, and other information sources (see chapter 3 for the periodical aspects). The 1988 edition of the *United Kingdom* volume lists over 1,800 newspapers, including daily and Sunday newspapers, weeklies, and local free newspapers. Separate sections list national newspapers (such as *The Daily Telegraph*), and the newspapers of London. English provincial newspapers and the newspapers of Wales, Scotland, and the Isle of Man and Channel Islands are listed in separate sections and are arranged within those sections by city. The individual entries include the title, year established, associated newspapers, address, telephone number, proprietors, editors and other key staff members, and circulation.

A county and city index is included, as well as a master index of the titles of all publications (both newspapers and periodicals) listed in the volume. Also, a list of publishing houses with the titles they publish is included, enabling the identification of groups of newspapers that are published by single companies.

For British newspapers, *Willings Press Guide* and *Benn's Media Directory: United Kingdom* provide much the same sort of comprehensive coverage.

There are many other directories that cover the newspapers of a single region or nation. A selected list of these publications, arranged by country, follows. Most of these directories are published in the predominant language of the nation, although many of the non-English publications have introductions and headings translated into English.

Australia:	*Australian Periodicals in Print.* Melbourne: D. W. Thorpe.
Brazil:	*Anuario Brasiliero de Midia.* São Paulo: Editora Meio & Mensagem.
China:	*China Press and Publishing Directory 1985.* Beijing: Modern Press.
East and West Germany:	*Stamm Leitfaden durch Presse und Werbung.* Essen, West Germany: Stamm-Verlag GMBH.
France:	*Annuaire de la Presse et Publicite et de la Communication.* Paris: Ecron Publicite.
Japan:	*Zasshi Shimbun Sokatarogu.* Tokyo: Media Risachi Senta.
Netherlands:	*Handboek van de Nederlandse Pers en Publiciteit: Gedrukte Media.* Schiedam: Nijgh Periodieken.
South Africa:	*Promadata, Promotion, Marketing & Advertising Data.* Rosebank: Clarion Communications Media.

For further information about other directories and most of those listed above, consult Eugene P. Sheehy's *Guide to Reference Books*, 10th edition, 1986 (Chicago: American Library Association).

Ethnic Newspapers of the United States

Some of the most difficult newspapers for which to locate information are ethnic publications produced in the United States, most of which are published in languages other than English. The *Guide to the American Ethnic Press: Slavic and East European Newspapers and Periodicals*, by Lubomyr R. Wynar (Kent, Ohio: Center for the Study of Ethnic Publications), was published in 1986 and lists publications of eighteen different ethnic groups, in categories such as the Russian press and the Polish press. Individual newspaper and periodical entries are listed alphabetically for each ethnic category. The entries include title, address, sponsor, editor, language, frequency, circulation, subscription price, and a brief description of the publication. Separate geographic and title indexes are included.

Two other works, although somewhat dated, are still the most helpful, and most recent, general directories of the entire field of United States ethnic newspapers. The second edition of the *Encyclopedic Directory of Ethnic Newspapers and Periodicals in the United States*, by Lubomyr R. Wynar and Anna T. Wynar (Littleton, Colo.: Libraries Unlimited), was published in 1976. Fifty-two separate sections cover the various ethnic presses. A title index is included. *The Oxbridge Directory of Ethnic Periodicals*, edited by Patricia Hagood (New York: Oxbridge Communications), was published in 1979. It covers newspapers and periodicals from approximately seventy different ethnic groups in North America. The entries are arranged by "ethnic classification," and a title index is included. (See chapter 3 for the periodical aspects of these directories.)

For coverage of ethnic newspapers, also consult some of the standard newspaper directories described earlier in this chapter such as the *Gale Directory of Publications*; the *Editor & Publisher International Year Book*; and *The Working Press of the Nation*, Volume 1, *Newspaper Directory*. All provide specialized information about foreign language newspapers published in the United States.

Other Sources of Newspaper Information

The Standard Periodical Directory (New York: Oxbridge Communications) is an annual that primarily covers periodicals published in the United States and Canada (see chapter 3). However, there is included a lengthy section of newspaper listings. Newspapers of the United States are listed first and are arranged by state and city. The Canadian newspapers are then listed in one alphabetical title arrangement, without a breakdown by province or city. The individual entries include title, address, telephone number, editor, publisher, other key staff members, year established, frequency, subscription price, circulation, and, in some cases, a very brief description of editorial content. Although this is not the best source for newspaper directory type information, it can be used if other more appropriate directories are not available.

The Serials Directory (Birmingham, Ala.: EBSCO Publishing), was established in 1986 and primarily covers periodicals and annuals published worldwide. However, there is a comparatively short section that lists approximately two thousand newspapers from around the world. The entries for these newspapers are arranged alphabetically by title. There is no access by country, state, or city. Individual entries include title, year established, language, frequency, address, and telephone number. Since there is no geographic access and since relatively few newspapers are listed, this directory should be used for newspaper information only when other more appropriate directories are not available.

The Europa Year Book (London: Europa Publications) is an annual reference work that provides general surveys of the nations of the world. A section titled, "The Press," is included for each nation, in which general background about the press in that nation is given. Listed in this section are the major newspapers of the nation with the following information: title, address, telephone number, year founded, when published (for example, morning or evening), editor, and circulation. This is perhaps the best source to consult for a concise list of the principal newspapers of any given country.

Notes

[1]*Benn's Media Directory: International*, 136th ed. (Tonbridge, U.K.: Benn Business Information Services, 1988), A9.

[2]*Willings Press Guide*, 114th ed. (East Grinstead, U.K.: British Media Publications, 1988), unnumbered page in the preliminary section.

[3]*Newspaper Directory*, 39th ed., Vol. 1 of *The Working Press of the Nation* (Chicago: National Research Bureau, 1989), unnumbered page in the preliminary section.

11

Union Lists of Newspapers and Other Sources of Newspaper Holdings Information

Just as no library can possibly have every periodical, no library can possibly have every newspaper. As was noted in chapter 9, more than 10,000 newspapers are currently published in the United States, and there is a world-wide total of over 54,000 currently published newspapers. Even the largest research libraries can subscribe to only a fraction of the total number of news-papers. For instance, the Library of Congress currently receives 487 news-papers from the United States and 1,161 from other countries. Of these, 363 United States newspapers and 1,115 foreign newspapers are retained perma-nently on microfilm, while the others are retained on a current month or current year basis only.[1] For researchers at the Library of Congress, this means that approximately 97 percent of all currently published newspapers must be found elsewhere.

Most libraries subscribe to far fewer newspapers than does the Library of Congress. A 1980 survey of twenty-three university libraries in the south-eastern United States showed the median number of current newspaper titles received in those libraries was eighty-five.[2] A 1985 survey of eighteen univer-sity libraries that are members of the Association of Research Libraries showed that they received a median number of forty-three international news-papers.[3] There are very good reasons why libraries receive relatively few news-papers. First, the cost of a newspaper subscription, especially for a foreign airmail subscription, can be extremely expensive. Second, with the exception of local news and advertisements, most newspapers from a particular region will cover basically the same news, thus resulting in much duplication between newspapers. For libraries, then, it is not necessary to subscribe to many news-papers from the same region. A library can serve the needs of its patrons for current news coverage by subscribing to a relatively small number of major national and international newspapers and the various local and nearby newspapers.

On a retrospective basis also, libraries can only collect a small percentage of the total number of newspapers that have been published. Since it is esti-mated that there have been over 300,000 newspapers published in the United States alone,[4] there is a large body of newspapers that is not widely available. In general, it can be stated that other than the major newspapers of national or international prominence, most of the files of particular newspapers will be located in the town, city, state or region in which they were originally published. Of course, there are exceptions to this rule since newspaper files have been known to show up in some very unlikely locations. Also, the development and growth of microfilming has made it practical for libraries to acquire files of newspapers that otherwise would have been unavailable or prohibitively expensive to purchase in original issues. Nevertheless, files of specific newspapers, whether on microfilm or in original issues, are, for the most part, available in only a limited number of repositories. The focus of this chapter is on the reference works and other sources that will provide the locations of newspaper files.

As with sources of holdings information for periodicals, newspaper locations and holdings information have traditionally been presented in printed union lists. Currently, though, the trend is toward making available such information through computer databases. This parallels the development of online access to periodical locations and holdings information and computer-output printed union lists. Undoubtedly, the future for newspaper locations and holdings information lies with the computer. At present, though, printed newspaper union lists must still be depended upon. What follows are descriptions of the standard printed newspaper union lists, then a description of computer-related aspects of this field, including the development and significance of the United States Newspaper Program.

Printed Union Lists of Newspapers of the United States

History and Bibliography of American Newspapers, 1690-1820. 2 vols. By Clarence S. Brigham. Worcester, Mass.: American Antiquarian Society, 1947; reprint, including "Additions and Corrections," Hamden, Conn.: Archon, 1962.

Originally published periodically in segments in the *Proceedings of the American Antiquarian Society*, from 1913 through 1927, this remarkable work was produced by Brigham while working on it during evenings, Sundays, and vacations.[5] The cumulated edition was not published until 1947, with a reprint edition issued in 1962. This work lists 2,120 American newspapers published from 1690, when the first American newspaper appeared, through 1820. The title entries are arranged by state and city, then alphabetically by title, disregarding the name of the town or city in the alphabetization. Entries include dates of publication, frequency, and a fairly detailed history of the newspaper. Depositories are listed by name, not by symbol, and the holdings are shown. The depositories listed include approximately five hundred libraries and over one hundred private owners. Two indexes are provided, one of titles and the other of the names of printers.

The "Additions and Corrections" section that appears in the 1962 reprint edition, was originally published in the April 1961 issue of the *Proceedings of the American Antiquarian Society*. It lists nine new titles, and some updated holdings information is given for the titles listed in the original edition. New biographical facts about publishers, printers, and editors are entered, along with important changes in the historical accounts of newspapers.

When referring a patron to this source, be certain to explain that the bulk of the information presented was collected over sixty years ago. Even the updating section in the reprint edition is now a quarter of a century old. Therefore, much of the information presented, particularly regarding holdings, may no longer be accurate. This work can also be misleading in that it was compiled before the rise of microfilming, which revolutionized the handling and collecting of newspapers in libraries. Patrons should be advised to also consult *Newspapers in Microform: United States, 1948-1983* (described later in this chapter), which may provide more updated information for any particular newspaper listed in "Brigham." The private collections listed in this work are probably now inaccessible, for the most part, and patrons should be informed of this fact. As Brigham wrote in the original cumulated edition, "There is little doubt but that many of the newspapers listed in this Bibliography under private ownership will not be in existence twenty-five years hence."[6]

Though some of the information in this work is now outdated, this is still an excellent source. The listings of these early American newspapers, along with their histories, provide a valuable resource, and although the holdings listed may no longer be strictly accurate, they do serve as a general guide to where these newspapers may be available.

A work that can be used in conjunction with "Brigham" is *Chronological Tables of American Newspapers, 1690-1820*, compiled by Edward Connery Lathem (Barre, Mass.: American Antiquarian Society and Barre Publishers, 1972). This work provides chronological access to the titles listed in the original cumulated edition and in the "Additions and Corrections" section of the reprint edition.

American Newspapers, 1821-1936: A Union List of Files Available in the United States and Canada. Edited by Winifred Gregory. New York: H. W. Wilson, 1937; reprint, New York: Kraus Reprint, 1967.

This monumental work lists files of United States and Canadian newspapers from 1821 through 1936 available in depositories in those two nations. The depositories include libraries, county courthouses, newspaper offices, and private collections. This union list was published ten years before Brigham's work (see earlier in this chapter) was published in a cumulated edition. Together, "Brigham" and "Gregory" provide coverage of United States newspapers published from 1690 through 1936.

The title entries in *American Newspapers, 1821-1936* are listed geographically by state and city, with the Canadian entries listed last, by province and city. Within the listings for each city or town, the entries are arranged alphabetically by the first important word in the title of the newspaper, disregarding the name of the city or town, names of the days of the week, or words that indicate periodicity such as "daily" or "weekly." Each entry includes frequency, dates of publication, and any necessary notes regarding variant titles, title changes, or mergers. Newspapers are listed under their latest titles, with cross-references from previous titles. Depositories with files of a newspaper are indicated with a symbol, followed by the dates held by that depository. A key to the library symbols appears in the front of the volume.

Also included is a three-page section titled, "A Bibliography of Union Lists of Newspapers," compiled by Karl Brown and Daniel C. Haskell. Another short segment, "Notes on Newspapers Published in Foreign Countries Found in Libraries of the United States and Canada," provides listings of libraries with significant holdings of newspapers from various foreign nations.

All of the limitations due to age that were described for the "Brigham" book are also applicable for "Gregory." *American Newspapers, 1821-1936* is now over fifty years old. Thus, much of the holdings information is no longer accurate. This union list was also compiled before the introduction of widespread microfilming of newspapers. When showing a patron this work, be certain to point out its age and limitations and to also suggest *Newspapers in Microform: United States, 1948-1983* (described next in this chapter) as a source to search for more updated holdings information. In addition, it should be explained that it may be difficult or impossible to locate some of the depositories listed in this work. The names of many institutions have been changed, others have moved to different cities, and most of the private collections either have different owners or no longer exist. In locating the current addresses and phone numbers for libraries and other depositories listed in "Brigham" and "Gregory," two of the most valuable sources are the *American Library Directory* (New York: R. R. Bowker) and the *Directory of Historical Societies and Agencies in the United States and Canada* (Nashville, Tenn.: Association for State and Local History). With these limitations in mind, "Gregory" is still useful as a guide to newspapers that have been published in the United States and Canada and as a somewhat reliable guide to the institutions that are likely to have files of these newspapers.

Newspapers in Microform: United States, 1948-1983. 2 vols. Washington, D.C.: Library of Congress, 1984.

This two-volume set, which was published along with a volume for foreign newspapers (described later in this chapter), has a rather misleading title. The designation, "1948-1983," is thought by many first time users of this work to indicate that only newspapers published in those years are included. Actually, all United States newspapers available on microform, regardless of year, are within the scope of this publication. The "1948-1983" designation refers to the time period in which reports from libraries and commercial firms were received for inclusion in this volume. Thus, in showing this source to a patron, it should be stressed that the prominently displayed "1948-1983" has no bearing on the dates of the newspapers included.

The current edition of *Newspapers in Microform* is the successor to a number of other similar publications that have emanated from the Library of Congress since 1941. For those interested, this publishing history is recounted in the introduction to the current edition. The purpose of this work is to identify microform editions of American newspapers and to indicate where the master negative(s) and service copies are available. All types of microform editions are within the scope of this work, including microfilm, microfiche, micro-opaque, and microprint. As was previously mentioned, this work is compiled from reports submitted by commercial microfilming firms and from libraries, with the reports of over one thousand contributing firms or libraries included. Although most of the contributing libraries are in the United States and Canada, there is a good representation of contributors from other nations such as Australia and the United Kingdom.

The newspaper entries are arranged geographically, by state and city, with the individual entries for a town or city arranged alphabetically by title. Each entry contains the standard name of the newspaper, dates of publication, frequency, and any continuation notes. The symbols of libraries or commercial firms that have the master negative(s) or service copies available are listed, along with an indication of the dates they own. Many union lists of newspapers or of periodicals enter publications that have changed titles under either the earliest or latest entry and provide cross-references from the variant titles to the main entry. *Newspapers in Microform*, however, employs successive entry cataloging, which results in individual entries for all separate titles in the life of a newspaper. So, it is necessary to pay close attention to, and to follow through on, all "continues," "continued by," and, "merged with" notes.

A title index is included, which can be very useful when a patron is searching for a newspaper, but knows only the name of the newspaper, and that name does not reflect the place of publication. Another special feature of this work is the inclusion of newspapers for which no microform is reported. These newspapers are apparently those that either preceded or succeeded other newspapers that are listed in this work as being available on microform. Also be aware that there was a significant omission in this edition's "Symbols of Contributors." The symbol, "McP," is not in the list. This symbol stands for the Bell & Howell Micro Photo Division, which is now part of University Microfilms International (Ann Arbor, Mich.) and is probably the most prominent American newspaper micropublisher.

When used together, the *Newspapers in Microform: United States, 1948-1983*, "Brigham," and "Gregory" provide blanket coverage of United States newspapers. *Newspapers in Microform* is especially useful as an update to the other two union lists. It also facilitates the interlibrary loan process for newspapers on microform. Keep in mind, though, that although many libraries are covered by these union lists, there are thousands of libraries that are not covered. Until the United States Newspaper Program is successfully completed (see later in this chapter), these three union lists should continue to provide the best general coverage for United States newspapers.

The German Language Press of the Americas. 3 vols. By Karl J. R. Arndt and May E. Olson. Munich: Verlag Dokumentation, 1973-1980.

Volume 1 of this set is titled, *History and Bibliography 1732-1968: United States of America* and appeared in a third, revised edition in 1976. This volume lists approximately five thousand German-American newspapers, giving dates of publication, title changes, and names of editors and publishers. The arrangement is by state and city, with a brief historical statistical summary of the status of the "German-American element" provided for each state. Individual title entries also give a list of all holdings located. The files of over five hundred libraries and historical societies are listed, as well as approximately fifty prominent European libraries.

Volume 2, which was published in 1973 covers German language newspapers published in the countries of Argentina, Bolivia, Brazil, Canada, Chile, Costa Rica, Cuba, the Dominican Republic, Ecuador, Guatemala, Guyana, Mexico, Paraguay, Peru, Uruguay, and Venezuela. Also included is a section of United States listings which acts as an addenda to the first volume. The arrangement is by country and city. Individual entries include dates of publication, title changes, names of editors and publishers, and holdings from libraries throughout the United States and around the world.

Volume 3 is a collection of essays about the history and influence of German language newspapers and periodicals in the Americas.

Many union lists have been compiled to cover the newspapers of a single state. Such works can be quite useful in that they frequently report holdings from smaller libraries that might not be included in national union lists. Some examples of this type are *Guide to Ohio Newspapers, 1793-1973*, edited by Stephen Gutgesell (Columbus, Ohio: Ohio Historical Society, 1974), and *Directory of New Jersey Newspapers, 1765-1970*, by William C. Wright and Paul A. Stellhorn (Trenton, N.J.: New Jersey Historical Commission, 1977). *A Bibliography of Iowa Newspapers, 1836-1976* (Des Moines, Iowa: Iowa State Historical Department, Division of the State Historical Society, 1979) was compiled by the Iowa State Pilot Project of the Organization of American Historians — Library of Congress United States Newspaper Project. This was the pilot project, funded by the National Endowment for the Humanities, that served as the first step of the United States Newspaper Program (described later in this chapter). As such, this state project was used as a test to determine the resources necessary to create a national newspaper database. It resulted both in the creation of computer records for the newspapers of Iowa and in this printed union list. As the United States Newspaper Program progresses, many more state union lists undoubtedly will be published.

Printed Union Lists of Foreign Newspapers

Newspapers in Microform: Foreign Countries, 1948-1983. Washington, D.C.: Library of Congress, 1984.

This is the companion publication to *Newspapers in Microform: United States, 1948-1983* (described earlier in this chapter). As with its companion, the "1948-1983" refers to the years in which reports were received from libraries and commercial firms for inclusion in this list. The date designation has no relation to the dates of the newspapers included in this work, and that fact should be explained to patrons using this union list for the first time.

This work includes newspapers from all countries other than the United States that are available in any type of microform (microfilm, microfiche, micro-opaque, and microprint). The listings are based on the reports of holdings from hundreds of United States and foreign libraries. The number of newspaper entries varies widely from country to country. The stated explanation for this is that within "many developing nations there is no obvious urgency about reducing newspapers to microform, and there is no particular reason why the state library of a central European nation should report its holdings of microfilmed newspapers to the Library of Congress."[7]

The entries are arranged geographically by country and city and alphabetically by title within cities. Titles in Cyrillic, oriental, and other nonroman scripts are transcribed. Individual entries give frequency, publication dates, and any information about title changes. However, the abundance of question marks after publication dates found in this work indicates that much of the information has not been substantiated. Libraries reporting holdings of master negatives and service copies of microforms for newspapers are listed by symbol, along with an indication of the dates held. Be aware that, as with its companion volumes covering United States newspapers, this volume has omitted the symbol "McP" from its "Symbols of Contributors." As mentioned previously, this symbol stands for the Bell & Howell Micro Photo Division, which is now a part of University Microfilms International.

Newspapers in Microform: Foreign Countries, 1948-1983, should be the first source consulted in a search for libraries with holdings of specific foreign newspapers.

World List of National Newspapers. Compiled by Rosemary Webber. London: Butterworths, 1976.

This is a union list of national newspapers held in British libraries. British and Irish newspapers with a national circulation or that carry a significant amount of national news are included. All known holdings of foreign newspapers are also listed. The holdings of approximately 150 British libraries are represented in this work.

The arrangement of the individual entries is alphabetical by the title printed on the masthead of the newspaper. The entries include place of publication, dates of publication, frequency, and any title change information. Holding libraries are represented by symbols, followed by an indication of the dates held. Both microform and original issue holdings are listed. Since the arrangement is by title, an index by country is included, although this index does *not* provide access by cities within countries.

Latin American Newspapers in United States Libraries: A Union List. Compiled by Steven M. Charno. Austin, Tex.: University of Texas Press for the Conference on Latin American History, 1968.

This work, which was compiled at the Library of Congress, lists 5,500 Latin American newspapers owned by seventy reporting libraries in the United States. Newspapers published in the following countries are included: Argentina, Bolivia, Brazil, Chile, Colombia, Costa Rica, Cuba, the Dominican Republic, Ecuador, El Salvador, Guatemala, Haiti, Honduras, Mexico, Nicaragua, Panama, Paraguay, Peru, Puerto Rico, Uruguay, and Venezuela. The arrangement is geographical by country and city and alphabetical by title within each city. Individual entries include frequency, dates of publication, and any applicable continuation notes. Reporting libraries are identified by symbols, with their holdings enumerated in a detailed manner. Both microform holdings and files of original issues are reported.

The German Language Press of the Americas.
See description earlier in this chapter.

There are also available some union lists devoted solely to the newspapers published in a single "foreign" country or the newspaper holdings in the libraries of a single "foreign" country. An example of the first type is *Philippine Newspapers: An International Union List*, compiled by Shiro Saito and Alice W. Mark (Honolulu, Hawaii: Philippine Studies Program, Center for Asian and Pacific Studies, University of Hawaii, 1984), and published as *Philippine Studies Occasional Paper No. 7*. This work lists 432 Philippine newspapers and reports holdings from approximately thirty-five repositories in Australia, Canada, England, the Philippines, and the United States.

An example of the second type of foreign newspaper union list is *Newspapers in Australian Libraries: A Union List*, 3d edition (Canberra: National Library of Australia, 1975). This work is comprised of two volumes, the first of which is titled, *Overseas Newspapers*, and lists foreign newspapers in Australian libraries. The second volume is titled, *Australian Newspapers*, and lists domestic newspapers in Australian libraries.

The United States Newspaper Program and Other Online Sources of Newspaper Holdings Information

In 1969, the Committee on Bibliographical and Research Needs of the Organization of American Historians (O.A.H.) proposed that a revision of Gregory's *American Newspapers, 1821-1936* was needed. With grant support from the National Endowment for the Humanities, the Organization of American Historians began planning, in the years of 1973 through 1975, for such an update. Although at first it was thought that another printed work would be the outcome of such a project, it soon became evident that constructing a national newspaper database covering the entire history of United States newspaper publishing would be far superior to any revision of *American Newspapers, 1821-1936*.[8]

The Library of Congress became involved in the project, and a second National Endowment for the Humanities grant funded the Iowa Pilot Project. In the course of the project, approximately 1,200 Iowa institutions, including libraries, historical societies, museums, county courthouses, and newspaper offices were surveyed. The project resulted in the publication of a printed bibliography, *A Bibliography of Iowa Newspapers, 1836-1976* (see description earlier in this chapter), along with the creation of MARC computer records for the newspapers. In all, 6,500 newspaper titles were identified and cataloged, including those for which no holdings could be located.[9]

The National Endowment for the Humanities (NEH) decided in 1978 to coordinate the United States Newspaper Program, which by that point was being seen as both a cataloging and preservation effort, in addition to its original purpose as a national newspaper union list.[10] In 1982, NEH distributed a three-phase program guideline for grant applications for the development of state programs. The three phases of any state program are:

1. Planning for the comprehensive state project.

2. Bibliographical control, including the surveying, cataloging, and input of newspaper holdings into the CONSER database on OCLC.

3. Preservation of important and endangered newspaper files.[11]

To begin the program, six major national repositories, including the American Antiquarian Society and the Center for Research Libraries, were invited to submit proposals, that were subsequently approved, so that the database could be rapidly built. The Library of Congress also put a renewed emphasis on cataloging its own collections.[12] Since then, over two dozen state, or United States territory, projects have been awarded funds. Some projects, such as those for Hawaii and Utah, have already been completed through the cataloging phase. Harold Cannon, the Director of the Endowment's Office of Preservation stated that the program's original estimate of 300,000 records nationwide to be created by this project may be exceeded and that the project will probably "take another twenty years or more to complete."[13] When newspapers are cataloged as part of the United States Newspaper Program, their MARC records become a part of the CONSER database (see chapter 14 for descriptions of CONSER and the MARC serial record) and are accessible through the OCLC system. All OCLC member institutions can search for these records and display the symbols of repositories with holdings of a particular newspaper. OCLC also maintains the online union list of locations and holdings of newspapers held by institutions in the United States Newspaper Program. The records in the union list give detailed information regarding individual newspapers in specific repositories. Holdings are noted as either being on microform or in original issues. This is a help in facilitating interlibrary loans of newspapers. The online union list is accessible to all United States Newspaper Program member institutions and to all other OCLC member institutions that are a part of any union list maintained on the OCLC system.

In addition to online access, OCLC has produced microfiche and printed union lists based on the records created as part of the United States Newspaper Program. In 1985, the first *United States Newspaper Program National Union List* was published in eight paperback volumes and in a microfiche edition. The 35,000 records that had been created to that point were included, along with location and holdings information. Indexes provide access by beginning date, place, intended audience, and language.

The second edition, which was published on microfiche in 1987, contains 56,684 titles along with 104,820 summary holdings statements and 128,226 copy-specific holdings statements. This edition reflects the information entered into OCLC as of April 1987, by fourteen state projects, the Virgin Islands project, and the national repositories that were recruited for the program. The main body of the work consists of the individual newspaper entries arranged alphabetically by title. Both this union list and the entire United States Newspaper Program employ successive entry cataloging. Thus, every title change in a newspaper's history results in a complete cataloging and holdings record. The individual entries provide dates of publication, the publisher or publishing company, frequency, relevant "continues" and "continued by" notes, any other applicable notes, and the OCLC record number. Holding libraries are indicated by symbols, and their holdings, in microform and/or in original issues, are enumerated. Indexes are included that provide access by beginning date of publication, place of publication, language, and intended audience.

When referring a patron to this source, it is essential to explain that this is a work in progress and not a complete union list. Patrons should still be advised to consult the other major American newspaper lists described earlier in this chapter.

In addition to the United States Newspaper Program records and other newspaper records available through OCLC, other online systems make available MARC newspaper records, along with holdings information. Three of these other major bibliographic networks are the Research Libraries Information Network (RLIN), the Western Library Network (WLN), and the University of Toronto Library Automation System (UTLAS).

In using any online system, searches for newspaper records should be performed in the same manner as searches for other serial records. However, online newspaper record searching is complicated by the large duplication of titles. There have been dozens, if not hundreds, of newspapers with titles such as the *Sentinel*, or the *Star*, or the *Times*. Before starting an online search for newspapers, try to establish the beginning date of the newspaper, and limit the initial search to serials beginning in that year. Also, the two editions of the OCLC-produced *United States Newspaper Program National Union List* (described earlier in this chapter) provide access by title, place of publication, beginning date, language, and intended audience. Before searching OCLC for records of United States newspapers, this union list can be consulted. Since OCLC record numbers are given for the newspapers, it provides direct online access to the needed record.

In dealing with online MARC records, be aware that holding libraries should only be identified from the 850 field of the record or from a separate display of holding locations. The presence of a library's symbol in the 040 field of the record indicates an involvement in the creation of the record and does not indicate that the library has holdings of the newspaper. Also, do not assume that a library has a complete set of a newspaper based solely on the fact that the library's symbol is on the record as a holding location. A library's symbol can be placed on a record even if the entire holdings consist of only one issue of that newspaper.

Other Aspects of Reference Work
with Union Lists of Newspapers

Another type of reference source, although not strictly a union list, can be quite helpful in locating newspaper holdings. This type of source lists the newspaper holdings within one library or institution. Probably the most well known of this type of work is the British Library's eight-volume *Catalogue of the Newspaper Library, Colindale* (London: British Museum Publications for the British Library Board, 1975). Another example is *A Check List of*

American Eighteenth Century Newspapers in the Library of Congress, new edition (Washington, D.C.: Government Printing Office, 1936).

Occasionally, a search for a newspaper in the various sources described earlier in this chapter will uncover no record of the newspaper. In such cases, search for the title in some of the standard union lists of serials such as the *Union List of Serials in Libraries of the United States and Canada* and other sources described in chapter 4. Such "phantom newspapers" will frequently turn out to be periodicals. If the publication is, indeed, a newspaper, and it is not listed in any available newspaper union list, do not abandon the search. The various national union lists report the holdings of many libraries, but certainly not all libraries are covered. The assumption should be made that if a file of a particular newspaper exists, it will probably be in the town or city in which the newspaper was published. Consult the *American Library Directory* (New York: R. R. Bowker) and the *Directory of Historical Societies and Agencies in the United States and Canada* (Nashville, Tenn.: American Association for State and Local History) to locate telephone numbers and addresses for local libraries and historical societies. If these local institutions do not have a set of the newspaper in question, they may be able to provide a reference to another local repository or collector. On the other hand, they may just be able to confirm that the newspaper existed but that no known files of the newspaper remain.

Another possible location in which to find a file of a newspaper is in the office of the newspaper itself. This, of course, applies only to newspapers that are currently in print or that have merged with another newspaper that is still in print. A newspaper publishing company will usually retain an archival set of its publication and will frequently provide some level of access to that set. *Newspaper Libraries in the U.S. and Canada*, 2d edition, edited by Elizabeth L. Anderson (New York: Special Libraries Association, Newspaper Division, 1980) gives information relating to this for most of the larger newspapers published in the United States and Canada. An update to this work was published under the title, *The International Directory of News Libraries and Buyer's Guide, 1985-86* (Bayside, N.Y.: LDA Publishers, 1985). For newspapers not listed in these sources, consult the standard newspaper directories described in chapter 10 to determine if the newspaper is still being published and to locate an address and telephone number.

Finally, be cautious in the use of newspaper union lists as tools for referral. Just as when using periodical union lists, never state flatly that a library has a certain newspaper for a certain date, or range of dates, based solely on the reported holdings in a union list or other source of holdings information. Always state that a library is reported as having the date, or range of dates, but that the reader should contact the library first to confirm that they actually do have the newspaper and date(s) needed and that it is currently available. When possible, the serials reference staffer should make this contact for the reader, as an extension of reference service. It is extremely frustrating for a researcher to make a lengthy trip to another library to consult a newspaper, only to find that the microfilm of the date needed is out on interlibrary loan, or that the library never had the date to begin with.

This chapter has included descriptions of several standard newspaper union lists and other sources of newspaper holdings information. There are many other sources that have not been mentioned here. Some of these other sources may be found listed in Eugene P. Sheehy's *Guide to Reference Books*, tenth edition, 1986 (Chicago: American Library Association). Other references to newspaper union lists are in *Union Lists of Serials: A Bibliography*, compiled by Ruth S. Freitag (Washington, D.C.: Library of Congress, 1964). Another older listing is the three-page, "A Bibliography of Union Lists of Newspapers," compiled by Karl Brown and Daniel C. Haskell, which appeared in *American Newspapers, 1821-1936*.

Notes

[1]*Newspapers Received Currently in the Library of Congress*, 11th ed. (Washington, D.C.: Library of Congress, 1988), v.

[2]Janell Rudolph and Kit Byunn, "Academic Library Newspaper Collections: Developing Policy," *College & Research Libraries* 43 (January 1982): 80-81.

[3]Stanley P. Hodge and Marilyn Ivins, "Current International Newspapers: Some Collection Management Implications," *College & Research Libraries* 48 (January 1987): 52-53.

[4]George Clack, "Preserving Yesterday's News," *Humanities* 8 (January/February 1987): 25.

[5]Clarence S. Brigham, *History and Bibliography of American Newspapers, 1690-1820* (Worcester, Mass.: American Antiquarian Society, 1947; repr., Hamden, Conn.: Archon Books, 1962), ix.

[6]Ibid., 1189.

[7]*Newspapers in Microform: Foreign Countries, 1948-1983* (Washington, D.C.: Library of Congress, 1984), vii.

[8]Harold Cannon, "The National Endowment for the Humanities and the United States Newspaper Program," *Cataloging & Classification Quarterly* 6 (Summer 1986): 7-8.

[9]*A Bibliography of Iowa Newspapers, 1836-1976* ([Des Moines, Iowa]: Iowa State Historical Department, Division of the State Historical Society, 1979), i-iv.

[10]Larry E. Sullivan, "United States Newspaper Program: Progress and Prospects," *Microform Review* 15 (Summer 1986): 159.

[11]Donald F. Wisdom, "Newspaper Program Developments," *Library of Congress Information Bulletin* 42 (23 May 1983): 168.

[12]Cannon, "National Endowment for the Humanities," 8.

[13]Ibid., 8-9.

12

Newspaper Indexes and Abstracts

Library patrons use newspapers for two major purposes. The first use falls into the realm of current awareness. For the most part, patrons read recent issues of newspapers to keep up-to-date regarding current events and news. Such usage is not research oriented. Library staffers are usually not called upon to provide reference assistance to such users, except in cases when an issue of a newspaper is missing or a given newspaper is not subscribed to by the library, and the patron demands an explanation.

The second major use of newspapers in libraries falls into the realm of research, which may be historical and may involve the use of newspapers from decades or centuries ago. On the other hand, research with newspapers may center around a current topic and require the use of more recent issues. In either historical or current research, the patron seeks certain information from newspapers. Most inexperienced researchers do not know how to conduct such a search, and even experienced researchers can run into problems. The reference librarian, or other staffer responsible for serials reference service, should be able to provide assistance to such a library patron.

As with those who perform any type of research, newspaper researchers arrive at the library in various degrees of preparedness. Some already possess exact citations to articles that they need to locate. In such cases, one needs only to determine if the library owns the newspaper and the date(s) needed. If the library does not have the newspaper or date(s) needed, then a reference staffer can determine what other libraries might have it by using the standard sources of newspaper holdings information (see chapter 11). Other researchers know that they need a particular article or column from a specific newspaper, but they do not know the date or page number. Some may want to retrieve all of the articles that a specific newspaper has printed regarding a particular topic or event. Still others desire to locate any articles that have appeared in any newspaper on a specific topic or event. In assisting a newspaper researcher who does not have exact citations to articles, a reference staffer must first determine if there are any indexes that may be of help to that researcher.

Newspaper Indexes

A newspaper index is a systematically arranged list of articles, or other printed items, that provides enough information to identify and trace the items. Whereas most periodical abstracting and indexing services cover the articles in many periodicals, the majority of newspaper indexes are devoted to individual newspapers. The main point of access for most newspaper indexes is subject. Some also provide author indexing, but this is usually just for columnists and not for the regular reporters. There is no newspaper index that covers everything that appears in a newspaper. While most index all the general news articles and columns in a specific newspaper, others cover only the articles relating to a local region or city. Some indexes cover death notices, while many others do not. For the most part, advertisements, syndicated features, accounts of individual sports games, and photographs or illustrations are not covered in newspaper indexes.

In addition to printed newspaper indexes, many newspapers are available through online, full-text retrieval systems. For many types of inquiries, an online search is more efficient, and is preferable, to searching through printed indexes. For some newspapers, there is no printed index equivalent to an online system. Thus, online searching is the only alternative to performing a manual issue-by-issue, page-by-page search of a newspaper. A reference staffer must be aware of all newspaper searching alternatives in order to provide the best advice to the patron.

The first point that must be kept in mind regarding newspaper indexes is that there are no indexes for most newspapers. This fact comes as a rude shock to many patrons who assume that it will be a relatively easy chore to locate a specific article for which they do not have an exact citation. For example, if a patron is searching for a specific article or column from a 1968 issue of *The Washington Post*, and a date, or approximate date, of the item is not known, then such a search may prove to be quite lengthy and frustrating. There simply is not available a general index to *The Washington Post* prior to 1971. If the item in question regards an event of national importance, then some techniques can be employed to ascertain an approximate date of publication of related articles (described later in this chapter). Otherwise, there is not an index volume that can be pulled off the shelf and quickly consulted for a date and page number. Many patrons are incredulous when presented with the information that a newspaper is not indexed. The reference staffer can do little but present accurate information on what is and is not indexed and to suggest possible searching alternatives, when appropriate. Often, though, there is no alternative but to search through issue after issue until the needed item is found.

Indexing is available for only a small portion of the total number of newspapers that have been published and that are currently in print. In the United States alone, it is estimated that there have been 300,000 different newspapers published.[1] The worldwide total is unknown, but undoubtedly is huge. With the worldwide total number of newspapers reaching into the hundreds of thousands, and perhaps more than a million, one might expect to find a correspondingly large body of newspaper indexes. Unfortunately, that is not the case. Two fairly recent bibliographies of newspaper indexes, Anita Cheek

Milner's three-volume *Newspaper Indexes: A Location and Subject Guide for Researchers,* and the *Lathrop Report on Newspaper Indexes: An Illustrated Guide to Published and Unpublished Newspaper Indexes in the United States & Canada* (both described later in this chapter), list a total number of newspaper indexes in the hundreds. Thus, an extremely small body of newspaper literature is indexed.

The sad reality is that most newspapers are not indexed, because of two major reasons. First, the indexing of a newspaper is a very labor-intensive process, and therefore is quite expensive. This applies both to current and retrospective indexing. As an example, a South African librarian initiated a project to index two Cape Town newspapers for a number of years from the late 1800s and the early 1900s. After completing one year of indexing, he reported that he "was horrified at the amount of time it took and the number of entries that were generated." The indexing for one year (1871) took twenty months to complete and resulted in 35,000 entries typed on over seven hundred pages.[2] A second major reason that newspaper indexes are not produced is that there is not a big enough market for them. The only libraries that will purchase an index for a given newspaper are those that retain a permanent file of that newspaper. So, when a North Dakota librarian began to index the *Grand Forks Herald*, he found that only eleven institutions would purchase the finished product.[3]

Newspaper indexes produced by commercial firms, such as *The Official Washington Post Index* and the *Los Angeles Times Index*, are the most well-known and widely-circulated. Often, such indexes are produced by a firm that also produces the microform edition of the newspaper in order to make that microform edition more attractive to librarians. Commercial indexing of newspapers is available in all types of formats including print, microform, CD-ROM, and as part of online databases.

Other newspaper indexes are produced by libraries or historical societies as a public service, with profit not being a motivating factor. In most cases, these institutions index the local newspaper. Frequently, these indexes are not published and exist only as a card file at the library or historical society. Other such indexes are printed and distributed. Some examples of this type of index are the Cleveland (Ohio) Public Library's *Cleveland News Index* and the Duluth (Minn.) Public Library's *Duluth News-Tribune & Herald Index.*

A final class of newspaper indexes are those compiled by the staff of a newspaper either for distribution or for in-house use only. *The New York Times Index* is a prominent example of such a work.[4] Traditionally, the "morgue" of a newspaper provided subject access as a clippings file of items that had been printed in the newspaper. Public access to such files and other in-house manual indexes is generally quite limited. Increasingly, though, newspapers are abandoning the clippings files and are building databases consisting of full-text articles that have been printed in the newspaper. This has been beneficial to librarians and to researchers since many of these databases eventually become available for public online searching through services such as NEXIS, VU/TEXT and DataTimes (described later in this chapter).

Since most newspapers are not indexed, experienced researchers and librarians have learned how to most effectively use nonindexed newspapers. However, often an item in a nonindexed newspaper can only be located by searching through every page of issue after issue. Such searching is tedious and can be frustrating. Thus, it is not surprising that when given a choice, library patrons will opt to perform research in an indexed newspaper rather than a comparable nonindexed newspaper. A survey at the University of Illinois newspaper library showed that, from 1972 through 1976, 68.7 percent of all newspaper requests were for indexed newspapers.[5]

Since library patrons seek out and make constant use of newspaper indexes, serials reference staffers must be very familiar with such indexes. The remainder of this chapter is devoted to descriptions of, and suggestions for the use of, major types of newspaper indexes and major specific newspaper indexes in all formats, including systems that make accessible the online retrieval of newspaper articles.

Printed Newspaper Indexes

Palmer's Index to The Times Newspaper (Hampton Wick, U.K.: Samuel
Palmer) and *The Times Index* (Reading, U.K.: Research Publications).

In 1785, *The Daily Universal Register* began publication in London. Three years later, it changed its title to *The Times* and grew to be one of the most respected newspapers in the world. Over two hundred years after its inception, *The Times* remains as one of the most influential newspapers currently published.

Researchers and librarians are fortunate in that indexes exist for the entire run of this newspaper, making it the world's oldest continually-indexed newspaper. In fact, for a number of years in the first half of the twentieth century, there are two different indexes available. The first indexing of this newspaper was *Palmer's Index to The Times Newspaper*, which began in 1868. Retrospective and current indexing was undertaken, and eventually the *Palmer's* set covered from October 1790 through June 1941. In 1906, *The Times* began to publish its own index, despite the existence of *Palmer's* index. This "official" index has been issued under various frequencies of publication and has had numerous titles throughout the years, including the *Annual Index to the Times, The Official Index to the Times, Index to the Times,* and its current title, *The Times Index. The Times* has also produced an index to the years of 1785 through 1790, a period not covered by *Palmer's*, with the exception of the last quarter of 1790. For the years in which both indexes are available, 1906-1941, the "official" indexing of *The Times* is considered to be far superior to *Palmer's*.[6]

The Times Index is currently published on a monthly basis, with annual cumulations. In addition to providing coverage of *The Times* and *The Sunday Times*, this work also indexes the following publications, which are usually treated as periodicals in libraries:

The Times Literary Supplement

The Times Educational Supplement

The Times Higher Education Supplement

This additional coverage began with 1973. When directing a patron to this index, mention that many of the citations are to articles in these supplements. Also point out the abbreviations key in the front of the work so that patrons can be aware of some of the unusual abbreviations that are found in many of the citations. Abbreviations such as "sP," which stands for "speech in Parliament," can be found on practically every page.

One other peculiarity that reference staff should be aware of concerns the 1978 and 1979 editions of this index. From December 1, 1978, through November 12, 1979, *The Times* suspended publication due to a labor dispute. During this period, however, indexing of *The Daily Telegraph, The Sunday Daily Telegraph*, and the *Telegraph Sunday Magazine* is provided. Thus, a continuous newspaper index is sustained throughout this time span.

Reference staff should also be aware of a fairly common problem that surfaces with indexes to *The Times*. Some inexperienced researchers will consult this source, thinking that it is an index to *The New York Times*. Since *The Times* index does not prominently display the word "London," this is an easy mistake for a novice to make. So, if a patron states that an article cited in *The Times Index* is not to be found in the newspaper, that patron should be asked first if they are using *The Times* of London or *The New York Times*.

The New York Times Index. New York: The New York Times.

Founded in 1851, the *New York Daily Times* (later, *The New York Times*) quickly established itself as a reputable and authoritative newspaper. It rose above its competitors, "and no rival equaled it in developing the technique of careful reporting."[7] *The New York Times* is seen as the unofficial newspaper of record for the United States. Thus, it is one of the first sources library patrons choose to consult when they search for newspaper accounts of major events.

The New York Times Index covers the entire publishing history of the newspaper, back to 1851. It began publication on a regular basis in 1913, although indexes for some earlier years had already been published. Eventually, a complete backfile of indexes was compiled and printed. The first seven years of this index is in handwritten form and consists of the original indexing. From September 1858 through 1912, some of the volumes consist of the contemporary indexing done at the time, and others consist of modern indexing compiled recently. Due to the varying types of indexing and arrangement, the early years of *The New York Times Index* can be difficult to use. For detailed explanations of those early years, consult *Guide to the Incomparable New York Times Index*, by Grant W. Morse (New York: Fleet Academic Editions, 1980), and "A Corrective Supplement to Morse's *Guide to the Incomparable New York Times Index*," by Douglas H. Shepard (*Reference Services Review*, Vol. 9, no. 4, October/December 1981, p. 33-35).

The New York Times Index is valuable not only as an index to the articles in the newspaper, but also as a ready reference source to national and international events. Over the past forty to fifty years, the article summaries have developed into informative abstracts, in which the key data from articles are presented. Thus, this index is a detailed, subject-access summary of the news. In that capacity, it can also serve as a guide to articles covering events of national importance that may have appeared in other nonindexed newspapers. A manual search within a nonindexed newspaper can be narrowed by establishing the date of an event through the use of *The New York Times Index*.

The main purpose of this work, though, is to serve as a guide to the contents of *The New York Times* late edition, which is the edition that is microfilmed. The index is printed twice a month, with quarterly and annual cumulations. The entries are listed chronologically under subjects and personal names. So it is possible to use the index as a chronological overview to the news in any particular subject area. The individual entries include abstracts of the articles followed by an indication of the length of the article—"(L)," "(M)," and, "(S)," standing for long, medium, and short. These length abbreviations are frequently misinterpreted by readers to stand for a day of the week or the section of the newspaper. The rest of the entry gives the date, section, page, and column. For instance, "Ja 14, III, 9:5" means that the article appeared on January 14, in the third section, on page nine, column five. The section is always referred to by a roman numeral, even if the actual newspaper of that date uses letter designations for the sections.

Perhaps the most confusing aspect of this index for inexperienced users is its heavy usage of "see also" cross references. A majority of the headings have these cross references, which refer the user to other headings and specific dates in the index, where a complete entry will be found. Unfortunately, the cross-reference concept is alien to many novice users. Instead of following through on the cross reference, such a user may make a note of the date given and then try to locate the article by browsing through that issue of the newspaper. For example, in the 1984 index, the only notation under the heading "Abominable Snowman" is, "See also Monsters Je 6." An inexperienced user will frequently then get the microfilm for June 6, 1984, and scan through the issue trying to find the article. If the user had followed through on the cross-reference, the June 6 article entry listed under "Monsters" provides an abstract, along with the exact section, page, and column. So, reference staff should always take the time to explain this index to inexperienced users and to mention common mistakes that are made in its use.

There are two other major printed sources that can be used by those searching for items in *The New York Times*. The first is the *Personal Name Index to 'The New York Times Index' 1851-1974* (Succasunna, N.J. and Verdi, Nev.: Roxbury Data Interface, 1976-1983), which is a twenty-two volume index to personal names that have appeared in *The New York Times Index*. For each name, this work gives the date(s) and page number(s) of *The New York Times Index* on which the name appeared. One using the *Personal Name Index* must then use *The New York Times Index* to determine the date and page number of the item about this person in the newspaper itself. A three-volume supplement of the *Personal Name Index*, covering 1975-1979, has also been published.

The other major supplementary index is *The New York Times Obituaries Index* (New York: The New York Times), which has thus far been issued in two volumes. The first volume was published in 1970 and covers 1858 through 1968. The second volume was published in 1980 and covers 1969 through 1978. Together, these two volumes provide date, page, and column numbers for approximately 389,000 obituaries that were printed in *The New York Times* from 1858 through 1978.

In the early 1970s, the Bell & Howell Company began publishing individual printed indexes to a number of major newspapers. Some of the first newspapers covered included *The Washington Post* (beginning with 1971), the *Chicago Tribune* (beginning with 1972), and *The Times-Picayune* of New Orleans (beginning with 1972). Bell & Howell and University Microfilms International (UMI) have now merged, and the indexes are published by University Microfilms International. Since its inception, this series has grown to cover many other newspapers, including:

The Atlanta Constitution and *The Atlanta Journal*

The Boston Globe

The Christian Science Monitor

The Denver Post

The Detroit News

The Houston Post

Nashville Banner and *The Tennessean*

St. Louis Post-Dispatch

San Francisco Chronicle

USA Today

The Washington Times

UMI also publishes the *Black Newspapers Index*, which covers approximately ten major Black newspapers from across the United States. In addition, printed indexes are available to the short-lived English language edition of *Pravda* and to *The Guardian*, of England.

Most of the Bell & Howell/UMI indexes have had a succession of titles. For instance, the index to the *Los Angeles Times* was first known as *Bell & Howell's Newspaper Index to the Los Angeles Times* and then changed titles to *Newspaper Index. Los Angeles Times*. Later, it changed back to *Bell & Howell's Newspaper Index to the Los Angeles Times*. As of 1986, the title is *Los Angeles Times Index*.

Most of the indexes produced by UMI can also be accessed online through a service called Newspaper Abstracts Online. In addition, UMI offers a CD-ROM-based retrieval system, Newspaper Abstracts Ondisc.

The previously-mentioned Bell & Howell index to *The Washington Post*, which carried, at different times, the titles *Bell & Howell's Newspaper Index to The Washington Post* and *The Washington Post. Newspaper Index*, was published from 1971 through 1981. In 1979, Research Publications (Woodbridge, Conn.) began publishing *The Washington Post* on microfilm, and, concurrently started publishing *The Official Washington Post Index.* Thus, for the years of 1979 through 1981, indexes to *The Washington Post* were published by both Bell & Howell and by Research Publications. *The Official Washington Post Index,* published by Research Publications, has continued and is currently issued monthly, with annual cumulations.

In addition to the indexes already mentioned, there are several other important printed newspaper indexes. Among these are:

The Wall Street Journal. Index. New York: Dow Jones. Covers 1955-   .

Index to the Honolulu Advertiser and Honolulu Star-Bulletin. [Honolulu, Hawaii]: Hawaii State Library. Covers 1929/1967-   .

The New-York Daily Tribune Index. New York: The Tribune Association. Covers 1875-1906.

Virginia Gazette Index, 1736-1780. By Lester J. Cappon and Stella F. Duff. Williamsburg, Va.: Institute of Early American History and Culture, 1950.

Canadian News Index, formerly, *The Canadian Newspaper Index.* Toronto: Micromedia Limited. Covers seven newspapers, 1977-   .

Zeitungs-Index. Munich: K. G. Saur. Covers approximately a dozen German newspapers, plus one Austrian and one Swiss newspaper, 1974-   .

Indian Press Index. Delhi: Delhi Library Association. Covers over a dozen Indian newspapers, 1968-   .

Annual Index to the Financial Times, which cumulates the *Monthly Index to the Financial Times.* Reading, U.K.: Research Publications. Covers 1981-   .

There also exist hundreds of other printed newspaper indexes. Many of them cover only a limited period of time. Others are specialty works and index only certain aspects of a single newspaper or group of newspapers. Some examples of these indexes are the *Index to Marriages and Deaths in the New York Herald, 1835-1855,* compiled by James P. Maher (Baltimore: Genealogical Publishing, 1987), and *Michigan in the Civil War: A Guide to the Material in Detroit Newspapers, 1861-1866,* compiled by Helen H. Ellis (Lansing, Mich.: Michigan Civil War Centennial Observance Commission, 1965).

To determine if any type of published, or unpublished, index exists for a particular newspaper, one should first consult the *Lathrop Report on Newspaper Indexes: An Illustrated Guide to Published and Unpublished Newspaper Indexes in the United States & Canada,* compiled by Norman M. Lathrop and Mary Lou Lathrop (Wooster, Ohio: Norman Lathrop Enterprises, 1979-1980), and the three-volume work, *Newspaper Indexes: A Location and Subject Guide for Researchers,* by Anita Cheek Milner (Metuchen, N.J.: Scarecrow Press, 1977-1982). The *Lathrop Report* lists indexes of United

States and Canadian newspapers found in libraries and in other repositories within those two nations. Each index is described in detail, including scope, style and format, and availability. Also included is a reproduction of a sample section of the index. The *Lathrop Report* has six indexes of its own, including those which allow access to the entries for the newspaper indexes alphabetically, geographically, and chronologically.

The three volumes compiled by Milner list indexes of newspapers from all countries of the world that are available in libraries across the United States. Although the scope is international, the overwhelming majority of indexes included are for those of American newspapers. Each volume has two major sections. The first section lists, by state or foreign country, indexed newspapers, with an indication of the years indexed and repositories where the indexes are located. The second major section lists the repositories and provides addresses and other information, such as fees for photocopying and interlibrary loan availability.

Taken together, the Lathrop and Milner works are the most exhaustive listing available of published and unpublished newspaper indexes available in the United States.

Newspaper Indexes Published in Microform

The *National Newspaper Index* is produced by the Information Access Company and is similar to the *Magazine Index* and to the *Business Index*, also produced by the same company (see chapter 5). Like the other two indexes, the *National Newspaper Index* is stored on one large reel of 16mm microfilm and is housed within a self-contained viewing machine. It gives coverage of *The Wall Street Journal* (Eastern and Western editions), *the Christian Science Monitor, The Washington Post*, the *Los Angeles Times*, and *The New York Times* (late and national editions). The microfilm reel is updated monthly and contains over two years of indexing. This index began in 1979, and retrospective indexing not on the current reel of microfilm can be accessed through a microfiche edition.

As with most Information Access Company products, this index is easy to use. It is also very convenient to have over two years of indexing for these five newspapers cumulated into one index. The monthly updating allows this to be just as current, or even more current, than the printed indexes for these newspapers. The disadvantage to this index is that for many of the headings there are dozens and dozens of entries listed under various subheadings covering the two-year time span for the five newspapers. When a patron is searching for any articles on a subject, this is not much of a problem. However, when a patron needs to locate one specific article from one of these newspapers, searching in this index is not the most efficient approach. In such cases when the patron is searching for a particular article and knows the newspaper and approximate date, it is usually best to start the search in the printed index to that newspaper, if that index is available.

There is another major problem with this index to which all reference staff should be alerted. Both the national and late editions of *The New York Times* are covered in this index. A typical citation might read, "World Bank loans stir ire of U.S. farm groups. 8 col. in. The New York Times—June 5'87 p27(N) pD1(L) col 1." This indicates that the article will be found on page 27 of the national edition and on page one of section D in the late edition. The first problem is that most patrons and many reference staffers don't understand the meaning of "(N)" and "(L)," and assume that they refer to section designations. A more serious issue is that only the late edition of *The New York Times* is microfilmed. Once a library receives a reel of microfilm, which is usually within a few months after the original issues are published, the hardcopy issues are generally discarded, regardless of whether those hardcopies were from the late or national editions. Consequently, once the microfilm is received, only the late edition is available, and all citations to articles in the national edition are useless and very confusing to the patron.

The *National Newspaper Index* is also available as an online database and as one of Information Access Company's CD-ROM-based InfoTrac indexes.

There are very few newspaper indexes in other microform formats. However, there are some such indexes, and often, they are only available for distribution in the microform format. An example of a microfilm index is *The Florida Times-Union Index* (Jacksonville, Fla.: Jacksonville Public Library), which provides coverage of most years from 1895 to the present. An example of a microfiche index is the *Burlington Free Press Index*, compiled at the University of Vermont (White River Junction, Vt.: Computac), and issued on microfiche since 1984. One should also be aware that some major newspaper indexes are also available in microform editions. For instance, University Microfilms International sells a microfiche edition of *The New York Times Index*, and Research Publications offers a microfilm edition of *The Times Index*.

Online Newspaper Indexes and Full-text Retrieval Systems

In 1969, the management of *The New York Times* announced that it planned to make its computerized index files available by subscription. This did not become a reality until 1972, when *The New York Times* Information Bank was made available to subscribers. This current events database was a pioneering effort in that most of the other bibliographic databases of the time were concerned with science and technology.[8] The Information Bank indexed and abstracted articles from *The New York Times* and from a number of other newspapers such as *The Washington Post*, the *Los Angeles Times*, the *Chicago Tribune*, and the *San Francisco Chronicle*. In addition, many business and general interest periodicals were indexed. In the intervening years, numerous changes have occurred regarding the Information Bank, including a name change to "INFOBK." It is also now a part of Mead Data Central, the same company that produces the NEXIS database. INFOBK remains as a database of index terms and abstracts only, and it apparently is not used nearly as much as the full-text NEXIS system.[9]

The past decade has witnessed the widespread emergence of newspaper databases that offer full-text searching combined with the retrieval of articles online. Commercial systems such as NEXIS, VU/TEXT, and DataTimes are available to provide access to these databases. A field that was in the pioneering stage just twenty years ago, has now, in some cases, reached the point of overkill. As an illustration of this, a recent article about full-text retrieval of *The Washington Post* stated that the newspaper is commercially available through nine online information systems.[10]

Many of the full-text databases that are now available were first developed as in-house systems for use by the employees of the newspapers. These databases took the place of the traditional newspaper clippings file, or "morgue," and were often developed in conjunction with electronic editing operations. Once a database is established in-house, the next step is to make it available for public searching. This is attractive to newspapers since the database can be partially funded by the revenues generated by public searching.[11]

NEXIS is perhaps the most well known online newspaper retrieval system. It is owned by Mead Data Central, of Dayton, Ohio, and provides full-text retrieval of a handful of major newspapers including *The New York Times, The Washington Post, The Christian Science Monitor*, the *Los Angeles Times*, and the *Financial Times*, of London. Also included in the "Newspaper Files" group are a number of newspaper format periodicals such as the *American Banker* and *Computerworld*. NEXIS also has a "Wires File" group which allows full-text retrieval of items from approximately twenty wire services, including the Associated Press and United Press International. Several other files are available through NEXIS, including those which provide access to dozens of magazines and newsletters, many of which are related to business.

VU/TEXT grew out of the electronic editing system that was installed in the mid-1970s for two Knight-Ridder newspapers, *The Philadelphia Inquirer* and the *Philadelphia Daily News*.[12] This system now provides online full-text retrieval of over thirty newspapers, six wire services, and several other non-newspaper databases. Many of the newspapers in VU/TEXT have no printed indexes. So, if one wishes to conduct current subject searches of newspapers such as *The Philadelphia Inquirer, The Charlotte Observer*, or the *Akron Beacon Journal*, an online VU/TEXT search is the only alternative to an issue-by-issue, page-by-page physical search of the newspaper itself. Also, as can be noted by some of the titles mentioned, VU/TEXT carries many smaller and less prominent newspapers, which are just the types of newspapers that have traditionally not been indexed.

DataTimes had its foundation in the databases of *The Daily Oklahoman* and the *Oklahoma City Times*. It now offers full-text access to over two dozen newspapers, including some of national importance such as *The Washington Post*, and *USA Today*. Newspapers from Canada and Australia are also available, as well as many other business-related databases.

In addition to the online retrieval systems that provide access to numerous newspaper databases, other newspaper databases are available individually. For instance, the InfoGlobe database provides full-text access to *The Globe and Mail*, of Toronto, from November 1977 to the present. Newspaper Abstracts Online is a file available through DIALOG that gives access to abstracting information produced by University Microfilms International. Over twenty major newspapers are covered, including *The New York Times,*

The Wall Street Journal, USA Today, and the English language edition of *Pravda.* Also available through DIALOG and through BRS is the *National Newspaper Index* file, which is the online version of the microform editions of this Information Access Company product.

Newspapers that are available in online, full-text retrieval systems are different than their printed equivalents, and they must be used differently. Whereas a microform or printed newspaper file can be scanned, this is not possible with online systems. However, there are many types of searches that would be otherwise impossible with access only to the printed or microform newspaper itself or to the newspaper and its printed index. Another advantage of online full-text newspaper retrieval is that a library can provide access to newspapers without actually owning a hardcopy or microform file.

Full-text searching is a powerful and productive tool, when properly used. When improperly used, such searching can be a powerful detriment to research. This is particularly true in cases when a search has not been adequately narrowed and focused. A vague, general search of a full-text file can result in hundreds, or thousands, of irrelevant hits. In formulating full-text searches, always take care to search for the most specific and unique words that may have appeared in the article(s) and to qualify (by newspaper, author, range of dates, etc.) as much as possible. Considerably more skill and experience is required to be a competent full-text newspaper searcher than is required to be a competent searcher of printed newspaper indexes.

Be aware that online, full-text versions of newspapers do not correspond exactly to the print equivalents. This is due to what has been called the "minefield of inclusions, exclusions, and exceptions" that characterize various full-text newspaper files.[13] It is essential that a searcher be familiar with what is, and is not, included in any full-text version of a newspaper to avoid futile searching.

A final reminder about online full-text newspapers regards the dates that are available. Most of these databases have been established in the past decade. Therefore, most online newspapers are available only for recent years. There are very few newspapers available online with coverage prior to 1980, and many are only available back to the mid-1980s. It is unlikely that there will be any great movement to put retrospective years of newspapers into online databases. Thus, for the researcher using newspapers prior to the dates available online, the only indexing will be in printed or microform indexes or in unpublished indexes.

CD-ROM Newspaper Indexes

The recent emergence of CD-ROM technology has impacted on many areas of reference work, and is likely to play an increasing role in the future. This technology is just beginning to be applied in the area of newspaper indexing and full-text retrieval. Information Access Company's *National Newspaper Index* (microform editions described earlier in this chapter) is now available as a CD-ROM InfoTrac database. In 1988, the Alde Publishing Company, of Minneapolis, Minn., introduced a full-text, CD-ROM version of the 1986 and 1987 editions of the English language edition of *Pravda.*

NewsBank, of New Canaan, Conn., offers the NewsBank Electronic Index, a CD-ROM system which provides access to newspapers from over 450 United States cities, with the articles being available in full-text as part of a companion microfiche set. University Microfilms International offers a CD-ROM system, Newspaper Abstracts Ondisc, which allows access to articles in over half a dozen major newspapers. Undoubtedly, many new CD-ROM indexes and full-text retrieval systems will be introduced in the coming years.

Other Types of Newspaper Indexing

A traditional manner in which subject access has been provided to newspaper articles is through clippings files, in which the articles of a single newspaper, or of several newspapers, are arranged into files by subject. Although clippings files are being rapidly supplanted by full-text retrieval systems, they can still be found. Also, public or academic libraries often become the final repository for the clippings files of newspapers that have gone out of business. Consequently, researchers and librarians still must deal with this old fashioned form of newspaper subject access.

A modern, published version of the clippings file is the type of publication that is a compilation of newspaper articles. For instance, the Social Issues Resources Series (Boca Raton, Fla.), produces looseleaf volumes on various subjects which are comprised of reprints of articles from newspapers and other sources. *Editorials on File* (New York: Facts on File) is a twice-monthly "editorial survey" which reprints selected editorials and editorial cartoons from newspapers of the United States and Canada. *The New York Times Biographical Service* (Ann Arbor, Mich.: University Microfilms) is another periodical that reprints newspaper articles. It is a monthly compilation of biographical feature stories, profiles, obituaries, and other items of general biographical interest that originally appeared in *The New York Times.*

Some newspapers, or portions of newspapers, are indexed in periodical indexes. Thus, there is indexing for *The Wall Street Journal* on the *Business Index*, and recent indexing of *The New York Times* on various InfoTrac periodical indexes. Other examples include coverage of *The New York Times Book Review* and *The New York Times Magazine* in the *Readers' Guide to Periodical Literature*, and the selective coverage of *The Times* and *The Guardian* in the *British Humanities Index.*

There are some well-indexed periodical publications that provide English language translations of newspaper articles from foreign newspapers. Chief among these is the Joint Publications Research Service (JPRS) *Report* series, which covers twelve regions of the world (see chapter 6). Access to the articles is through the *Transdex Index*, published by University Microfilms International. Other periodicals that provide English language translations of foreign newspaper articles include the *World Press Review* and *The Current Digest of the Soviet Press*. Both of these publications are covered in a number of periodical indexing and abstracting services.

Newspapers for Which Indexing
Is Not Available

There are hundreds of printed and microform newspaper indexes. Additionally, online indexes or full-text retrieval capabilities are available for a significant number of newspapers. However, most newspapers are not indexed. This can come as a shock to some library patrons who naively assume that all newspaper information is easily accessible. It often seems that the only alternative left to a patron searching in a nonindexed newspaper is to perform a laborious issue-by-issue, page-by-page search of the newspaper. Before a patron embarks on such a search, the serials reference staffer should determine if the search can be performed in any other manner.

The first step is to confirm that an index truly does not exist for the newspaper in question. As described earlier, the initial sources to check for this are the *Lathrop Report on Newspaper Indexes: An Illustrated Guide to Published and Unpublished Newspaper Indexes in the United States & Canada* and the three-volume *Newspaper Indexes: A Location and Subject Guide for Researchers*. Even though these are the two most extensive listings of newspaper indexes, many more indexes undoubtedly exist that are not listed in these works. To search further for the existence of such an index, contact the newspaper itself if it is still in publication, or if it has merged into a current newspaper. Addresses and telephone numbers can be located in the *Gale Directory of Publications* or in the *Editor & Publisher International Year Book* (both described in chapter 10). Also consult *Newspaper Libraries in the U.S. and Canada*, edited by Elizabeth L. Anderson, 2d edition (New York: Special Libraries Association, Newspaper Division, 1980), or its update, *The International Directory of News Libraries and Buyer's Guide, 1985-86* (Bayside, N.Y.: LDA Publishers, 1985). Both list the availability of indexes in those libraries.

Should the newspaper no longer exist, or if an inquiry to the newspaper elicits no information about an index, attempt to locate a local library or historical society and inquire. Local United States and Canadian libraries can be identified in the *American Library Directory* (New York: R. R. Bowker), and historical societies can be identified in the *Directory of Historical Societies and Agencies in the United States and Canada*, 12th edition (Nashville, Tenn.: American Association for State and Local History, 1982). If staffers in these institutions are not aware of an index, then one can safely assume that one does not exist.

When searching for articles about a news event in a newspaper that is not indexed, the date of the event can often be established by using other standard sources. The two major sources are the American weekly, *Facts on File*, published since October 1940, and the British monthly, *Keesing's Record of World Events*, formerly known as *Keesing's Contemporary Archives*, which has been published since July 1931. A supplement to the latter, titled, *Synopsis of World Events*, covers 1918 through June 1931. The date for an event can also be established by using the index to another newspaper. The most prominent index for this purpose is *The New York Times Index*, although most any newspaper index can be used in the same manner. For news events of a more local interest, use an index to a newspaper from the same state or region as the nonindexed newspaper. A nearby newspaper would be more likely to carry news of an event of just regional interest.

Some newspapers such as *The Washington Post* and *The New York Times* carry extensive daily tables of contents. Since printed indexes to newspapers are usually not available until weeks after the publication of an issue, these tables can be effectively employed by those searching for items in recent issues. This can be used as an alternative to an online search, since, in many cases, either a library does not have access to an online system or searching may cost more than the patron is willing to spend.

Unfortunately, for many patrons desiring to locate items in nonindexed newspapers, there is no alternative except to search each page of every issue of the newspaper. Items of only local interest, such as marriage and death notices or short news articles, may be found only through this laborious, eye-straining, and often frustrating page-by-page search. There is little that a serials reference staffer can do in these cases other than to help the patron clearly define and narrow the search.

Notes

[1]George Clack, "Preserving Yesterday's News," *Humanities* 8 (January/February 1987): 25.

[2]Peter Ralph Coates, "The Retrospective Indexing of Two Colonial Newspapers," *The Indexer* 13 (April 1983): 183.

[3]Michael Knee, "Producing a Local Newspaper Index," *The Indexer* 13 (October 1982): 102.

[4]Susan Spaeth Cherry, "Yesterday's News for Tomorrow," *American Libraries* 10 (November 1979): 591.

[5]William J. Maher and Benjamin F. Shearer, "Undergraduate Use Patterns of Newspapers on Microfilm," *College and Research Libraries* 40 (May 1979): 258-59.

[6]Doreen Morrison, "Indexes to *The Times* of London: An Evaluation and Comparative Analysis," *The Serials Librarian* 13 (September 1987): 99-101.

[7]Edwin Emery and Michael Emery, *The Press and America: An Interpretive History of the Mass Media*, 5th ed. (Englewood Cliffs, N.J.: Prentice-Hall, 1984), 152-53.

[8]Marydee Ojala, "First There Was the Information Bank," *Online* 11 (January 1987): 113.

[9]Sharon Peake Williamson, Manager, Public Communications, Mead Data Central, letter to the author, 13 October 1988.

[10]Susan H. Veccia, "Full-Text Dilemmas for Searchers and Systems: The Washington Post Online," *Database* 11 (April 1988): 13.

[11]Jim Hunter, "Going Online with VU/TEXT," *Serials Review* 13 (Winter 1987): 11.

[12]June Holbert and Donna Willmann, "VU/TEXT Information Services, Inc.," *Serials Review* 13 (Winter 1987): 8.

[13]Veccia, "Full-Text Dilemmas," 14.

13
Other Aspects of Reference Work with Newspapers

Newspapers, as a class of library materials, have traditionally posed preservation and storage problems. The storage problems have revolved around the sheer bulk of a file of hardcopy newspapers and the space required to house such a file. Preservation problems arose from the introduction, in the latter part of the nineteenth century, of inexpensive newsprint. Newspapers printed on such newsprint suffer rapid deterioration.

By 1914, the New York Public Library had recognized these problems and had begun to respond to them. The library, at that time, was subscribing to newspapers from across the United States and around the world, but was retaining only New York City newspapers in bound volumes. All other newspapers were kept on a most recent two months basis only, with issues discarded after they reached the three-month stage.[1] It was obvious that the bound newspapers wre quickly deteriorating. Twice a day the janitor had to sweep up pieces of brittle newspapers that had flaked off from the bound volumes.[2]

The New York Public Library embarked on a program in which tests were conducted of twenty-two methods to preserve newspapers.[3] It was decided the most effective was a procedure in which Japanese tissue paper was pasted to both sides of a newspaper sheet, thus encasing it. However, it was estimated that such a procedure would cost approximately $420 a year (in 1914 dollars) for one daily newspaper.[4] Although viewed as promising, this type of treatment was too expensive for wide application. Eventually, five New York City newspapers agreed to pay for such a continuing preservation program that lasted fifteen years. By the early 1930s, it was realized that preservation using tissue paper only served to delay the deterioration process, and the newspapers that had been treated in this manner were still disintegrating.[5]

Microphotography, although first developed in the nineteenth century, did not come into widespread commercial use until 1928, when the Eastman Kodak Company marketed Checkograph, a system by which cancelled checks could be microfilmed.[6] At the time that the New York Public Library was coming to the realization that the tissue paper method of preservation was ultimately ineffective, a salesman from Kodak's newly-formed Recordak subsidiary visited the Library and inquired about possible library applications of microfilm.[7] So in May 1934, the Newspaper Division of the Library began to provide newspapers on 35mm microfilm to its patrons. At first, only a few months of three different New York City newspapers were available, and could be read on three Recordak projectors.[8] This experimental project, which set the stage for a revolution in the storage, preservation, and use of newspapers in libraries, was described by the chief of the Newspaper Division in a 1937 article.

> It did, of course, seem rather strange to use a mechanical device in place of a book. Some librarians today seem to dread the thought of using films and believe a projector is an extremely complicated affair. Some of the Newspaper Division staff had similar ideas, but we were in such desperate straits at that time, crowded for space, with many of our bound newspapers rapidly disintegrating before our eyes, that something had to be done and the film seemed to be a possible solution for our problems.
>
> The projector, we found, was not a complicated piece of mechanism at all, although the visits of the repair man were not infrequent in the early days, but quite easy to use. It was a very simple matter to place a roll of film on one spindle, bring it between two flat pieces of glass and insert one end of the film in a small aperture in a second spindle. Readers could not be trusted to do this, except in a few cases.[9]

It was soon realized that microfilm was the answer to the problems that libraries had encountered with newspapers. The storage space required for a microfilm edition of a newspaper was just a fraction of the space required for the same dates in bound volumes. As was reported in that 1937 article, a five-year file of *The New York Times* in bound volumes occupied fifty-nine cubic feet, while the microfilms for the same period occupied only one and a half cubic feet, and the cost of the microfilm was about the same as binding the original newspaper issues.[10] Microfilm also proved to be an acceptable long-term preservation medium. From a patron's viewpoint, using microfilm was seen as preferable to using bound volumes. As an eminent American historian had written, in an era before the development of microfilmed newspapers, "Next to manuscript material, the physical and mental labor of turning over and reading bound volumes of newspapers is the most severe, and I remember my feeling of relief at being able to divert my attention from ... this back-breaking and eye-destroying labor."[11] Microfilm eliminated the physical demands of working with bound volumes, although eye strain, even today, is still a side-effect with which newspaper researchers must cope.

Two major events in the development of newspaper microfilming took place in 1938. The Foreign Newspaper Microfilm Project was begun by the Harvard University Library, and University Microfilms was founded.[12] By 1948, the field had grown to such an extent that the first edition of *Newspapers on Microfilm: A Union Check List* was published by the Association of Research Libraries. This later evolved into *Newspapers in Microform*, which is currently published by the Library of Congress (see chapter 11). In the late 1940s and early 1950s, many state libraries and state university libraries initiated projects to microfilm local newspapers.[13] Commercial micropublishers, such as University Microfilms International, over the years have filmed thousands of other newspapers. The state projects formed as part of the United States Newspaper Program (described in chapter 11) include a preservation phase. Nationwide, this should result in the microfilming of thousands of other United States newspapers.

Microfilm has revolutionized the collection, storage, and use of newspapers in libraries. The small amount of space now required for the storage of a newspaper file has allowed even those libraries with severe space limitations to maintain such files. Microfilming has also made possible the universal availability for purchase of complete files of newspapers. The interlibrary loan of newspapers has been made feasible by microfilm. Microfilming of newspapers has also resulted in more commercial indexing of newspapers. Since the microfilm edition of an indexed newspaper is more attractive to a library than a similar newspaper that is not indexed, some commercial micropublishers have also engaged in the publishing of newspaper indexes.

One example can show how microfilm has completely changed the collection of newspapers in libraries. In 1914, the New York Public Library was binding newspapers from New York City only. All other newspapers were kept on a current issues-only basis. Today, that same library's newspaper collection consists of over 95,000 microforms of newspapers along with 22,000 bound volumes.[14]

Practical Aspects of Reference Work with Microfilmed Newspapers

One aspect of reference work in this area is determining if particular newspapers are available in microfilm editions. Currently, the two best sources to use for such a search are the Library of Congress publications, *Newspapers in Microform: United States, 1948-1983* and *Newspapers in Microform: Foreign Countries, 1948-1983* (both described in chapter 11). Although the titles of these works would seem to indicate that the years of coverage are limited, this is not the case. The confusing notation "1948-1983" refers only to the years in which information was received from reporting libraries for inclusion in the volume. There is no date limitation on the years of publication for the newspapers listed in these two works. The entries for newspapers in these union lists note the libraries or commercial micropublishers with service copies and the master negative of the microform. The dates held, and the type of microform is also noted.

The *United States Newspaper Program National Union List* (also described in chapter 11) provides information about the microform editions of newspapers. For each newspaper listed, holding libraries are indicated along with an indication of the extent of the holdings. The format of the holdings is noted, as either original issues or microform. If a holding library has the master negative of the microform edition, this is also indicated.

Various micropublishing companies also publish their own catalogs of newspaper titles. A prime example of this is the University Microfilms International catalog, *Newspapers in Microform*. It lists more than seven thousand newspapers available for sale on microform.

Although patrons often resist using microforms of periodicals, books, and other items, there is comparatively little resistance to the use of newspapers on microform. This is because bound volumes are very difficult to handle and hardcopy newspapers deteriorate quickly. A survey conducted at twenty-six institutions in 1968 and 1969, concerning the attitudes of patrons toward microforms, showed that users prefer to use microforms of newspapers as opposed to hardcopy. Microform editions of newspapers were also found to be satisfactory for "browse searching."[15] This user acceptance makes the job of the reference staff easier. Nevertheless, there still are some patrons who are reluctant to use microfilm of newspapers. This reluctance is often caused by the patron having never used microforms. A positive attitude on the part of the staff member, coupled with a demonstration of how to use the microform reading equipment, will help to put resistant users at ease. At the outset, the inexperienced user should be told of the possibilities of making photocopies from the microfilm. This is necessary since many novice researchers think that photocopies can be made only from hardcopy. They will resist using microforms because of that often-unstated reason.

In chapter 7, the subject of periodicals on microform was covered, and general suggestions about working with microform collections were given. Since these suggestions also apply to newspaper microfilm collections, they are repeated as follows. Reference staff working with a microform collection should become very familiar with all of the microform reading and photocopying equipment that is available for users of the collection. Such staff should know how each type of machine operates and be able to correct minor problems with the equipment (changing bulbs, adjusting exposure for photocopies, etc.). Also, staff must become experienced at handling the problem of film that has been wound backwards on a reel and that of microfilm that has been improperly threaded on a reading machine and will not rewind.

There are problems and peculiarities that relate specifically to newspapers on microfilm. One major problem that can be extremely confusing to a patron and to a librarian alike is the microfilm edition of a newspaper that covers more than one edition of that newspaper. One of the most prominent examples of this practice is found in the microfilm edition of the *Los Angeles Times*. What one usually first encounters for each date on this microfilm is a complete, page-by-page reproduction of the entire newspaper, which is fairly straightforward. After this, though, follows a collection of assorted pages from different geographic editions of the newspaper for that date. Apparently, every page that is different from the original edition is filmed. As an example, the date of Saturday, November 28, 1987, was chosen at random, and the microfilm was examined. For that date, there first was filmed a regular edition of the newspaper for that day, where all is in order and complete, with one exception. Part V, the "View Weekend" section first has pages 1, 2, 3, and 10, followed by a blank stretch of film. Next, pages 4, 5, and 6 of part V are on the film, which is followed by the next section of the newspaper. So, pages in part V are out of order, and pages 7 and 8 are missing, with no explanation.

After the entire first edition, there is the front page again, which is identical to the first front page, except that this one states "Valley Edition" and the table of contents box is slightly different. This is followed by a number of pages from different sections of the Valley edition. For instance, part III, the sports section has only pages 1, 2, 20, 24, 25, 26, and 27. This type of pattern is followed for all of the other editions. For this November 28, 1987, edition of the microfilm, there are four separate front pages and four different sports section front pages, not to mention the seven different special sections of automotive ads and numerous supplements.

A patron who fast forwards the microfilm and ends up in the middle of an issue can quickly become bewildered and frustrated by the *Los Angeles Times* microfilm and others that are similar to it. The best advice to offer to someone in this situation is to locate the first front page for the date needed, then slowly proceed through the film. If the patron is searching for a cited article, it will most likely show up in that first edition on the microfilm.

Another filming oddity that can be very confusing to patrons is evidenced by the well-known colonial United States newspaper, *The Virginia Gazette*, published in Williamsburg. A few different competing newspapers by this title were produced by different printers at the same time in that same city. The microfilm of this title "solves" the problem by putting more than one edition on the same reel of film. For instance, on the reel that covers the years 1772 and 1773, the edition that was printed by Alexander Purdie and John Dixon is included along with the edition printed by William Rind. First on the reel is the entire run of 1772 issues of the Purdie and Dixon edition, followed by all of the 1772 issues of the Rind edition. This is then followed by all of the 1773 issues of the Purdie and Dixon edition, and continues in that manner. There is no explanation of this arrangement at the beginning of the reel. The only indication of anything out of the ordinary are the markers on the film showing where the different editions begin. Needless to say, this can be very confusing to an uninitiated patron.

A major problem in dealing with newspapers on microfilm is that most microfilm editions are missing issues or sections of issues. *Newspapers in Microform: United States, 1948-1983* states, "The reader is cautioned that almost no microfilm of a newspaper is actually complete, even for current runs."[16] In other words, expect that any microfilmed newspaper will have gaps, sometimes to a very significant degree. This is because a micropublisher can only film issues that are available. Missing issues are often unobtainable. This problem is most evident with older newspapers or with current newspapers from Third World nations. However, virtually all microfilm newspaper files are susceptible to this problem. Most libraries do not have the staff time available, or the inclination, to check frame-by-frame each reel of a newspaper as it is received on microfilm. Usually, once a reel of film is received, the corresponding hardcopy issues are discarded. Consequently, if the film is incomplete, and the hardcopy has been discarded, the access to that missing section or missing issue is, for all practical purposes, lost forever.

Newspapers in Bound Volumes

Although bound volumes are now viewed as an archaic storage medium for newspapers, they still exist, especially at large research libraries such as the Library of Congress, where these volumes were bound before the advent of newspaper microfilming. The first point to keep in mind about these volumes is that it is physically demanding to service and to read them. Since these volumes can be quite bulky and very heavy, there is a chance of being injured when lifting or carrying them. Also, due to their size, weight, and bulk, the photocopying of these volumes can be dangerous to both the volume and to the person doing the photocopying. In addition, the paper within these volumes is often in an advanced state of deterioration, and rough handling can destroy a page or an issue. For these reasons, self-service photocopying should be restricted. Where available, a library's copy center can normally do a much better job anyway, with less damage to the volume. An alternative to photocopying that some patrons find attractive is to take high quality photographs of the pages needed. These photographs can then be enlarged to a size where the print is readable.

Syndicates and Wire Services

An issue of a newspaper comprises articles, columns, and other items from various sources. Local news articles and local features are generally written by reporters and feature writers employed by, or freelancing for, the newspaper. Prestigious, well-circulated newspapers can also afford to have a staff of national and even international reporters. Smaller newspapers, however, must depend upon wire services, also known as news services, to provide the national and international news that is printed. Even major newspapers rely upon wire service copy to cover stories not handled by their own staff writers. Virtually all American newspapers also purchase syndicated materials to fill out a newspaper issue. The two major areas in which syndicates predominate are comic strips and columns produced by a single writer on a continuing basis.

Wire services exist to provide news reporting, for a fee, to anyone who subscribes. Newspapers that wish to provide international or national coverage subscribe to one or more of these services. Two of the leading news services are the Associated Press and United Press International, but there are literally dozens of others. News services are listed in the *Editor & Publisher International Year Book* in a section titled "News, Picture and Press Services." They can also be found listed in *The Working Press of the Nation*, volume 1, *Newspaper Directory*, and in the *Gebbie Press All-in-One Directory* (all described in chapter 10).

Many wire services are available in full-text online retrieval systems. For instance, NEXIS provides access to a number of wire services, including the Associated Press and United Press International. This access is both a blessing and a curse to library reference staff. The online, full-text availability of these services allows relatively easy access to the information they contain. There are problems associated with this access. First, when a patron receives the results of a cross-file search in a system such as NEXIS and only the citations to the articles are printed, there will be references to articles that appeared in various publications and references to articles that are on the wire service databases. These references to articles from news services can be vexing to a patron, since it is not clear where these articles were published. Usually, the most efficient way to obtain a copy of the article is to have another online search done and have the full-text printed out.

Another problem that frequently occurs is that a patron has already obtained a full-text printout of an article from a wire service database but still desires to have a photocopy of the article as it was printed in a newspaper. This is the same type of problem as that posed by a patron who knows that an article was transmitted by a certain wire service on a particular date and needs to obtain a photocopy of the article as it appeared printed in a newspaper. Unfortunately, there is no easy way to determine which newspapers printed, in full, individual wire service stories. First it must be decided if newspapers in a certain state or region would have been more likely than others to have carried such a story. At that point, a search in the entries for daily newspapers from that area in the *Editor & Publisher International Year Book* should be conducted. These entries do indicate which wire services each newspaper receives. In most cases, the search from that point forward consists of actually looking through the issues of the newspaper possibilities in an effort to locate the article.

In addition to wire services, newspapers depend upon feature syndicates to provide material such as comic strips, puzzles, and columns. There are sources that can be employed to identify the various syndicates and syndicated features. An issue of the weekly *Editor & Publisher* is published every year, usually in July, with a separate supplement titled, *Syndicate Directory*. The syndicates are listed by name, with addresses, phone numbers, and names of key contact people given. Another section lists the features by author, giving the name of the feature and the syndicate. A final section classifies the features by general subjects. Both the *Editor & Publisher International Year Book* and *The Working Press of the Nation*, volume 1, *Newspaper Directory*, also have sections that give listings of feature syndicates.

The most common type of reference inquiry about syndicated features relates to syndicated columnists. Patrons often wish to find columns by a certain columnist but do not know in which newspapers that column is, or was, carried. Currently, the best source for this type of information is *Syndicated Columnists*, 3rd edition, by Richard Weiner (New York: Richard Weiner, 1979). Although this is not an exhaustive listing, and is somewhat dated, this work provides a good history and survey of the field. Weiner has also compiled the *Syndicated Columnists Directory* (New York: Public Relations Publishing) beginning with an edition for 1982. Another source that may be of limited help in this type of search is *The Working Press of the Nation*, Volume 4, *Feature Writer and Photographer Directory*. A final point to keep in mind about syndicated columns is that the same column may appear on different days in different newspapers. Thus, if a specific column appeared on a certain date in one newspaper, this does not mean that it appeared in another newspaper on the same day. There may be a difference of several days or even weeks.

Special Aspects of Newspaper Reference Work

Patrons often inquire about the availability of translations of newspapers or of separate newspaper articles. Beginning in 1986, the Russian newspaper, *Pravda*, became available in an English translation from the Context Corporation, of St. Paul, Minn. What began as a translation of every issue, eventually became selected translations of one issue per week. In May 1988, this publisher suspended publication, with the intention of one day resuming publication. A microfilm edition and companion indexing service is available from University Microfilms International for the issues that were produced. A full-text, CD-ROM version of this translation for the years of 1986 and 1987 is available from Alde Publishing, of Minneapolis.

Other newspaper article translations into English are available in various compilation publications that are issued as periodicals. Foremost among these is the Joint Publications Research Service (JPRS) *Report* series, which provides translations of newspaper, periodical, and other articles in editions that cover twelve regions of the world. Many of the regional editions are further broken down into specific continuing reports on particular aspects of the region. (See chapter 6). Two other periodicals that publish English-language translations of newspaper articles are the *World Press Review* and *The Current Digest of the Soviet Press.*

As mentioned in the chapters about periodicals, many patrons regard any publication printed on newsprint or in newspaper format to be a newspaper. Consequently, they often refer to publications such as *Computerworld*, the *American Banker*, and other less recognizable periodicals as newspapers. From a reference standpoint, always be cognizant of the fact that what a patron refers to as a "newspaper" may actually be a periodical. So, if there's no record of a newspaper in standard newspaper sources then search for the publication in periodical and other serial sources.

Some patrons also assume that all publications produced under the aegis of a newspaper are also newspapers. Some examples of these types of publications are the *National Business Employment Weekly*, published by *The Wall Street Journal*, and *The Times Educational Supplement*, published by *The Times* of London. Libraries class both of these as periodicals, but many patrons expect to find them in a newspaper collection. Also be aware that some libraries, through the years, have also treated publications of this nature as newspapers. Thus, it is not unusual to find such periodicals listed in newspaper union lists and in other newspaper reference sources.

In newspaper reference, be mindful that many important newspapers are published in several different editions each day. Such editions may be relatively easy to distinguish, such as the Midwest, Southwest, and Western editions of *The Wall Street Journal*. Other editions of newspapers may be more difficult to distinguish, such as the early and late editions of the same newspaper, which are usually identical except for some updated news and sports information. Some newspapers also publish weekly compilation issues. An example is the National Weekly Edition of *The Washington Post*. As a rule, most patrons do not differentiate among editions. For instance, a novice researcher may have a citation to an article in the Western edition of *The Wall Street Journal* and search in vain for that article in the Eastern edition. Although this type of problem does not occur regularly, reference staff should know that it does arise occasionally.

Those responsible for newspaper reference may be asked by patrons where they can sell old, and supposedly valuable, issues of newspapers. Such requesters should be informed that very few single newspaper issues, or short runs of newspapers, have any great monetary value. Those that do have value will usually be bought and sold by dealers who specialize in out-of-print books. Classified telephone directories can be used to locate such dealers. One may also consult the *ABAA Membership Directory* (New York: Antiquarian Booksellers Association of America) and the *American Book Trade Directory* (New York: R. R. Bowker) to identify these dealers.

Related to this topic is the subject of reprint editions of famous newspapers. Some newspaper issues of historical importance have been reprinted so often that the likelihood of an individual having an original is very remote. Examples of frequently reprinted newspaper issues include the July 4, 1863, issue of *The Daily Citizen*, of Vicksburg, Miss., which was originally printed on the back of wallpaper, and the *New York Herald* of April 15, 1865, which carried an account of the assassination of President Abraham Lincoln. The Library of Congress has produced a series of information circulars that deal with eighteen newspaper issues of historical importance that have been widely reprinted. Distinguishing characteristics are described, so that a reprint edition can be differentiated from an original issue. Requests for these information circulars should be addressed to: Serial and Government Publications Division, Library of Congress, Washington, D.C. 20540.

A popular type of birthday gift is a full-page reproduction of the front page of a newspaper from the day a person was born. The copies provided by self-service microform photocopiers are usually not of a quality associated with gifts, and often an entire page cannot be covered in one copy and must be reproduced in a number of separate copies. In such cases an institution's copy center may be able to provide a high-quality, full-page reproduction. Also, University Microfilms International can provide full-page reproductions, either framed or unframed, of any United States newspaper listed in their catalog, *Newspapers in Microform*. There are also dealers who sell complete issues of old newspapers. Advertisements for these dealers can often be found in *The New Yorker* magazine.

Notes

[1]Harry Miller Lyndenberg, "Preservation of Modern Newspaper Files," in *The Library within the Walls* (New York: H. W. Wilson, 1929), 251.

[2]Keyes DeWitt Metcalf, *Random Recollections of an Anachronism* (New York: Readex Books, 1980), 276.

[3]Ibid.

[4]Lyndenberg, "Preservation," 254.

[5]Metcalf, *Random Recollections*, 276.

[6]Allen B. Veaner, "History of Micropublishing," in *Microforms in Libraries: A Reader* (Weston, Conn.: Microform Review, 1975), 14-15.

[7]Metcalf, *Random Recollections*, 277.

[8]Louis H. Fox, "Films for Folios," *Library Journal* 62 (1 May 1937): 361.

[9]Ibid., 362.

[10]Ibid., 363-64.

[11]James Ford Rhodes, "Newspapers as Historical Sources," in *The Library within the Walls* (New York: H. W. Wilson, 1929), 247.

[12]Veaner, "History of Micropublishing," 15.

[13]Lawrence S. Thompson, "Microform Publication," in *Encyclopedia of Library and Information Science*, vol. 18 (New York: Marcel Dekker, 1976), 107.

[14]The New York Public Library, Astor, Lenox and Tilden Foundations, *Annual Report for the Year Ended June 30, 1987* (New York: The New York Public Library, Astor, Lenox and Tilden Foundations, 1988), 39.

[15]Donald C. Holmes, "Excerpt from *Determination of User Needs and Future Requirements for a Systems Approach to Microform Technology*," in *Microforms in Libraries: A Reader* (Weston, Conn.: Microform Review, 1975), 415.

[16]*Newspapers in Microform: United States, 1948-1983* (Washington, D.C.: Library of Congress, 1984), x.

14

Serials Cataloging and Its Effect on Reference Service

As a class of materials, serials are quite different from monographs. This is understood by all who have ever used both books and periodicals. Despite this undeniable reality, libraries have traditionally handled serials as if they were merely recalcitrant monographs. This is nowhere more evident than in the cataloging of serials. The bibliographic description produced for a book during the cataloging process will generally be accurate forever. On the other hand, a currently-published serial is subject to constant change. Thus, "Only after a serial has finally died can the cataloger describe it in peace."[1] Unfortunately, living serials are the titles that receive the most use, and it is these titles that are most inadequately covered in current serials cataloging practice.

Patrons use library catalogs to:

1. Determine if the library has a certain item;

2. Identify works by a particular author in the library's collection;

3. Determine which editions of a specific work are in the library's collection; and,

4. Identify materials the library has on a particular subject.[2]

Bibliographic records for serials can only provide the patron with some of this needed information. For instance, an entry in a library's catalog for a serial will indicate that the library does have the publication. However, unless a holdings note is added, the patron will not know which volumes, issues, or dates are in the collection. Serial cataloging records also do not indicate which authors have published items in the serial. Finally, the subject headings assigned to a serial must, of necessity, be somewhat general or vague, and often give only an inkling of the contents.

The basic cause for this inadequacy of serial cataloging records is that no library can afford to, nor feels the need to, separately catalog each issue of a periodical, or other serial, except in cases where each issue is virtually a separate monograph. It has traditionally been thought that a single bibliographic record that describes a serial in general is sufficient for the purposes of the library catalog. This is made possible, and practical, by the existence of other sources of serials information, some of which have been referred to as "complementary records."[3] The main complementary record for any serial is the check-in, or accessioning, file record where issues or volumes of a publication are recorded as they arrive in a library. Such a record displays the holdings of a serial in the library and also shows changes in frequency of publication. (See chapter 15 for a further discussion of check-in files and procedures.)

In addition, there are commercially-available works that serve to supplement a serial cataloging record and to provide the most updated information about that serial. The prime example of this type of work is a serials directory, such as *Ulrich's International Periodicals Directory*, which annually updates the most important facts of publication regarding serials. The frequency of publication or the place of publication stated in the bibliographic record for a serial will frequently be outdated and no longer correct. This is true whether it is found on a printed catalog card or in the database of a bibliographic utility or in any other form. The most current publishing information about any serial can usually be found in the publishing statement printed in the most recent issue of the serial. If such an issue is not readily available, then serials directories can be depended upon to update the bibliographic record in the library's catalog. The bimonthly periodical, *Archaeology* (ISSN 0003-8113), a publication of the Archaeological Institute of America, can be used as an example. As of December 1988, the OCLC cataloging record (number 1481828) showed the address for this periodical as "260 W. Broadway, New York, NY 10013." This was apparently based on information from the October 1975 issue, as noted in the record, but it is no longer accurate. The 1988-89 edition of *Ulrich's International Periodicals Directory* gives the address as "15 Park Row, New York, NY 10038." The September/October 1988 issue of *Archaeology* does give the "15 Park Row" address as the location to send manuscripts, books for review, and advertisements. However, two other addresses are also provided. A Boston address is given for the Archaeological Institute of America, and a Boulder, Colo., post office box address is given for subscription service.

Another class of information sources that serve to supplement the serial bibliographic record are abstracting and indexing services. A serial will normally have broad subject headings assigned to it in a cataloging record. Such headings may be as nonspecific as "Business — Periodicals" or "Science — Periodicals." These subject headings are of little help to a patron searching for articles on a specific topic such as family corporations in the business field or lymphocyte receptors in the science field. Herbert S. White has argued against the classification of periodicals, stating, "Every article is different, and, presumably, it is these we ought to classify."[4] This is exactly the purpose served by abstracting and indexing services, which provide specific subject access. Many services also provide alternate forms of access, such as by author.

Given the shortcomings and inherent inadequacies of bibliographic records for serials, why are serials cataloged at all? It is necessary to catalog serials so that each can be identified and differentiated from other publications. Catalog records do differentiate two or more serials with the same title. The data elements such as place of publication, date of first publication, volume numbering, and the subject headings that are assigned provide a distinction between two publications with the same title. For instance, the *National Reporter*, published in Washington, D.C., covers topics having to do with espionage and intelligence service, while the *National Reporter*, published in Canada, carries law reports from certain Canadian courts. Classification is also essential in libraries where serials are shelved by call number. In other libraries, periodicals are shelved by title or main entry in an alphabetical arrangement, and a call number is not needed. However, in these situations, serials still must be cataloged to determine the main entry under which the serials are to be shelved.

From the reference standpoint, all serial cataloging records should be viewed with a healthy degree of skepticism. It cannot be stressed enough that living serials are constantly changing, thus making it impossible to produce a perfect bibliographic record that will remain so indefinitely. As a serials cataloger has lamented, "No matter how meticulous one's cataloging is, it won't remain accurate for long."[5] Also, reference staff should take great care in referring a patron to a library's subject catalog to find periodicals in a certain subject area. Broad subject headings such as "History—Periodicals" or "Medicine—Periodicals" are merely "gigantic approximations" of the contents of a serial.[6] For a novice researcher, such a subject catalog can be misleading in that it gives the impression it might be the best, most detailed, topical approach to periodicals. An effective reference interview will find that most patrons who begin by asking for periodicals in broad subject areas actually are searching for articles on quite specific topics. In these cases, patrons will most often be better served by using an abstracting or indexing service rather than using the subject headings in a library's catalog.

Current State of Serials Cataloging

Over the years, there have been many changes in the manner in which serials are cataloged. There are two particular areas of contention that provide fertile ground for disagreement regarding serials cataloging practices. The first such area concerns the main entry for a serial. The second concerns whether a serial that has changed titles should be cataloged under its earliest title or latest title, or if there should be successive separate records for every title in the life of a serial. The current cataloging code, *Anglo-American Cataloguing Rules, Second Edition*, edited by Michael Gorman and Paul W. Winkler (Chicago: American Library Association; Ottawa: Canadian Library Association, 1978), also known as *AACR2*, address both of these longstanding issues.

AACR2 directs that many serials that would have previously been cataloged under corporate main entries should now be cataloged with title main entries. This is a departure from the previous code, under which many serials were cataloged with a corporate main entry. Examples of this are the entries, "Canadian Education Association. *Information bulletin*," and, "Society of Petroleum Engineers of AIME. *Journal*." Under *AACR2*, the main entry of such a publication would be its title. For the most part, this change has been for the better, since the majority of patrons look for a serial by title, and many complex corporate main entries have been replaced by title main entries.[7] On the other hand, entries for generic titles such as *Bulletin* and *Journal* have mushroomed, frequently resulting in more difficult searches for specific publications. Another complicating factor is that *AACR2* still allows corporate main entries for serials in the following cases:

1. Works of an administrative nature dealing with the issuing corporate body itself.

2. Some types of legal and governmental works.

3. Records of the "collective thought" of the issuing corporate body.

4. Reports on the "collective activity" of a conference.[8]

So, even though *AACR2* has resulted in a greater number of title main entries, a reference staffer still cannot tell a patron to search in the serials catalog, or in an alphabetically arranged periodical shelving section, under title only. Some serials are still listed under the issuing corporate body. Most catalogs will, however, provide cross-references from title added entries to corporate main entries where needed.

AACR2 states, "If the title proper of a serial changes, make a separate main entry for each title."[9] This is the essence of successive entry cataloging, and it is the standard manner in which title changes are currently handled. However, there are other ways in which title changes have been treated in the past. Earliest entry cataloging specifies that the earliest title of a serial be cataloged, with notes provided on that single bibliographic record for subsequent titles. Added entries are provided in the catalog referring a patron from the subsequent title(s) to the earliest title. Latest entry cataloging specifies that a single bibliographic record be prepared for the latest title of a serial, with notes and added entries provided for earlier titles.[10] There are advantages and disadvantages for all three of these practices.

The main advantage of successive entry cataloging "is the simplicity it offers for description of complicated materials."[11] Each title has its own unique record, which is beneficial to serials check-in clerks. This unique record is also helpful to the majority of library patrons, who search for specific articles with references to the title of the serial at the time the article appeared — not what the periodical was initially, or later, titled. The main disadvantage of successive entry cataloging is that the description of the entire history of a serial is not available on one record. Although a successive entry record will provide linking notes indicating the title(s) that immediately preceded or followed, several searches may be necessary to construct the history of a serial. For example, *Portable 100*, a periodical for TRS-80 Model 100 computer users, began publication in September 1983. Shortly thereafter, it changed titles to *Portable 100/200*, and, with December 1985, changed again to *Portable 100/200/600*. In August 1986, it changed titles once more, this time returning to its original name, *Portable 100*. Thus, to reconstruct the short history of this periodical, four separate records must be located, two of which are for the same title. To further complicate matters, as of December 1988, there were records for three of these titles in OCLC, but there was no record for the second title, *Portable 100/200*. In cases such as this, where a record is missing, the continuity of linking notes is broken. This also can happen within a serials catalog for a single library, when a library has incomplete holdings resulting in a broken run of a publication.[12]

As might be expected, the advantages and disadvantages of earliest and latest entry cataloging are the opposites of those found with successive entry cataloging. Both earliest and latest entry systems allow for the entire history of a serial to be presented on one bibliographic record. Likewise, in union lists, this allows for holdings throughout the life of a serial to be shown under one entry. The major disadvantages of earliest or latest entry cataloging are that this type of system can be confusing to a library patron and it makes the serials check-in procedure more complex.

From the reference standpoint, be aware of all of these types of cataloging and be able to identify them. Today, most libraries will conform to the successive entry practice. Reference staffers must also remember that various standard serials reference tools employ different types of cataloging practices. As examples, the *Union List of Serials in Libraries of the United States and Canada* uses latest entry, while the *British Union-Catalogue of Periodicals* employs earliest entry, and *Newspapers in Microform: United States, 1948-1983* has successive entries.

Serials Catalogs

It has been stated that, "to organize serials collections is the first step in providing public service to patrons."[13] A vital second step in this process is the production and maintenance of a serials catalog that shows which serials are in a library's collection. In addition to listing the serial titles in a library, a serials catalog can fulfill some, or all, of the following functions:

1. Enumerate holdings of each serial.

2. Provide essential information about a serial such as the call number, publisher, place of publication and other publication data.

3. Show the physical location(s) of a serial in the library.

4. Provide general subject access to the serials in the library.

Serials catalogs are produced in various formats. The traditional catalog is in card format. These cards may be segregated from, or integrated with, the main card catalog of a library. Computer-output serials catalogs are now very popular, with such catalogs being produced on microform or as paper printouts. Many libraries have converted their card catalogs to online catalogs, and their serial records have also become available in that mode. Some automated serials check-in systems allow for public searching of the files, thus resulting in a serials catalog that is also a working accessioning file. In the future, some libraries may provide access to their serials catalogs through CD-ROM systems.

Regardless of the format, all serials catalogs provide special challenges for reference staff. The major problem is that it is difficult for many patrons to understand such a catalog and to grasp the various bits of information given in any particular entry. A reference librarian, writing in *The Journal of Academic Librarianship*, stated that in his reference activities, "the most frequently asked 'factual' questions ... concern the computerized serials list containing information about our 6500 current serial holdings and other previously received titles."[14] Most patrons are accustomed to rather straightforward searching in a library's catalog for book titles. Either a library has a book, or it doesn't. If it does, then all that's needed is a call number to retrieve it. Serials searching is a much more complex process. Titles may be listed in the catalog under title or under corporate entry. Even if a title is listed, the patron may be uncertain as to whether the library has the actual volume, issue, or date needed. In most libraries, periodicals can be shelved in a number of locations based on whether they are in bound volumes, or in loose, current issues. Microform files may be shelved in a separate location. Many serials are reference works, and the current edition may be found in a separate reference collection. The library may have two or more serials with the same title, and the patron may not know which is the one that is needed.

The detailed information given in a serials catalog is often confusing to a patron. Thus, reference staff are frequently called upon to explain catalog entries. There are some common misinterpretations made by patrons due to their lack of knowledge of serials and serials catalogs. The most prevalent mistake made is the assumption that if a serial title is listed in a library's catalog, then the library has a complete set of the publication. This is a problem especially in regard to serials catalogs where holdings are not shown. Another problem arises from the dates of publication shown on a serial cataloging record. For instance, the record may indicate dates of publication as, "Vol. 15, no. 1 (Jan. 1984)- " indicating that this particular serial title began with the issue carrying the designation, "Volume 15, number 1, January 1984," and that it presumably continues to be published up to the present. Unfortunately, many inexperienced patrons will assume that volume 15, number 1, January 1984 is the only issue that the library owns.

Another problem is that some patrons will search in manual catalogs for titles that begin with initialisms or acronyms as if those series of letters were words. Thus, instead of looking in the beginning of the "I" listings for *IEEE Spectrum*, a patron will look somewhere in the middle of the "I" listings, after *Ideals* and before the "Illinois" entries. If the patron does not find the acronym or initialism listed as a word, the assumption often will be made that the library does not own the serial. Patrons do make these mistakes, and experience other difficulties, in using serials catalogs. Therefore, reference staff should always be aware of this. When assisting a patron who is using the catalog for the first time, the reference staffer should take a moment to explain the catalog and to point out any idiosyncrasies that may be unique to that catalog or library. At the very least, a staffer should suggest that the patron again seek assistance if the search in the serials catalog is unsuccessful. This will give the reference staff a chance to confirm that the search was done correctly and to make referrals where possible.

MARC Serial Cataloging Records

The rise of online bibliographic utilities, most prominently OCLC, over the past two decades has revolutionized much of librarianship. Serials librarianship has seen great changes, particularly in the areas of union listing and cataloging. The change in cataloging is reflected in serials cataloging at Iowa State University. In 1978, the serials catalogers there still typed their cards since the serial records then available on OCLC were "sparse and incomplete."[15] Eight years later, a serials cataloger at the same library found "that the majority of on-the-job cataloging consisted of editing copy found on the library's bibliographic utility."[16] OCLC now contains over one million serial records,[17] with over 625,000 of them being high-quality records contributed by CONSER participants.[18] OCLC is also the "home" of eighty online union lists. Other online bibliographic utilities also provide similar access to serial cataloging records.

Reference staff use online serial cataloging records for two major purposes. First, they are used to identify holding locations of serials. A second major reference use is to obtain various types of bibliographic information about serials. The types of information that can be accessed include dates and place of publication, preceding and succeeding titles, and abstracting and indexing services in which the serial is covered. A reference staffer must understand the MARC (machine-readable cataloging) serial cataloging record and know the significance of several important fields in that record.

A MARC serial record is composed of a number of fixed fields at the top of the record, followed by many variable fields. Most serial records are two to four pages, or video display terminal screens, in length. For reference purposes, the variable fields are of utmost importance, and the number of these fields fluctuates from one record to another. It is essential that serials reference staff become familiar with the following fields, in particular.

010 – Library of Congress (LC) control number or pseudo control number. Records can be accessed directly by searching under this number. This identifier formerly was called the Library of Congress card number.

022 – International Standard Serial Number (ISSN). This unique number assigned to a serial allows direct online access to its record.

030 – CODEN designation. This is another unique identifier. Some systems allow direct access to a record by searching under this identifier.

222 – Key title. This is a unique title assigned by the International Serials Data System.

245 – Title statement.

246 — Varying forms of title, which appear on different parts of the serial.

260 — Imprint statement, including publisher and place of publication.

265 — Subscription address.

310 — Current frequency.

321 — Former frequency.

362 — Dates of publication and volume designations.

510 — Citation note. Publication(s) in which the serial has been abstracted or indexed.

515 — Numbering peculiarities note.

533 — Photoreproduction note.

580 — Linking entry complexity note.

650 — Subject added entry — topical heading.

651 — Subject added entry — geographic name.

780 — Preceding entry.

785 — Succeeding entry.

787 — Nonspecific relationship entry.

850 — Holding institutions listed by NUC symbols of those institutions reporting to *New Serial Titles*. Other holding institutions may be found listed in a separate locations display.

936 — Date/volume of latest piece used in cataloging.

CONSER

Certain aspects of serials reference work have become much more productive and efficient as the result of the monumental goals accomplished by the CONSER project. CONSER is an acronym, which at first stood for the Conversion of Serials Project, but, as of November 1986, stands for the Cooperative Online Serials Program.[19] The project was conceived in the Ad Hoc Discussion Group on Serials Data Bases, which first met informally in 1973. This group was interested in rapidly building a comprehensive North American database of serial titles.[20] Originally, CONSER was envisioned as a project of two or three years that would produce approximately 200,000 records, with those records contributed by no more than fifteen member libraries. OCLC was chosen to house and provide access to the CONSER records, and the participants began initial input into the database in 1976.[21]

By 1986, CONSER had amassed a database of more than 625,000 cataloging records.[22] This database also includes all of the records that have been created, and will include future records to be created, by the United States Newspaper Program (see chapter 11). Another CONSER undertaking was its Abstracting and Indexing Coverage Project, the purpose of which was to enhance CONSER records by adding notes for serials covered in the major abstracting and indexing services.[23] Such services that cover a serial are specified in notes in the 510 field of the MARC serial record.

ISSN and CODEN

An International Standard Serial Number (ISSN) is a distinctive number assigned to a serial so that the publication may be uniquely identified. ISSNs are composed of either eight digits, four before and four after a hyphen, such as "0261-9180," or are composed of seven digits and the letter "X," such as "0742-969X." When this program began operation in 1971, the numbers were assigned by the R. R. Bowker Company. These numbers are now assigned by national or regional centers operating within the International Serials Data System. The United States center is the National Serials Data Program at the Library of Congress.

As unique identifiers, ISSNs are very helpful in differentiating between two or more serials with the same title. They also offer a means of rapid access to the online record for a serial in the database of a bibliographic utility such as OCLC. In using ISSNs for online retrieval, it is surprising to find that more than one record may be retrieved for a single ISSN. This is often caused by duplicate records in a database for the same serial in different formats (print, microfilm, and microfiche).

There are a number of sources where the ISSN for a serial can be identified. First, and foremost, the ISSN of a current serial may be found printed on each issue of the publication. Although it is recommended that the ISSN be printed in the top right corner of the front cover,[24] it is likely to be found in any number of locations, including the title page or in the publishing statement. Many periodical directories also list ISSNs, most notably, *Ulrich's International Periodicals Directory* and *The Serials Directory*. All current ISSN registrations made by the National Serials Data Program are entered as MARC records in the CONSER database (see earlier in this chapter).[25] The ISSN is given in field 022 of the MARC record.

A CODEN is a six-character code that uniquely designates a serial publication. For example, the CODEN for the *Journal for College Science Teaching* is "JSCTBN," and the CODEN for *Michigan Botanist* is "MBOTAU." The CODEN system, which was conceived and widely implemented in the 1950s and early 1960s, has been used throughout its history primarily for scientific periodicals,[26] in conjunction with abstracts and citations, and is currently administered by the Chemical Abstracts Service. At one time, it was thought that CODEN would become a broadly applicable identification system that could be used in serials control.[27] However, the ISSN system has filled this function on a widespread basis and has overshadowed CODEN. Some online systems, most notably OCLC, allow serial record retrieval by CODEN designation. CODENs are listed in the 030 field of MARC serial records. *Ulrich's International Periodicals Directory* and *The Serials Directory* also contain CODEN designations.

Other Aspects of Serials Cataloging

A special cataloging procedure is applied to serials that are "analyzed." However, most serials are not even considered for this type of treatment. Analytics are usually appropriate only "for serials with clear monographic characteristics: each issue or volume has a specific and distinct subject focus, a sizable number of pages, is not generally indexed in standard indexes, and is likely to be cited as a monograph in the literature."[28] When a serial is analyzed, a library may choose to have the set "collected" or "scattered." If collected, each individual volume or issue of a serial is cataloged separately but given the class number of the serial, thus assuring that all issues will remain together. If scattered, each volume or issue is cataloged individually and a class number appropriate to its contents is assigned.[29] The result is that individual issues are dispersed throughout a library's collection.

The use of initialisms in the beginning of periodical titles, and as complete periodical titles, is quite common. Examples of such titles are *AAOHN Journal: Official Journal of the American Association of Occupational Health Nurses, RBER: Review of Business and Economic Research*, and *WWD: Women's Wear Daily*. Although these titles may be eye-catching and visually pleasing to the publisher and to the reader, they can cause problems in libraries. As was mentioned earlier, many patrons unfamiliar with library catalog filing practices will search in a manual catalog for an initialism as if it was a word and never look in the beginning of a letter segment. When the initialism is not found, the patron assumes that the library doesn't have the periodical needed. Other patrons will disregard the initialism entirely and search under the words for which it stands, even in cases where the initialism actually is the title.

From a cataloging standpoint, it can sometimes be very difficult to determine if the initial letters are actually part of the title, or if they constitute a logo for the publication. In some cases, the initialism may appear in different places, in relation to the title, throughout a periodical. As an illustration of this practice, a serials librarian wrote in 1979 that "the periodical whose cover reads *The Journal of General Education JGE* presents on its title page and with its editorial information the title *JGE: The Journal of General Education*, and uses as its running head and in its address the title *The Journal of General Education*."[30] The only advice that can be given to someone searching for such a title in a manual catalog is to look in all of the possible places in the catalog where the entry could possibly be filed.

Notes

[1]Paul S. Dunkin, *Cataloging U.S.A.* (Chicago: American Library Association, 1969), 62.

[2]Bohdan S. Wynar and Arlene G. Taylor, *Introduction to Cataloging and Classification*, 7th ed. (Littleton, Colo.: Libraries Unlimited, 1985), 4.

[3]Andrew D. Osborn, *Serial Publications: Their Place and Treatment in Libraries*, 3d ed. (Chicago: American Library Association, 1980), 212-15.

[4]Herbert S. White, "Oh, Why (and Oh, What) Do We Classify?" *Library Journal* 113 (15 June 1988): 43.

[5]Lori L. Osmus and Jeanne M. K. Boydston, "A Tale of Two Serials Catalogers: Their Education and Training," *Cataloging and Classification Quarterly* 7 (Summer 1987): 107.

[6]White, "Oh, Why," 43.

[7]Cindy Hepfer and Will Hepfer, "AACR2's Effect on Public Services," *The Serials Librarian* 12, nos. 1-2 (1987): 21.

[8]Michael Gorman and Paul W. Winkler, eds., *Anglo-American Cataloguing Rules, Second Edition* (Chicago: American Library Association, 1978; Ottawa: Canadian Library Association, 1978), 285.

[9]Ibid., 287.

[10]Jackie Zajanc, "Title Changes in an Automated Environment: The Last Shall Be First," *The Serials Librarian* 11 (September 1986): 15.

[11]Beth Reuland, "Successive Entry: Another Look," *Serials Review* 9 (Fall 1983): 92.

[12]Zajanc, "Title Changes," 19.

[13]Deborah J. Karpuk, "Reference Services, Serials Cataloging, and the Patron," in *Reference Services and Technical Services: Interactions in Library Practice* (New York: Haworth Press, 1984), 99.

[14]Mark Schumacher, "A View from the Trenches," *The Journal of Academic Librarianship* 13 (November 1987): 278.

[15]Osmus and Boydston, "Tale of Two Catalogers," 104.

[16]Ibid., 98.

[17]*OCLC Annual Report, 1987/88* (Dublin, Ohio: OCLC Online Computer Library Center, 1988), 4.

[18]Suzanne Striedieck, "Cooperative Online Serials Program," *Serials Review* 13 (Spring 1987): 55.

[19]Ibid.

[20]Jeffrey Heynen and Julia C. Blixrud, *The CONSER Project: Recommendations for the Future*, Network Planning Paper, no. 14 (Washington, D.C.: Library of Congress, 1986), 1.

[21]Ibid., 4-5.

[22]Striedieck, "Cooperative Program," 55.

[23]Jim E. Cole and Olivia M. A. Madison, "A Decade of Serials Cataloging," *The Serials Librarian* 10 (Fall 1985/Winter 1985-1986): 113.

[24]Linda K. Bartley, "ISSN and NSDP: A Guide for the Initiated," in *The Management of Serials Automation: Current Technologies & Strategies for Future Planning* (New York: Haworth Press, 1982): 175.

[25]Ibid., 172.

[26]Neal L. Edgar, review of *Serial Publications: Their Place and Treatment in Libraries*, 3d ed., in *Serials Review* 7 (April/June 1981): 63.

[27]Andrew D. Osborn, *Serial Publications: Their Place and Treatment in Libraries*, 2d ed. (Chicago: American Library Association, 1973): 132-34.

[28]Eleanor Ferrall and Mara Pinckard, "To Analyze or Not to Analyze: Who Makes the Decision?" *The Serials Librarian* 10 (Summer 1986): 55.

[29]Ibid., 55-56.

[30]Frank E. Sadowski, Jr., "Initially, We Need Some Definitions: The Problems of Initialisms in Periodical Titles," *Library Resources & Technical Services* 23 (Fall 1979): 366.

15
Serials Processing and Its Effect on Reference Service

As bibliographic entities, serials are the most complicated items in a library's collection. It then follows that in order to acquire, maintain, and provide access to serials, a significant number of specialized processing activities are required. Each of these processing activities has an impact on reference service. A breakdown in any of them results in later problems that usually must be handled by the public services staff. In contrast, when all serials processing activities are constantly performed correctly, a high level of reference service can be sustained.

In brief, serials processing activities fall into the areas of acquisitions, record-keeping, maintenance of the collection, and preservation. A serial's life within a particular library begins when a decision is made to start receiving the publication on a continuing basis. This is normally achieved through a paid subscription, which is often placed or maintained through a subscription agency. Once issues start to arrive, a check-in, or accessioning, clerk notes each issue received on a manual or automated accessioning record for the title. At some point after a serial has begun to be received, it will be cataloged (see chapter 14). A shelf location will be made for it in the serials collection, based on whether the library arranges serials by call number, title, or by some other classification. As issues are received, one at a time upon publication, they are noted in the record and then sent to the shelf location or to wherever else they may go via a routing assignment. When certain issues are not received, or if the serial inexplicably ceases to arrive, claims must be submitted, either directly to the publisher or to the subscription agency through which the subscription has been placed.

Once a number of issues have accumulated, a decision must be made as to whether they will be preserved. If they are to be preserved, a method of preservation must be chosen. The traditional form of preservation is through the binding of loose issues into volumes. An alternative to binding is the purchase of microform. If the issues are to be bound, then there will be a continuing process of replacing missing issues and pages that have been ripped out or otherwise mutilated. The binding process itself is an ongoing activity, with issues of a serial being bound usually on a yearly, or more frequent, schedule, depending upon the frequency of publication and the thickness of each issue.

Another continuing process is the payment of subscription fees, including any subscriptions to microform editions that are acquired as an alternative to binding. Of course, the commercial bindery must also be paid for its work on a continuing basis. Another serials processing activity that has become increasingly more important and widespread in the past two decades is the cancellation of subscriptions.

The balance of this chapter examines more closely the aforementioned processing activities and their effects on reference service.

Acquisition of Serials

The decision to add a serial to a library's collection is one that is usually made after careful consideration. Whereas the selection of a monograph results in a one-time outlay of funds, the beginning of a subscription to a serial results in a continuing commitment of funds to pay for the subscription and for processing activities related to the ongoing receipt and preservation of the publication. Since "the serial standing order or subscription is intended to continue until someone at the library acts to end it,"[1] such selection decisions can have financial repercussions for years, and even for decades. A portion of a study undertaken in 1978 and 1979 sought to discover the reasons why libraries place new subscriptions to scholarly and research journals. The results showed that four of the top five reasons involved recommendations, by individual users or user groups, to subscribe to the periodical.[2] So, in most cases, new subscriptions are apparently instituted because of user demand.

There are basically three standard methods for libraries to obtain serials. They can be acquired by purchase, through an exchange program, or as a gift. The purchase, or subscription, method is the manner in which most libraries obtain the majority of their serials. An individual interested in subscribing to one or more periodicals will normally submit subscription orders directly to the periodical publishers or to magazine fulfillment centers that handle subscriptions for certain periodicals. For libraries, though, it would be an accounting and paperwork nightmare if they were required to deal with a separate publisher or fulfillment center for each title acquired. This is where the subscription agency comes to the aid of the library.

> Traditionally, a subscription agency serves libraries by consolidating subscriptions to periodicals, serials, and journals. The library places its order with the agency, pays with one check, and lets the agency take it from there. The agency places the library's order with, and pays, the various publishers. The agency worries about chasing down missing journal copies, about duplications, and other headaches such as publications that change names (or ownership or subscription rates) or omit an issue or go out of business. The agency also deals with foreign currencies.[3]

Subscription agencies make their profits through discounts from publishers and by service fees charged to the libraries. Some serials, however, cannot be ordered through agencies. These include serials from publishers who refuse to deal with subscription agencies and publications that are available only through a membership in an association. Nevertheless, a library can substantially reduce its paperwork by placing orders through agencies.

From a reference standpoint, the "by-products" of a library's relationship with a subscription agency are very important. All of the major agencies issue catalogs of serial publications. The most prominent of these is EBSCO's annual, *Librarians' Handbook*, which can be effectively used as a serials directory (see chapter 3). Subscription agencies have also developed automated check-in systems, with Faxon's LINX system being one of the leading examples. With such systems it is possible to access the information in a library's serials record from terminals at multiple access points. Such systems also provide the possibility of customized printouts of titles in a library's collection.

In addition to acquisition through subscriptions, libraries also obtain serials through exchange programs and as gifts. Exchange programs, which are often established with foreign libraries, allow two institutions to either exchange available publications or to each subscribe to publications in their home countries that will be sent to their partner's library.[4] Serials that are obtained as gifts are usually sent free of charge from the publisher or are paid for by some individual or organization as a gift to the library. Individuals also may donate personal copies of issues of serials once they have read them. Since nothing is being paid for these gifts, the library has no recourse in the event that an issue is missed or if the title stops coming completely. Donated personal copies carry the added disadvantage of delayed receipt since the donor usually must read them first. Gifts are the least reliable method of serials acquisition.

Check-in Procedures

The most basic and fundamental processing activity regarding serials is the process of checking-in issues, or volumes, as they arrive in the library. This check-in function is also referred to as "accessioning" or just "checking." The purpose of this process is to maintain an accurate record of the issues, or volumes, of a serial that have been received in the library. Such information serves as one of the foundations of serials reference service.

The classic manual check-in file is sometimes referred to as a "visible file" or "Kardex." A separate record for each serial title received is kept in an alphabetical arrangement, by title or corporate main entry, attached to trays that slide in and out of large metal cabinets. Each individual record may consist of several check-in sheets, called over-riders or flimsies. Generally, the top sheet will be the one on which current receipts are noted, while the bottom sheets may contain the retrospective accessioning records and the record of permanent holdings in formats such as bound volumes or microform. An over-rider is a printed sheet approximately 3½-by-6 inches, and the most common type has lines printed on it in the shape of a grid. Each block in the grid represents an issue of the serial. There are several different types of over-riders, with the main difference being the number of squares on a sheet. For instance, there are separate over-riders designed to be used for serials with daily, weekly, or monthly frequencies of publication.

When an issue of a serial is received, the accessioning clerk must locate the appropriate record, which sometimes can be difficult, especially for generic titles or for those entered under corporate main entries. Although cross-references can be found in these files, they are normally not as widespread as those found in a library's public serials catalog. Once the correct record is found, the accessioning clerk places a check in the appropriate square, thus indicating that the issue has been received. In some libraries, the date of receipt may also be noted on the over-rider. Depending on the procedures of the particular library, the clerk may then perform any number of other functions, including:

Property stamp the item.

Write a call number on the item, or affix a label to the item and write a call number on the label.

Attach a routing slip to the item.

The last step in the check-in process is for the issue to be sent to its destination in the library. From a public service standpoint, it would be preferable that all periodicals, as soon as they are received and accessioned, be sent to one area. Unfortunately, the reality in most libraries is that current issues of periodicals are scattered in different areas of the library. They may also be routed to one or more individuals or offices prior to being sent to their designated shelving area. So, when a reference staffer is asked by a patron about a particular current issue of a serial, the check-in file must be consulted to determine if the issue has been received and, if so, where that issue should be located.

In the past decade, a number of automated serials management systems have been introduced. Many of these have been marketed by serial subscription agencies.[5] Automated serials management systems provide several advantages. In the check-in process, most of the manual activities can be eliminated, including the sorting and alphabetizing of periodicals, which is a standard procedure followed in manual accessioning operations.[6] Automated check-in also can help to reduce the number of errors made on an accessioning record, since a clerk can no longer "put a check mark in the wrong little square."[7] Records are also easier to read, as the peculiarities of the handwriting of various clerks will no longer be encountered. Although these factors are significant, other advantages provided by automated systems are of more importance. First, automated systems allow reference staff, and patrons, greater access to serials information. Second, these systems also allow greater control over the claiming of missed issues (see later in this chapter).[8] Automated serials management systems also aid in the binding process, and customized printouts regarding a library's serials collection are also possible with these systems. Another significant possibility offered by such systems is that of off-site check-in. That is, the issues of serials are accessioned at some place other than the library, and are then shipped together to the library, ready to be added to the collection or sent on routings. In most cases where this has gone into effect, subscription agencies have handled the off-site check-in.

Shelving and Access to Serials

A common question asked by patrons in many libraries is, "Where are your periodicals?" This rather simple inquiry can rarely be answered easily. In most libraries, unbound issues of periodicals are housed in one area, while bound volumes are stored in another area. The bound volumes may all be segregated into one portion of the library, or interfiled into the book collection. Microform editions of periodicals are most likely stored in another area. A large portion of the recent receipts of periodicals may not be available at all because they are at the bindery (see later in this chapter). In some libraries, only the most recent issue of a periodical is displayed, while other issues must be requested. In closed-stack libraries, such as the Library of Congress, practically all issues of periodicals, be they recent, dated, or ancient, must be requested by filling out and submitting call slips.

Even when a patron has found the area in which the unbound or bound periodicals are shelved, a number of impediments to easy access may surface. It is possible that the periodicals are arranged by call number. In such cases, the patron must have the call number in order to find the periodical on the shelf. In other libraries, periodicals are arranged on the shelf by title, or main entry. Patrons who are looking for a generic title such as *Bulletin* may not know enough about library practice or about library cataloging to also check in such arrangements under the name of the issuing corporate body.

In libraries where unbound periodicals and bound volumes of periodicals are shelved in separate areas, it is fairly common for novice library users to become confused. The whole concept of bound volumes of periodical issues may be unfamiliar to such a patron. Also, the concept of issues being sent away from the library to a bindery may be inconceivable to an inexperienced researcher. A reference staffer should be aware of this possibility and be prepared to offer the bibliographic instruction necessary to enable the patron to understand where the needed periodical issue currently is and when it might be returned from the bindery.

As with all other aspects of serials in libraries, the shelving and access to them is a complex matter that can be befuddling and frustrating to library users. Serials reference staff should try to maintain a high degree of empathy, especially when dealing with the novice researcher. Undoubtedly, a large percentage of users become frustrated with the periodicals retrieval process and leave the library without saying anything to the staff and without obtaining the materials they need. Although it is not always practical to do so, serials reference staff should make a habit of asking departing patrons if they have found what they need. This, of course, can result in more work for the reference staffer, but a professional should feel inclined to ensure that as many patrons as possible receive a full measure of reference service.

Binding and Microforms

Libraries, for the most part, acquire serials with the intention of permanently preserving them for their collections. Even though some newspapers or periodicals of a current awareness nature may be kept on a "current year" or other temporary basis, the majority will be retained permanently by a library. However, serials are usually published in formats that will not stand up to continued use over a number of years. The covers of most periodicals are just paper, and they are susceptible to creasing, ripping, and tearing. The binding of a single periodical issue normally consists of a few staples. Newspapers and many periodicals are published on newsprint, which easily tears and rapidly deteriorates. So, most serials cannot be permanently stored and used by library patrons in the format in which a library receives them.

Binding is the traditional method used to preserve serials. Normally, unbound issues of a serial are received by a library one at a time as they are published. Once a sufficient number of issues have accumulated, they can be pulled off the shelf and prepared for binding. The number of issues and date coverage in any bound volume is largely determined by the thickness of the individual issues and by the frequency of publication. It is preferable to have one bibliographic volume bound into one physical volume. This is often not practical, however, and one bibliographic volume frequently is bound into two or more physical volumes.

Serials librarians are advised that a volume should be sent to the bindery "as soon as all components to be bound are present ... even though the public is deprived of its immediate use."[9] The reason for this is that the sooner a volume is bound, the less likely there will be instances of torn pages, mutilated issues, and issues that have disappeared completely. Unfortunately, it is at just that point that the normal periodical will be receiving its peak usage, due to coverage in abstracting and indexing services.[10] Since a volume may be inaccessible for a few weeks up through a few months or more while it is being bound, this process has serious repercussions for public services staff. In situations where a needed periodical issue is at the bindery, the best that can be done by the reference staffer for the patron is to first estimate when the volume may return from the bindery, and then to try to locate another library with holdings of the publication. Exercise caution in referring a patron to another library for the same issue since its copy may also be at the bindery.

A major problem experienced with bound volumes of periodicals regards photocopying. Some volumes may be very thick or have narrow inside margins called "gutters." In either instance, it may be impossible to produce usable photocopies, although some patrons will attempt to produce a good copy, which often results in damage to the volume. Patrons in such a situation should be referred to a library's copy service.

Reference staff should be aware that in years past, a number of different binding practices have been in vogue. For instance, it is not unusual to find old periodical volumes with all of the separate title pages from issues removed or with all of the advertisements removed. Under some binding practices, the advertisements were removed from the individual issues and placed in a separate section at the rear of the bound volume. Of course, these practices can have an effect on today's researcher, especially when studying advertisements in the old periodicals. For the reference staffer, it should be kept in mind that some past binding practices were quite different than today's practice, and that what the patron is looking for may have been discarded when the volume was bound.

The main alternative to the binding of issues of periodicals is the acquisition of microform editions of the publications. Instead of binding, a library can subscribe to a microfilm or microfiche edition of a serial. Once the microform edition for a certain range of issues is received, the corresponding copies in hardcopy that were originally received are simply discarded. This has become a standard practice for the permanent retention of newspapers and is now becoming widely accepted as an alternate method for the preservation of periodicals. From the public service perspective, microform editions of periodicals provide two major advantages. First, the issues are never "at the bindery" and, therefore, unavailable. Second, articles or pages do not get ripped out of microform editions as they do from bound volumes and from unbound issues (see chapters 7 and 13 for further discussions of periodicals and newspapers on microform).

As mentioned earlier, some serials are received by a library for the purpose of providing current information only. The retention decision for such a periodical may be, "Keep Current Two Years," or, for a newspaper, "Keep Current Thirty Days." Some patrons have great difficulty in understanding such decisions. They assume that if a library receives something, it will be kept forever. So, in such instances, serials reference staff must patiently explain the basis for such decisions, and then attempt to find another library with holdings of the older issue(s) needed by the patron.

Other Aspects of Serials Processing

Claiming is a fundamental element in the serials acquisition process. Simply, a claim is a notice sent to a publisher or a subscription agency stating that a particular issue of a serial was not received or that a serial has stopped being received entirely. In essence, a library is saying that they have paid for the publication, but one or more issues have been missed. To be effective, claims must be submitted as promptly as possible. For instance, if the November issue of a periodical is received, but the October issue was never received, a claim should be quickly issued. These types of receipt problems are the easiest to discover since an accessioning clerk is looking at the record.

A more difficult problem to spot is a periodical that has ceased to be received. Unless reference staff become aware, usually through patron complaints, that the periodical is not up to date, the situation may not come to light until it is too late to claim the missing issues. It is important, then, that any receipt problems that come to the attention of the reference staff be immediately reported to those responsible for claiming. Also, it is essential for those who submit the claims to keep a clear record of such activities on the serial accessioning record, so that the reference staff can be aware of attempts to acquire missing issues. With automated serials management systems, claiming has become a more scientific, reliable practice. Most systems predict the arrival date of issues of serials, based on their frequency of publication and date that the last issue was received. When an issue is not received within the prescribed amount of time, the title will either be listed on a report of titles needing claiming, or a claim will automatically be generated.

A vexing problem for patrons and for public services staff is that issues of periodicals often disappear or are mutilated. Some issues are stolen, while others just get placed in the wrong pile and are temporarily lost. Others have articles or photographs ripped out. Some issues fall apart from continuous use, and pages are lost. When these types of situations are discovered, they should be reported to the staff member responsible for obtaining replacement issues and replacement pages. In most instances, replacements can be acquired. If the reference staff members notice a continuing problem with a particular publication, the library might need to change from binding the issues to purchasing a microform edition.

In the past two decades, rapidly increasing subscription prices, coupled with the inability of library budgets to keep pace, has resulted in a trend toward the cancellation of serial subscriptions. This is a new phenomenon, since the routine cancellation of subscriptions was "almost unknown, except in special libraries, before the early 1970s."[11] It has now become a widespread practice, and the pressures that have caused it show no signs of abating. The 1988 annual price survey of United States periodicals shows prices increasing at rates far in excess of the rate of inflation.[12] Scholarly journals issued by large European publishers constitute a major component of the problem to such an extent that their increases are being referred to as "blackmail" and that calls for a boycott of such publications have been made.[13]

The result of this situation is that libraries must cancel subscriptions. These cancellations are usually based either on an exhaustive review of titles by subject area in a library or on whether the titles considered for cancellation are available from a union list partner.[14] Reference staff may become involved in these cancellations in either of two ways. First, such staff members may be called upon to evaluate serial titles for possible cancellation. A second involvement occurs once a serial is cancelled, and patrons become aware of the cancellation. Public services staff should then be able to explain why subscriptions were cancelled and on what basis such decisions were made. There may also be a higher demand for interlibrary loan services and for accurate referrals to other libraries that still subscribe to the cancelled serials. For patrons who had formerly read periodicals that have been cancelled, it may be helpful to suggest other publications still being received by the library that cover the same topic.

Notes

[1]Marcia Tuttle, *Introduction to Serials Management* (Greewich, Conn.: JAI Press, 1983), 59.

[2]Herbert S. White, "Factors in the Decision by Individuals and Libraries to Place or Cancel Subscriptions to Scholarly and Research Journals," *Library Quarterly* 50 (July 1980): 302.

[3]N. Bernard Basch and Alice Sizer Warner, "Subscription Agencies: A New Look at an Old Service," *Library Journal* 113 (1 April 1988): 57.

[4]Tuttle, *Introduction to Serials Management*, 63-64.

[5]Basch and Warner, "Subscription Agencies," 58.

[6]Jean Walter Farrington, "The Serials Visible File: Observations on Its Impending Demise," *Serials Review* 12 (Winter 1986): 35.

[7]Basch and Warner, "Subscription Agencies," 58.

[8]Farrington, "Serials Visible File," 35.

[9]Milan Milkovic, "The Binding of Periodicals: Basic Concepts and Procedures," *The Serials Librarian* 11 (October 1986): 103.

[10]James S. Healey and Carolyn M. Cox, "Research and the *Readers' Guide*: An Investigation into the Research Use of Periodicals Indexed in the *Readers' Guide to Periodical Literature*," *The Serials Librarian* 3 (Winter 1978): 185.

[11]White, "Factors in the Decision," 287.

[12]Leslie C. Knapp and Rebecca T. Lenzini, "Price Index for 1988: U.S. Periodicals," *Library Journal* 113 (15 April 1988): 37.

[13]Thomas M. Gaughan, "Serials Prices Stir Rumbles in ARL; Privately, Library Directors are Talking 'Boycott,' " *American Libraries* 19 (April 1988): 328.

[14]October Ivins, "Serials Prices," *Serials Review* 14, no. 3 (1988): 62.

16
The Future of Serials Reference Work

Recent Developments in the Field

Over the past two decades, there has been considerable change in serials librarianship and in the provision of reference services related to serials. During this same period, however, the basic world of serials publishing has not been drastically altered. Newspapers still are published on newsprint and remain as a standard source of information. Printed periodicals, ranging from scholarly journals to magazines sold at newsstands, still are omnipresent in our culture and in our information chain. So, the printed serial, itself, has not changed significantly. What has changed are the processes employed by libraries to handle serials. In addition, technological advances have given rise to automated serials-related services that have changed forever the nature of serials reference work.

From the processing standpoint, the automation of serials cataloging activities has been the most important development. Serials catalogers now, in most instances, do not need to perform original cataloging. They simply locate the appropriate record for a serial in the database of a bibliographic utility, such as OCLC, and edit that record to suit the needs of the library. A cataloging record is thus created for the library in a fraction of the time that original cataloging would have consumed. With the creation and rapid building of the CONSER database, hundreds of thousands of high quality MARC serial records are available for both cataloging and reference functions.

The online networks that have grown as a result of these bibliographic utilities serve another purpose aside from the shared cataloging function. In essence, these databases are constantly changing and expanding online union lists. Staff are no longer dependent solely upon printed union lists, which in many cases are outdated, to identify libraries holding particular serials. The online serial records show such holding locations. In addition, many union list groups that formerly produced printed union lists can now have the exact holdings of their member institutions available through online files.

In the abstracting and indexing areas, the past two decades have witnessed vast, innovative changes. A researcher in years past, searching for articles on a subject, would have had available printed indexes and, perhaps, printed bibliographies on the topic. Today, that same researcher still has available the printed resources but also has access to indexing and abstracting in various other forms, including databases accessible through online and CD-ROM systems. Also, many newspapers and periodicals can be accessed through electronic full-text retrieval systems, which allow searching capabilities that could only have been dreamed of not too long ago.

These and other changes that have occurred in the recent past have been the result of advances in technology. Doubtless, future technological progress will affect the manner in which serials are handled in libraries. In particular, serials reference work will continue to evolve. At the same time, serials should become less of a mystifying and segregated area for reference staff. Publications of this sort will become more integrated into a total information-related approach in libraries, where the form of a publication will not be as important as the information contained therein.

The rest of this chapter will cover major trends and projected developments that will affect future serials reference work.

The Electronic Journal

Electronic publishing has been heralded as the scholarly communications medium of the future.[1] Such paperless publishing of journals on a widespread basis would significantly alter the communications process and have a considerable effect on libraries. An electronic journal is a publication "where the writing, editing, refereeing and distribution of an item are carried out without any paper intermediaries."[2] Electronic journals are not the same as electronic, full-text periodicals (see later in this chapter). In general, periodicals that can be retrieved electronically in full-text versions are simply the electronic versions of printed publications. The term "electronic journal," on the other hand, refers to a type of publication for which there is no print version. That is, no print edition exists unless a printout is made from the electronic version.

The primary advantage cited for electronic journals is the speed at which articles can be "published" and disseminated. With printed journals, articles often are published many months after they are written. Electronic journals offer online interaction among writers, editors, and readers. Theoretically, with an electronic journal, an article could be disseminated as soon as it is input into the database and accepted by the "publisher." With refereed publications, the review process can be substantially accelerated since there is no need to mail the manuscript back and forth among author, editor, and referees. The resulting rapid publication and distribution of articles would certainly be of great benefit, especially to scientists currently researching or conducting experiments. At present, electronic journals are not without their disadvantages, most of which derive from the tradition of printed scholarly communication. The major problem is in "introducing this form of publication within the structure of the current technical and scientific information exchange practices."[3] Electronic publishing raises a number of thought-provoking questions for those who would write the articles and for those who would use those articles. How will electronic publishing fit into the "publish or perish" system that predominates in the academic community? How should electronic articles be cited? If an article is revised once it has been electronically published, should both the original version and the edited version be available?[4] Will the readership of articles in an electronic journal be as wide and varied as that for a comparable printed journal? Especially, will the journal be available to those who are not members of the particular discipline to which that journal caters? Another related question is whether electronic journals will be accepted by readers in the future, since readers currently prefer the conventional printed journal over an electronic version of the same journal.[5]

The questions raised for libraries center around access to electronic journals. While it is relatively easy for a library to provide its users with a printed journal, access to an electronic journal may require special hardware and access fees. Libraries will need to decide if they will allow their patrons to have direct access to electronic journals or if library staff will access and print out articles needed from these publications. The prediction has even been made that libraries will need to print out entire electronic journals and then preserve them through binding.[6]

Presumably, if electronic journals become a major factor in the future, standards will come into place for electronic scholarly publishing. Thus, many of the questions that authors and researchers now have regarding this form of publication will be answered. Libraries will undoubtedly be driven by the demands of their patrons. If future users demand access to electronic journals, then such access will probably be made available, and library-related questions and problems will be handled at that time.

Full-text Newspapers and Periodicals

In the 1980s, databases providing online, full-text access to newspapers and periodicals have blossomed and grown immensely. Systems such as NEXIS, VU/TEXT, and DataTimes all allow full-text, online retrieval of a number of newspapers, periodicals, and wire services. As of 1987, the full-text of articles from 355 periodicals were available through DIALOG.[7] Such databases have become popular because, in addition to offering the entire text of articles, they allow for rapid online searches that would be impossible or impractical with the print equivalent. These systems also allow a library to provide access to the items contained in a publication without actually owning a file of the publication. The main drawback to this type of searching and access is that it is relatively expensive. An example given to support this is that it would cost approximately $75.00 to download (at 1200 baud) an issue of *Business Week*, while the newsstand price for the same issue is $2.00.[8]

The future of full-text retrieval may lie with CD-ROM technology. Librarians have embraced CD-ROM, and it seems as if its future in libraries is secure, unless it is superseded by a more advanced technology. CD-ROM is attractive to libraries for two major reasons. First, CD-ROM files are generally available by subscription for a set price, whereas charges for access to online databases vary by amount of usage. It is easier and more reassuring for a library's budget officer to allot a set amount of money for a CD-ROM subscription than to set aside a block of money to cover the fluctuating costs of online searching. The second major advantage is that CD-ROM files are designed with the library patron as the end user. Thus, library staff members are not required to serve as intermediaries in the search process.

Although the number of CD-ROM files containing full-text serials is quite limited at present, there is a good likelihood that such files will be more widely produced in the near future. Publishers now view full-text serials on CD-ROM, or in an online database, as an "after-market," in which the electronic product augments the print product, rather than replacing it.[9] Should this continue, libraries, of course, will need to decide in which format(s) to provide access. For instance, a print subscription could be discontinued and replaced by a CD-ROM subscription. Another approach would be to subscribe to neither the print nor the CD-ROM formats, but to only access articles from an online, full-text database on an as-needed basis. One other factor that could have a great effect in this area is if optical disk systems become widely available to libraries at a reasonable cost. Such systems are capable of displaying the actual images of articles and other printed items, not just the text. Despite all of these technological achievements resulting in heightened access, printed serials will continue to reign supreme for years to come and will simply co-exist with their equivalents in electronic formats.

Aspects of Future Serials Reference

There have been great changes in the indexing and abstracting of serials over the past one hundred years. In the late 1800s and early 1900s, many of today's standard indexing and abstracting services were established and began to flourish. The number of such services multiplied until, by 1975, it was estimated that there were two thousand abstracting and indexing services covering just the fields of science and technology.[10] By the mid-1970s, newspaper indexing had become more widespread, and the researcher could be offered more than just indexes to *The New York Times* or *The Times* of London. At about the same time, the online availability of databases of abstracting and indexing services emerged as an important factor for libraries and for researchers. The number of such databases has continued to grow, and the choices for searching have become increasingly more complicated.

The recent introduction of abstracting and indexing services on CD-ROM systems has been the latest development in this field. CD-ROM systems can be considered a hybrid of the printed abstracting and indexing service and of the online database. It is similar to the online database in that a vast amount of material can be searched electronically in a very short time. Also, with many CD-ROM systems, complex searches, that would be impossible or impractical to conduct using the printed version of an index, can be performed. On the other hand, CD-ROM systems are similar to printed abstracting and indexing services in that they are available on the library premises, and patrons can perform their own searches. In addition, as mentioned earlier, most CD-ROM services are available by subscription. From the financial standpoint, it is much easier for a library to deal with a subscription that provides unlimited usage for a set price than with a fluctuating monthly bill of online charges.

Because of these characteristics and the positive response of patrons, it seems as if CD-ROM has a very bright future as a format of choice for abstracting and indexing services. This will especially be true if standards are established to enable a library to set up a single workstation capable of handling all types of CD-ROMs. Should this become a reality, it is likely that libraries will subscribe to more CD-ROM services, while concurrently reducing the number of print subscriptions and providing less online searching of databases.

Another future possibility is that large libraries and library systems will acquire entire abstracting and indexing databases and load them into their own computer systems. Patrons will then be able to search the service on the library's own computer terminals. The Library of Congress has already successfully accomplished such a feat with the Magazine Index database from the Information Access Company. This could become a significant trend in the coming years.

Related to future abstracting and indexing is the future of serials cataloging. Traditional cataloging of serials results in publications being classified under broad subject headings, with no indication of the titles or authors of articles within issues of the serial. This traditional level of cataloging and the access it provides is adequate only for those users simply trying to locate serials in a certain field. However, most patrons need articles on very specific topics. It has been suggested that since every article in a periodical is different, each should be cataloged and classified separately.[11] At first glance, that idea might seem absurd. Yet, that is basically the service that is currently provided by abstracting and indexing services.

It is quite probable that, in years to come, online public access catalogs will offer just this type of article-level cataloging information for serials. In fact, the Colorado Alliance of Research Libraries is implementing such a system, with a goal of providing access to articles in over ten thousand journals. When searching the catalog, users can choose to search for both books and articles or for articles only.[12] Nontraditional serials cataloging of this sort will undoubtedly become extremely popular with patrons where it is available. Should it become a widespread practice, the very existence of some abstracting and indexing services would be threatened since libraries would no longer be dependent upon them for article-level access.

A possible future change in traditional serials cataloging would have a great effect on serials reference work. At present, successive entry cataloging is the standard that is generally followed. This means that every time a serial changes its title, a separate cataloging record must be created. It has been stated that the use of successive entry cataloging in an automated environment "is costly to libraries and confusing to users."[13] A call for the reevaluation of this practice has been sounded,[14] and a change to either earliest entry or latest entry cataloging may be in our future.

Other aspects of serials reference work will continue to change and develop as new technologies are implemented. As with abstracting and indexing services, serial directories have traditionally been published in printed form. Recently, though, the databases used to produce these directories have become accessible through online searching and in CD-ROM formats. The traditional printed directories provide limited points of access to the information contained within them, but the online and CD-ROM formats offer a multitude of searching possibilities. CD-ROM systems such as Ulrich's PLUS and The Serials Directory/EBSCO CD/ROM are destined to become standard reference sources if the prices for them become comparable to that of their print equivalents.

Union lists of serials will continue their migration from the printed format to electronic formats. At present, union lists are becoming increasingly available in online modes, especially through the OCLC system. These online union lists are a fantastic tool for reference staff to utilize. With their availability, there is no need to depend on long outdated printed union lists. Online union lists can be constantly updated with the most current accurate information regarding holdings and locations.

In the union listing area, one of the major future accomplishments that is eagerly anticipated is the completion of the United States Newspaper Program. The purposes of this program include the identification of every newspaper that has ever been published in the United States and the identification of all repositories holding the newspaper, along with an indication of those holdings. Once this project is completed, researchers and librarians will have access to an unprecedented body of information. Accurate referrals and interlibrary loan requests will be possible. The entire field of newspaper research will be enhanced and improved.

There are other trends that may emerge in the field of union listing. It is possible that union listing groups will begin to produce and distribute their lists in CD-ROM format. Another development that would have a huge effect on the whole field of union listing and resource sharing would be the establishment of the National Periodicals Center. Such an institution would act as a central clearinghouse for copies of periodical articles. It is a proposal that has been hotly debated for years. At present, the prospects for the establishment of such a center are not very promising, but perhaps this will change in the future.

Serials and the Organizational Structure of the Library

Serials departments and serials librarians exist in the present structure of most libraries to provide expertise in the cataloging, processing, and servicing of serials. The predominance of such departments and specialists has served to isolate serials within the organizational structure of the library. A "serials mystique" has also developed and is perpetuated by serials librarians.[15] Staff members who are not serials specialists may thus feel unnecessarily intimidated by serials and believe that difficult questions about them should be handled by a serials specialist. The tide has begun to turn, however. Propelled by the emergence of new technologies and their resultant library applications, serials are becoming more integrated into the total service offered by libraries, and the era of serials librarianship as a professional specialization may be nearing an end.[16]

Reference staff today must be able to handle serials questions, even those of a difficult nature. As stated in the opening sentence of this book, every reference librarian is a serials librarian. Although many reference librarians might dispute that statement, serials are a major part of reference work, and, in the future, serials will become an even larger responsibility for the reference staff. This is because the serials specialization in librarianship is destined to be eliminated. Since most serials cataloging can now be accomplished through the use of records found in the database of a bibliographic utility, it is already unnecessary to employ professional librarians specifically as serials catalogers within serials departments in most libraries. The relatively small percentage of titles that require original cataloging can, in most libraries, be handled within the traditional cataloging department. Other functions normally associated with serials departments such as ordering, check-in, and binding, are jobs that can be filled by clerks or technicians. There is no need for serials librarians to accomplish those tasks. In addition, it is possible that in the future there may be a trend to merge the functions currently carried on by serials departments with the standard acquisitions, cataloging, and binding-labeling operations already existing in libraries.[17] The reign of the separate serials department may be coming to an end, hastened by the rise of new technologies and the desire of libraries to economize on processing activities.

From the reference standpoint, serials have become increasingly important, especially with the developments brought on by automation. Many of the online databases and CD-ROM systems that are so visible in libraries are simply abstracting and indexing services in electronic formats. These systems have revolutionized serials literature searching and have focused attention on the importance of serials as a part of the library's collection. Serials are now "front and center" as a result of the emergence of these electronic systems.

Reference staff members need to be familiar with serials and with the various reference sources related to them. This will become a more critical requirement in the future as the number of serials librarians dwindles. At the same time, serials will continue to become more fully integrated into the overall information retrieval package that is offered by a library in the form of its collections and resources. Thus, serials will remain at the forefront, and inquiries regarding them will continue unabated. Even difficult serials questions will need to be handled by the reference librarian. It is hoped that this book can serve as the foundation for the provision of such reference service.

Notes

[1]F. W. Lancaster, *Toward Paperless Information Systems* (New York: Academic Press, 1978), 105-13.

[2]John Gurnsey, *The Information Professions in the Electronic Age* (London: Clive Bingley, 1985), 131.

[3]Murray Turoff and Starr Roxanne Hiltz, "The Electronic Journal: A Progress Report," *Journal of the American Society for Information Science* 33 (July 1982): 201.

[4]James R. Dwyer, "Evolving Serials, Evolving Access: Bibliographic Control of Serial Literature," *Serials Review* 12 (Summer/Fall 1986): 61.

[5]O. L. Standera, "Electronic Publishing: Some Notes on Reader Response and Costs," *Scholarly Publishing* 16 (July 1985): 296-97.

[6]John Lubans, Jr., "Scholars and Serials," *American Libraries* 18 (March 1987): 181.

[7]Roger Summit and Ann Lee, "Will Full-Text Online Files Become 'Electronic Periodicals'?" *Serials Review* 14, no. 3 (1988): 7.

[8]Ibid., 9.

[9]Richard W. Boss, "Electronic Technology and Serials," *The Serials Librarian* 13 (December 1987): 99.

[10]Bernard Houghton, *Scientific Periodicals: Their Historical Development, Characteristics and Control* (London: Clive Bingley, 1975), 85-86.

[11]Herbert S. White, "Oh, Why (and Oh, What) Do We Classify?" *Library Journal* 113 (15 June 1988): 43.

[12]Gary M. Pitkin, "Access to Articles through the Online Catalog," *American Libraries* 19 (October 1988): 769.

[13]Jackie Zajanc, "Title Changes in an Automated Environment: The Last Shall Be First," *The Serials Librarian* 11 (September 1986): 21.

[14]Sue C. Lim, "Successive Entry Serials Cataloging: An Evaluation," *The Serials Librarian* 14, nos. 1-2 (1988): 68.

[15]Don Lanier and Glenn Anderson, "Dispelling the Serials Mystique," *The Serials Librarian* 5 (Summer 1981): 15-17.

[16]Tony Stankus, "The Year's Work in Serials, 1986," *Library Resources & Technical Services* 31 (October/December 1987): 315-16.

[17]Michael Gorman, "Dealing with Serials: A Sketch of Contextual/Organizational Response," *The Serials Librarian* 10 (Fall 1985/Winter 1985-1986): 16-17.

Author/Title Index

Subject Index